Advance Praise for *Prank the Monkey*

"Sir John Hargrave has taken pranking to the next level...It's safe to say that I have become a blubbering fanboy."

—Maddox, author of *The Alphabet of Manliness*

"Easily the funniest thing I've read in the last six to eight minutes."

—Drew Curtis, FARK.com (updated every six to eight minutes)

"The CIA and the FBI should get ahold of John Hargrave—not to arrest him but to have him run things. He is some kind of mad, intrepid genius, a cross between a psychopath and a revolutionary. He's part Thomas Jefferson and part Dr. Evil (if Dr. Evil was a good guy). This is a fascinating, comedic book and beautifully written as well."

—Jonathan Ames, author of *Wake Up, Sir!*

"The ultimate prankster, Hargrave sees the world through the eyes of a child. A child your mom kept you away from but who you secretly wanted to be."

—Ze Frank, creator of zefrank.com

"Devilishly creative... Sir John Hargrave's exploits have given 'balls' a new meaning."

—Legendary prankster Alan Abel

"Wickedly entertaining...It's hard to imagine anyone trumping this prankster for a very long time, if ever."

—George Ouzounian, creator of The Best Page in the Universe

Advance Rejection for *Prank the Monkey*

"I'm afraid Al doesn't have the time to read and endorse manuscripts—especially at this point when he's deep in gearing up his next album."

—Publicist for "Weird" Al Yankovic

"Dave is tied up in other projects through the end of the year, so he can't take on blurb requests right now."

—Handler for Dave Eggers, author of
A Heartbreaking Work of Staggering Genius

"I'm afraid I don't have time to read or blurb your book, as I am working on my own book now."

—John Hodgman, author of *The Areas of My Expertise*

"Unfortunately his schedule does not allow him to really read the book, so we will have to pass."

—Press lackey for Penn Jillette, author and magician

"Thanks so much for the Marlins tickets, but I really meant it when I said Dave doesn't do blurbs."

—Assistant to Dave Barry, humorist and extremely rich man

PRANK
the
MONKEY

The ZUG BooK of PranKs

Sir John Hargrave
Illustrations by Al Natanagara

CITADEL PRESS
Kensington Publishing Corp.
www.kensingtonbooks.com

CITADEL PRESS BOOKS are published by

Kensington Publishing Corp.
850 Third Avenue
New York, NY 10022

Designed by Jeffrey Rutzky

All Kensington titles, imprints, and distributed lines are available at special quantity discounts for bulk purchases for sales promotions, premiums, fund-raising, educational, or institutional use. Special book excerpts or customized printings can also be created to fit specific needs. For details, write or phone the office of the Kensington special sales manager: Kensington Publishing Corp., 850 Third Avenue, New York, NY 10022, attn: Special Sales Department; phone 800-221-2647.

10 9 8 7 6 5 4 3 2 1

Printed in the United States of America

Library of Congress Control Number: 2006934740

ISBN-13: 978-0-8065-2780-2
ISBN-10: 0-8065-2780-3

Dedication

The professors of the Miami University English department would not allow me to test out of their Introductory Composition class, because they didn't think my writing skills were strong enough.

This, my first book, is dedicated to them.

Contents

Introduction   1

Corporations

The Wal-Mart Prank   7
Signing My Life Away   18
Starbucking the System   30
Shirt-Changed   41
Fight the Power (Company)   50

Spammers

Good Morning, Vietspam   62
The V1@GRA Prank   70
Hot Rod   81
Chick Juice   93
Going Postal   109

Celebrities

The Celebrity Sincerity Test   122
I Kissed Bill Gates   146
The Making of Michael Jackson's Thriller   156
Hurley-Whirler   176
Kutcher in the Lie   187

Government

Royal Pain in the Ass   208
Congress Is a Joke   221
The Untied Nations   240
Highway to Hell   255
The Boston Tax Party   263

Death

The John Hargrave Memorial Concert   278

Acknowledgments   303

PRANK the MONKEY

The ZUG BooK of PranKs

Introduction

I WAS BORN on April Fool's Day.

This was a fact not lost on the burly Boston police officer glaring angrily at my driver's license. "April Fool's Day," he growled through a larynx glued partially shut by glazed doughnuts. "What is this, some kind of fake ID?"

"No sir," I responded. We were being held in the dingy back room of a CVS drugstore, the place where they brought the shoplifters to work them over. My cameraman and I sat across from each other at a tiny, filthy table. There was barely enough room for the police officer to squeeze inside. The guy was built like a cold storage warehouse.

"So what were you *doing?*" he asked for the twelfth time.

"I run a comedy Web site," I explained again. "We do pranks on large organizations that we think deserve it..."

"You're saying CVS deserved shoplifting?" interrupted the cop.

"Look," I reasoned, "the anti-theft gates at the front of CVS drugstores always seem to go off when you're buying something embarrassing, like Monistat-7 or hemorrhoid cream. We were *testing* the anti-theft gates with sample items. We wanted to see if they actually stopped shoplifters, or just embarrassed honest customers."

The cop mulled this over for a while. "Who do you think you are, Roger Moore?" he asked.

It took me a second to realize he meant *Michael*

Moore, the documentary filmmaker, not *Roger* Moore, the actor who played James Bond.

"I'm more of the Sean Connery type," I cracked. This was a stupid thing to say, but I was hoping the cameras in our bag were still rolling. Years later, I would learn the fine art of dealing with the police when they were called in to stop our pranks, but I was still a novice.

The policeman glared at me, then left to confer with his partner. "Sorry about all this," I said to my cameraman, who actually wasn't my cameraman at all, but a fan of my humor Web site, ZUG.com. I had met Dinesh only an hour before, when he had suddenly barged into my office at the technology company where I worked my day job. He had been traveling to Boston on business and thought it would be funny to show up unannounced, just to say how much he liked the site. I was annoyed that he would show up without any notice, interrupting my busy schedule—but now, at least, I was getting some revenge.

"All right, up, BOTH OF YOU," bellowed Officer Hamsteak, barging into the room.

"Easy," cooled his partner from just outside the door. "Take it easy." They really do play good cop/bad cop. This still happens, in real life.

"Turn around," he ordered. "Against the wall."

I still didn't think we would actually be arrested. I had been in numerous scrapes with authority figures throughout my pranking "career," but it seemed ridiculous that a police officer would arrest me for this silly comedy stunt. But when he slapped a pair of handcuffs on me and began reading my rights, I felt a dam of adrenaline exploding into my bloodstream, flooding me with fear and remorse. I was a white male professional with a good career and a happy marriage, but now I saw a blanket of horror smothering my future. *Will I lose my job? Will I be able to post bail? What is bail, anyway?* They're not gentle with the handcuffs, even for comedy writers. The metal cut into my skin as the cops led us through the mall, handcuffed and shamed. But as bad as things were, I knew they could get worse: *I could be seen by a co-worker.* My office was just down the street, so my co-workers made frequent visits to this mall for lunch and shopping. The cops kept us at the front entrance for fifteen or twenty minutes, waiting for the paddy wagon to arrive (no kidding, they actually brought a paddy wagon). I prayed fervently that I would not see anyone I knew.

If a person's life can be summed up in a single moment, this was mine: as Dinesh and I were being pushed into the back of the police van, I looked over and saw three of my co-workers, *including my boss's boss,* walking toward the mall. It was extraordinary timing: I saw them just as my head disappeared behind the door, a split second before they saw me. The incident perfectly captured the dual life I have created for myself: I'm part of the system at the same time I'm fighting against the system. I'm working for The Man one minute, then sticking it to him the next.

On life's karma scorecard, I figure I'm netting out even.

What Is a Prank?

Let's get one thing straight: *a prank is more than a practical joke.* The bucket of water balanced above the doorframe, Saran Wrap stretched across the toilet seat: these are *practical jokes*, the domain of fraternities and fools. A *prank*, on the other hand, deflates the pompous, rights a wrong, or brings down the powerful (and the bigger the buffoon, the funnier the fall). A practical joke maintains the existing power structure. A prank turns it on its head.

A good prank doesn't have to bring down The Man, but it does have to get a laugh at The Man's expense. And here I speak with authority, because I *am* The Man. I have a comfortable home in the suburbs, a day job in middle management, a wife and child. I take great pride in my lawn, and I occasionally wear a tie. When I am pranking these institutions, they believe I'm legit, *because I am.* When I'm forging credit card receipts, they glance at the unlimited credit Amex gold card and don't think twice. When I'm taking Viagra in church, I have no problems, because I attend every Sunday.

I'm undercover. I'm *deep* undercover. I've got a mortgage, a three-year-old, and a weed whacker. They have no idea who I am. I even got my MBA from one of the nation's top-rated business schools so I could learn all their tricks. I know every corporate deception, every bureaucratic maneuver, and I will not hesitate to use their methods against them.

Thus, my weird schizophrenic life: honest citizen by day, professional liar by night. When the phone rings, I have no idea whether the caller is expecting to speak with John Hargrave, or the President of Paraguay. I am a pro at cons.

Why Prank?

It's not that I have a problem with authority; it's that I have a problem with *senseless* authority. I have no problem with rules, just *ridiculous* rules. It's like the pool rules. I was at the pool the other day. Have you read those rules lately? Out of the twelve pool rules, I was breaking *four*, and that was in front of my toddler son. I was engaging in horseplay, chewing gum, diving off the side, and I hadn't taken a cleansing shower. I haven't taken a cleansing shower since 1972. And: no horseplay?! *What the hell is the point of a pool, if not horseplay!?* Without horseplay, it's known as a BATH.

Who makes the pool rules? The usual suspects: humorless corporations, bloated attorneys, faceless bureaucrats. The same people who create the voicemail trees that lead to automated messages that ultimately hang up on us. The ones who buy, sell, and occasionally *misplace* our personal data, while always protecting their own. After all, the rich and powerful enjoy a human shield of receptionists, handlers, press agents, public relations executives, and "customer care professionals." They could give a rat's ass about our privacy, because they're safely sealed away in their ivory towers and corner offices.

But that's exactly why I do it. *I do it for us.* I prank the rich and give a laugh to the poor. I'm like a retarded Robin Hood.

Prank the Monkey

So sit back and enjoy a few chuckles at the expense of the world's biggest, dumbest, and most deserving targets. Let's have some fun with the people and institutions that deserve so much more than a practical joke.

They deserve a prank.

CORPORATIONS

The Wal-Mart Prank

 WE KNOW THAT WAL-MART IS BAD FOR US, but we still shop there.

I'm as a guilty as you are. Even though I know Wal-Mart drives the little guy out of business,[1] replacing my quaint town stores with enormous, impersonal blue warehouses[2] staffed by handicapped, non-unionized[3] wage slaves[4] who sell merchandise that may be manufactured by sweatshops in Bangladesh,[5] I *still shop there.* What can I say? I love a bargain.

What really bothers me about Wal-Mart is the *censorship.* The world's most powerful retailer refuses to sell books and CDs it deems morally objectionable. They returned George Carlin's 2004 book after discovering it featured a parody illustration of Carlin sitting at the table of the Last Supper.[6] They refused to sell *The Daily Show's America (The Book)* because it contained parody illustrations of naked Supreme Court Justices.[7] Even Sheryl Crow got rejected, not because her music sucks, but because her self-titled album contained *anti-Wal-Mart lyrics.*[8]

I could overlook all this, except for one thing: *I'm writing a book.* I've got to move 5,000 copies just to turn a profit on this mofo. I need Wal-Mart, with its *$288.2 billion* in annual sales, built on the tender backs of third-world child laborers, to pimp my writing. But how could I get this risqué comedy book into a retailer that prefers to stock books like *The Precious Moments Bible* and *Chicken Soup for the Latter-Day Saint Soul: Stories Celebrating the Faith and Family of Latter-Day Saints?* It wouldn't be easy, even if I changed the name to *Prank Thy Monkey.*

1. "An Empire Built on Bargains Remakes the Working World," *Los Angeles Times,* November 23, 2003.

2. "Preservationists Call Vermont Endangered by Wal-Mart," *New York Times,* May 25, 2004.

3. "Wal-Mart: The High Cost of Low Price," Robert Greenwald, Director, November 2005.

4. "Is Wal-Mart Good for America?", PBS *FRONT-LINE,* November 16, 2004.

5. "Praise Uncle Sam and Pass the 18p an Hour," *London Observer,* June 20, 1999.

6. "Carlin's No Joke for Wal-Mart," *CNN Money,* October 28, 2004.

7. "Behind the Robes, Stewart Finds Controversy," *USA Today,* October 20, 2004.

8. "Wal-Mart: Impact of a Retail Giant," PBS *NewsHour,* August 20, 2004.

Part I: Reasoning

I did a little Internet research and found that Wal-Mart actually outsources its book buying to an Illinois company called Levy Home Entertainment. From there, it was a simple matter to track down the e-mail address of their primary book buyer, Rob Connor.

I sent Rob a few e-mails, asking him if Wal-Mart would be willing to read through my manuscript, highlighting or deleting any portions they might find offensive. I pictured a Wal-Mart Morality Council, consisting of several white guys in their fifties, all wearing fezzes, who might take a looksee through my book and tell me what Wal-Mart found funny.

Rob quickly grew tired of this line of questioning, and asked me to stop e-mailing him. Geez! Touchy. I decided to call Rob personally, to sort out the misunderstanding. I called Levy Home Entertainment's main number, which was listed on their Web site, and asked to speak with Rob.

ROB CONNOR: Rob Connor.

JOHN HARGRAVE: Hi, Rob. My name is John Hargrave, and we've been trading some e-mails. I have to say, your last note was a little bit rude. I'm just trying to make a book that's family-friendly and that Americans will enjoy.

RC: *(testily)* Then you have to do that with the publisher. We do not read books, or copy, or proof, or anything like that. *You have to do that with your publisher.* And I tried to make that very clear with you on about two or three occasions, but *you didn't seem to get the message.*

JH: I don't understand. Doesn't Wal-Mart have a committee, or a...

RC: *(rudely interrupting) NO.* Wal-Mart does not have a committee to read every book that goes into their stores.

JH: Then how do you know if they're any good?

RC: *(pause)* It's up to your *editor* to read your book.

JH: Well, how does Wal-Mart decide what to reject?

RC: *(pause)* It's when they get customer complaints regarding the book.

JH: But Wal-Mart rejects books before they've even hit the shelves. How could a customer complain about a book that hasn't been released?

RC: When Wal-Mart gets customer complaints is when they withdraw a product from the marketplace.

JH: Well, let me just run some of these ideas by you...

RC: *NO!* No, no, no! Not at all! Thank you! I don't have time for it! We don't do that!

JH: For instance, there are several jokes about breast cancer.

RC: Were you listening to what I just said?

JH: Yeah, but the jokes are crucial to the plot.

RC: *Were you listening to what I just said?*

JH: Uh-huh.

RC: WE DON'T EDIT. WE DON'T... *(calming himself)* Ah, look, this is an editorial process. We are not in the business to be editors.

JH: Okay. There's a whole section about my penis also.

RC: Thank you, John! Get a publisher! Get an editor!

JH: Do you think that pornography involving unicorns would be okay?

RC: Get a publisher, get an editor. That's their job to do what you're asking us to do. It is not our job.

JH: I call it "uniporn."

RC: I'm very busy at this moment. Thank you. *(hangs up)*

▲ Target.

Sheesh! Some people have no sense of humor, especially when you call them at 4:55 on a Friday afternoon. Suffice it to say that I wasn't very happy with the outcome of this discussion. So I decided to *force* Wal-Mart to sell the books that it seeks to censor.

Part II: Brute Force

Maybe if I could prank Wal-Mart into selling me a banned book or CD, I thought, it would be like tearing down the Berlin Wall or the Iron Curtain. Free speech! Free love! Free samples in aisle 5! They'd sell my book, somewhere between the eggs and the laundry hampers! Profit!

Like so many of the targets you'll read about in the following pages, Wal-Mart's strength is its size, but that's also its weakness. At your local bookstore, for instance, they'd probably notice if you walked in with a carton of banned books and put them on the sale rack next to *The Purpose-Driven Life.* But Fred, the elderly Wal-Mart greeter, just grinned and nodded at me as I walked in with the box of books I had purchased weeks earlier from Amazon.com. Wal-Mart greeters search your bag going *out*, but not going *in*. I was shoplifting, in reverse.

Getting the merchandise on the shelves was easy. They've got a bewildering array of suppliers, so they had no idea if that guy in the tie was legitimately stocking shelves. I always wear a suit when pulling off any high-stakes pranks, since people are less likely to question a well-dressed troublemaker. I walked around the section for a while, straightening the books and CDs, as if I were a regional manager.

▼ Apparently, these books are more dangerous than the guns they sell over in Sporting Goods.

No one gave me a second glance, even when I started taking pictures.

The only difficult part of the prank was forging the Wal-Mart price tag that I had affixed to the items. Wal-Mart is legendary for its focus on strict inventory control, which means that all Wal-Mart merchandise is meticulously labeled with computerized bar codes. A few days beforehand, I had visited Wal-Mart and peeled a tag off a Harry Potter book. (*Switching* price tags is illegal, but not *removing* them.) Then I went home and scanned the tag into Photoshop, where I forged a pretty good replica of the bar code. It wouldn't scan correctly into Wal-Mart's registers, but then again, *neither do half the items in my basket when I check out.*

▲ Close enough.

I took my merchandise up to the Wal-Mart counter, where I was helped by a young man named Jeff, whose multiple facial piercings nicely accented his blue button-down Wal-Mart vest. He scanned my paper towels and socks, then got to the first book. The register beeped angrily. He ignored the register's complaints and bagged the book anyway. The second book did the same thing. He punched some keys and gave me this book for free also.

He scanned in a few more items, then got to the Sheryl Crow CD. This time he scanned in the *legitimate* UPC code on the back of the CD, not my fake bar code sticker. The register rang it up correctly, *then immediately voided it out.* It was as if the register could not tolerate the selling of merchandise

forbidden by the Wal-Mart thought police.

Jeff finished ringing up my goods.

"Your total comes to $36.33."

"Wow," I said. "That's a pretty good bargain, even for Wal-Mart. You sure everything rang up correctly?"

"Hmm." He looked over the receipt. "I didn't charge you for the CD."

"Or the books," I added helpfully.

"I'll thcan them again," he said. His tongue-stud gave him a slight lisp.

We pulled the unscanned merchandise out of the bags, and I gave him another try. He scanned the UPC codes, but the register spat back the purchases, refusing to contaminate itself with moral filth. Finally, he did that little Commander Data move, typing in a bunch of numbers on the keypad really fast to override the system, and the computer accepted my books. Apparently, there's some kind of Censorship Filter that can be turned off, because the computer finally relented and *sold me the forbidden items!*

The whole stunt was so easy that I had to go back and do it again, this time with pornography.

Part III: Booty Force

Wal-Mart does have a "Men's" section on its magazine racks, but this is filled with sports and fitness magazines, *Guideposts,* that sort of thing. I carefully laid out my hand-selected pornography, though I realize now that I made the critical error of putting

Playgirl next to *Penthouse.*
Clearly, *Playgirl* should have
gone in "Women's,"
next to *Family Circle.*

"Excuse me," a middle-
aged woman asked me as I
was arranging pornography.
"Do you know where I can
find the Air Wicks refills?"

"You'll want to look
in Household," I responded
without a moment's hesitation.

▲ Men's Business.

She looked confused. "This *is* Household," she
said, pointing to the aisle beside us.

"Right," I said. "You want the *other* Household,
down fourteen aisles, on your right." See, she was
thrown off by the tie. A tie is the prankster's best
defense.

"Do you know how often I'm supposed to refill the
Air Wicks?" she asked.

"I'm not sure, but Brenda will know," I said. "Find
Brenda in Household II. She's like the Air Wicks
expert."

"Okay," she said, smiling. "Thanks!" I felt kind of
bad about wasting her time, but then figured it was
probably the best service she'd get at Wal-Mart all day.

I approached the counter with my pornography
and related items. I was helped by Sheila, a portly
young cashier who scanned in my Kleenex and socks,
then got to the nudie mags. The register beeped furiously as she pulled the bar code over the scanner.
She looked curiously at the title, *Big Black Butts,*

then continued to pass the magazine over the bar code reader. She turned over the magazine and peered at the back cover, which featured a full-page photo of a generous African-American woman perched atop a beach ball.

"What's the price on this?" she asked me.

"Priceless," I said.

She looked over the magazine for a price, running her finger over a headline that read VALENTINE'S DAY SPECIAL EDITION: 8 HEART-SHAPED HEINIES TO HIT!

"$8.99," I said, finally locating the price. "Minus the 10 percent everyday discount on magazines."

"$8.99 minus 10 percent," she said, trying to calculate this in her head. I was trying to figure it out myself. Both of us were distracted by the giant bumfarm staring at us from the back cover. It was like a cow trapped in a Naugahyde sofa.

"I'll give it to you for $7.00," she finally said, punching it into the register. ENTER DESCRIPTION, the register said, and she punched in "111111."

"Hey, could you put in a proper description for these magazines?" I asked as she tried to find the price on the *Playgirl*. "I need it spelled out on the receipt, for tax purposes."

She looked around furtively. She knew that something was wrong, but couldn't put her finger on it.

"No. I...I don't want any kids behind you to see this."

```
        WAL★MART®
      ALWAYS LOW PRICES.
          Always
      WE SELL FOR LESS
          ALWAYS

ST# 2902 OP# 00001735 TE# 16 TR# 05460
GV FF SKIM M 007874235189 F    2.47 O
PUFFS CUBE   003700033531      1.28 X
EGGS         081390500064 F    0.73 O
       WAS 1.46 YOU SAVED 0.73
NYLON SOCK N 008041446600      0.96 N
KY WM LIG 1  038004008944      3.87 X
111111         DO3 QTY 1       7.00 X
MMMMMM         DO3 QTY 1       8.00 X
GV CEREAL    007874235889 F    1.77 O
GV CEREAL    007874235889 F    1.77 O
SENSOR RAZOR 004740012831      2.94 X
               SUBTOTAL       30.79
       TAX 1   5.000 %         1.15
               TOTAL          31.94
       AMEX TEND             31.94

ACCOUNT #4006
APPROVAL #568452
TRANS ID -
VALIDATION -
PAYMENT SERVICE -
          CHANGE DUE          0.00
```

I looked behind me. There was an eighty-year-old guy in a motorized shopping cart.

"What kids?" I asked, but it was too late. She had already charged me $8.00 for the *Playgirl*, and put in the description as MMMMMM. I thought that was an appropriate description for pornography. I would have preferred "MMMMMM, YEAH," but it didn't matter. My mission was accomplished.

I got Wal-Mart to sell me the stuff they said was too dangerous to sell me. It's not exactly Tiananmen Square, but I think it's a step toward free speech in our nation's most powerful retailer. And maybe now that they've sold some of these controversial works, Wal-Mart will consider selling *my* book as well.

In fact, now I've got Wal-Mart exactly where I want them: If they *don't* carry my book, it shows they can't tolerate criticism of their company. If they *do* carry it, maybe I can finally make enough money to start shopping somewhere upscale, like Linens 'n Things. ☺

Did Wal-Mart end up carrying this book? Log on to the official Prank the Monkey Web site to find out: www.prankthemonkey.com/walmart

Signing My Life Away

IN MY LIFETIME, I HAVE MADE nearly 15,000 credit card transactions. I purchase almost everything on plastic. What bugs me about credit card transactions—I mean, besides supporting a faceless industry that encourages reckless spending and debt—is the *signing*. Who checks the signature? Nobody checks the signature.

Credit card signatures are a useless mechanism designed to make you *feel* safe, like airport security checks. These companies don't give two rats' asses about our security. It seems like every month I read a news story about one of these corporations losing millions of customer records by misplacing a laptop, or dropping a backup tape off the back of a truck. There are no legal penalties, so why should they care? In my mind, if you lose 40 million Social Security numbers, your CEO is put to death. End of story. Once we put the death penalty in place, *then* we'll see companies protecting our privacy. Until then, we've got the cheesy credit card signatures.

My question was this: *how crazy would I have to make my signature before someone would actually care?* This is the signature on the back of my credit card:

Even my normal signature looks like it was drawn by an epileptic weasel. I am an *arteest*, and my signature must reflect that. *But how* arteestic *could I get before someone would notice?*

Part I: Large and In Charge

I spent several weeks seeing how wacky I could make
my signature before someone would pay attention.
First, I decided to get a little artistic.

Then I decided
to get *wicked*
artistic:

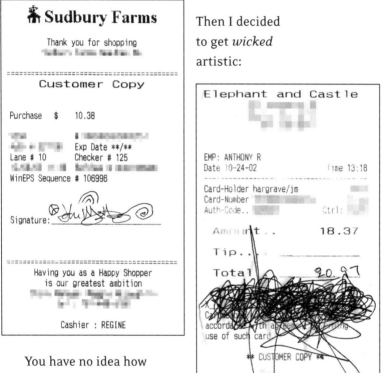

You have no idea how
strange it is to have a counter
clerk watch you scribble fiercely
on a piece of paper, as if you
wished to purge the evil that is your signature.
Then I smiled and handed him back his pen.

Next time I bought something that required a
signature, I considered just creating a rectangle of

solid black. Then I thought a grid might be weirder:

Only the most SuDoku-obsessed nerdboy would actually use a grid for his signature, but the kid at the pizza place didn't look twice. What if I went the other way? How *minimal* would my signature have to be before someone would notice?

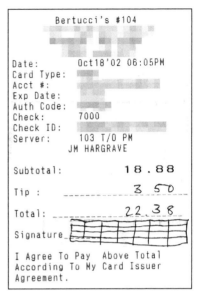

Part II: Minimally, in Cursive

Next I tried the old standby, "X." I was kind of nervous about this one, and had a long story prepared about how I had recently been involved in a motorcycle accident, and during my sixteen months in traction had only been able to sign with an X, a signature which grew on me. At the last minute, I chickened out and added an additional squiggly:

Signing X, incidentally, is not a bad idea; it's quick and easy, and if someone wants you to "sign on the X," *it's already signed.*

Next, I took a suggestion from one of my readers, and tried signing with a stick figure. Before the server came back to my table, though, I decided it looked too lonely, so I tried drawing a little landscape. I forgot that I have the artistic ability of a piece of toast.

Finally, I know of no law that says your signature has to be in your own alphabet. So I found a Web site that converted my name to Egyptian hieroglyphics. Although "John Hargrave" was too long to remember, "John" was just snake, bird, caterpillar.

On my way out the door, I realized it would

Rec: 69
Terminal: 3

SKIPJACK'S NEWTON
55 NEEEDHAM STREET

CARD TYPE   ACCOUNT NUMBER

00 TRANSACTION APPROVED

TRANS TYPE: Credit Card SALE

CHECK :   55.55
TIP :   .
TOTAL :   66.55

X

CARDHOLDER WILL PAY CARD ISSUER ABOVE
AMOUNT PURSUANT TO CARDHOLDER AGREEMENT

DUNKIN DONUTS
                    000001
                    0001
P130450
EGG & CHZ $2.09
P130450
EGG & CHZ $2.09
MD COMBO #2 $2.73
  MD HOT COFFEE
  1 MUFFIN
MD COMBO #2 $2.73
  MD HOT COFFEE
  1 MUFFIN
MDSE ST $9.64
TAX1 $0.48
***TOTAL $10.12
CREDIT $10.12
CHANGE $0.00

CREDIT $10.12

TIP AMOUNT
TOTAL   10.12
GUEST SIGNATURE

X
I AGREE TO PAY ABOVE TOTAL AMOUNT
ACCORDING TO CARD AGREEMENT

have been funnier if I had signed it "Ra."
Which got me to thinking—
what if I didn't even sign
with my own name?

Part III: The Name Game

First, I lobbed a slow ball:

The guy at the deli
didn't say anything, probably because I am mistaken
for Mariah Carey all the
time. Except for the goatee
and the back hair, we are
like twins.

Next I decided to try:

```
COWLICKS DELI PRO

TERMINAL I.D.:
MERCHANT #:

                        ITEM #: 003
SWIPE              EXP. DATE
SALE

   DATE: JUL 01, 2003  TIME: 12:31
                       AUTH NO:

TOTAL                  $5.78

JM HARGRAVE
x   Mariah Carey

   I AGREE TO PAY ABOVE TOTAL
   ACCORDING TO CARD ISSUER
   (MERCHANT AGREEMENT)
```

```
        Masala Art
       Dining Room


Exp Date:   XX/XX
Auth Code:
Check:
Table:     6/1
Server:    410 Sameer
           JM HARGRAVE

Subtotal:    10.50

TIP          1.50

TOTAL       12.00


SIGNATURE  BEETHOVEN

           THANK YOU
```

▶ The composer or the dog; you decide.

I cheated on
this one, leaving it
on the table and
high-tailing it out
of there. I expected
a phone call from
someone, maybe
Beethoven's
Hollywood agent,
but once again
I discovered that
no one cared.
Except, possibly,
Lassie, who could
use the publicity.

Drunk with power, I signed this on my next food shopping trip:

I think that's a somewhat effeminate signature for the leader of the gods, but I was in a hurry. The kid at the Trader Joe's looked strangely at the receipt, then back up at me, as if to say, *"Are you really him?"* I trucked out of there before he could ask, and in my haste to escape, nearly ran over an eight year-old standing in the doorway. I apologized, which was a dead giveaway, since the real Zeus would have just fried the kid with lightning. I'm such a fake Zeus.

Where could I go from here?

Part IV: Signature Moments

Next, I went to my readers for suggestions. Many folks said they wrote "PLEASE CHECK ID" on the back of their credit cards, but what if I tried writing that on the credit card receipt itself?

Apparently, "PLEASE CHECK ID" on your credit card is about

as effective as "PLEASE HANDLE GENTLY" on your airport luggage.

Another reader told me that she once signed a credit card receipt "Mickey Mouse" at Disneyland, because she was so fed up with not having her signature checked. She ended up getting the item for free; it never showed up on her statement.

I signed this purchase "Porky Pig," but I *did* have to pay for it. So maybe that trick only works in Disneyland.

```
DUNKIN DONUTS
                              000001
                              0001
P003086
SM ORIG BLEND                  $1.39
MDSE ST                        $1.39
TAX1                           $0.07

***TOTAL                      $1.46
CREDIT                         $1.46
CHANGE                         $0.00


CREDIT                         $1.46
 TIP AMOUNT    _____
  TOTAL    _____  /.46
GUEST SIGNATURE

X    Porky Pig
I AGREE TO PAY ABOVE
TOTAL AMOUNT ACCORDING
TO CARD ISSUER AGREEMENT
(MERCHANT AGREEMENT IF
 CREDIT VOUCHER)
```

Finally, one reader suggested, "Try signing the slip as: *I stole this card.*"

I'm thinking of changing my name to "I Stole This Card." It's got a nice ring to it, and boy, wouldn't my mom be confused when I sent her a Mother's Day card?

```
BROOKLINE ASSC INTL

              BATCH: 651
            S-A-L-E-S  D-R-A-F-T
REF:
CD TYPE: MASTERCARD
TR TYPE: PURCHASE
DATE:    JUL 01; 03  15:14:38

TOTAL                  $10.00
ACCT:                  EXP:
AP:
NAME: HARGRAVE

CARDMEMBER ACKNOWLEDGES RECEIPT OF GOODS
 AND/OR SERVICES IN THE AMOUNT OF THE
TOTAL SHOWN HEREON AND AGREES TO PERFORM
   THE OBLIGATIONS SET FORTH BY THE
CARDMEMBER'S AGREEMENT WITH THE ISSUER

X   I stole this card

TOP COPY-MERCHANT  BOTTOM COPY-CUSTOMER
```

This was crazy. Surely there was *some* way to make them check the signature. Maybe I just needed to up the ante. So I started thinking: what was the most ridiculous purchase I could charge?

Part V: You Have to Give Me Credit

I chose the enormous national retail chain Circuit City for my final credit card experiment. I confidently strode in, asking for their most expensive television: the Hitachi 42-inch plasma HDTV.

The middle-aged Indian fellow manning the TV department had thick black hair sprouting from his ears, but that didn't block the sound of cash registers ringing in his head. "Yes," he nearly cried, "we have those in stock!"

I had checked their inventory on the Internet earlier that day, so I knew exactly how many they had. "The 42HDT51?" I asked, idly fiddling with my cuff links. I had model numbers *and* a suit. I could have made sausage out of baby meat and gotten away with it.

"Yes, sir!" said the Indian clerk, punching on his computer. "We have, ah, *three* in stock."

"I'd like all of them," I said without hesitation.

The guy almost crapped his pants. "Do you have a truck to carry them home?" he asked.

"Yes," I lied. "Yes, I have a truck." (I did have a *hand*-truck, back home in my garage.)

"That's great!" he said. "Great, just great."

Shaking his head at this sudden good fortune, he punched in my order, which, when tallied with all the optional service plans and recommended cables, came to well over $16,000.

I have to admit that my heart was pounding as I handed him my credit card. I was definitely playing with fire. He ran the charge card through, then asked me to sign the electronic touchpad. I tried to sign "I DO NOT AUTHORIZE THIS TRANSACTION," but apparently there's some kind of memory buffer in these things, and the touchpad stopped recording my input after "I DO NOT AUTHORI." So what if you have a really long Arabic name, like Fawzi Bin Abd Al-Majid Shubukshi, or Mohammed Abdul-Jabbar-Shamaladingdong? Not only are the signature machines *useless*, they're *racist*.

I had to literally try the signature *four times*, while the guy stood breathing over my shoulder. It was excruciating, and it smelled like curry. Finally I settled on "NOT AUTHORIZED," then took a picture of the screen, while trying to carry on a conversation like this was totally normal.

"So, who you rooting for in the big game?" I asked nonchalantly as I snapped another picture of the screen.

"Oh, ha," he laughed nervously. "Ah...what are you doing, sir?" he asked.

"What?" I asked him, which is always a safe response when challenged.

"Why did you sign 'NOT AUTHORIZED'?"

"Hmm?" I asked. "What?"

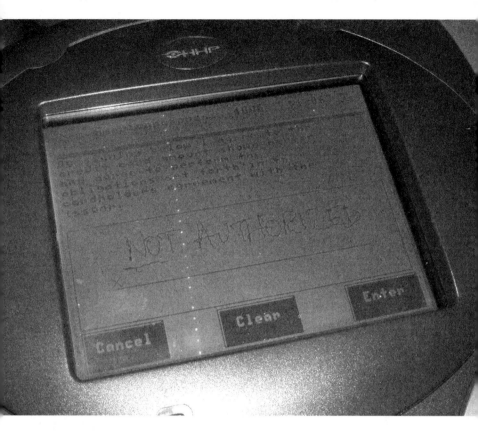

"Let me call a manager," he said, voiding out the transaction. A few moments later, a middle-aged guy with a ponytail and goatee came over to see what was wrong. They exchanged some hushed words, and then he rang through my purchase again. "Can you sign the screen, please?" he asked, glaring at me.

Again I signed "NOT AUTHORIZED" to my $16,800 purchase.

"What is that?" he asked.

"That's my signature," I said.

"You can't sign it 'NOT AUTHORIZED.'"

"Why not?"

"Because you need to sign your name."

"Well, I recently changed my signature," I said hopefully. "It now looks a lot like 'NOT AUTHORIZED.'"

"It's got to match the back of your card," the manager said.

"Oh," I said. "No problem." I took the card back from him and wrote "NOT AUTHORIZED" on the back of my credit card. I had heard that this trick sometimes works, but this guy was too smart for me.

"No, no," he said as I started writing. "That doesn't count."

"It's never had to match before," I said. "No one has ever cared."

"Well, I'm sorry if we've overlooked the signature in the past," he said. "But we can't accept this. Do you want to try again?"

"You mean try to forge the signature so it matches the back of the card?"

"Can't you just sign your real name?" the Indian clerk pleaded, watching his commission slip away. "We can let you try again."

"Guess what?" I said, changing course. "This is the first time anyone has verified my signature in years. I want to congratulate you guys. You've really made me feel good about buying things at Circuit City." I hit CANCEL on the signature screen. "Thanks!" I cheerfully waved good-bye as I walked out of Circuit City, empty-handed.

So there you have it. As long as you're not buying $16,000 worth of TVs, no one cares how you sign your credit card receipts. I guess the lesson is: There are some things money can't buy. For everything else, there's forgery.

Starbucking the System

AS THE OLD JOKE GOES, there are so many Starbucks—over 10,000 locations worldwide—that soon the only place to build *new* Starbucks will be inside of *existing* Starbucks. Then I thought: Why should that be a joke? I developed the following business proposal, which I sent in to Starbucks headquarters.

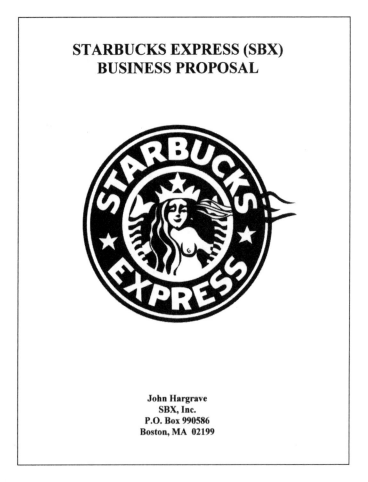

**STARBUCKS EXPRESS (SBX)
BUSINESS PROPOSAL**

John Hargrave
SBX, Inc.
P.O. Box 990586
Boston, MA 02199

EXECUTIVE SUMMARY

Let's be honest: there are so many Starbucks locations that soon the company is going to run out of room for new ones. Starbucks also faces increasing competition from fast food chains like Dunkin' Donuts and McDonald's, which serve premium coffee more quickly and cheaply. It is the perfect time for STARBUCKS EXPRESS (SBX), a quick-serve Starbucks franchise located *within* existing Starbucks franchises.

CONCEPT

Currently, Starbucks serves a bewildering array of coffee-based drinks. However, my research indicates that 38% of your customers simply order a plain coffee [**Exhibit 1**]. Why make these customers wait in line behind the man that wants a ginger-infused half-caf 2% creamsicle mochiatto?

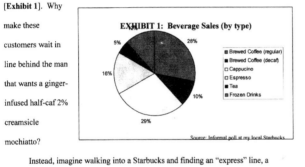

EXHIBIT 1: Beverage Sales (by type)

- Brewed Coffee (regular)
- Brewed Coffee (decaf)
- Cappucino
- Espresso
- Tea
- Frozen Drinks

Source: Informal poll at my local Starbucks

Instead, imagine walking into a Starbucks and finding an "express" line, a STARBUCKS EXPRESS line! SBX would serve <u>only</u> regular and decaf coffee; no specialty or mixed drinks. The SBX franchise would be discreetly placed in a corner of the restaurant, eliminating the need for the large, expensive leather chairs that bring in no

All jokes aside, this is a great idea. Starbucks is running out of ways to grow its business. Unless they want to start opening coffeehouses inside day care centers, or injecting coffee directly into the tender membranes of developing fetuses, a "quick-serve counter" is their best hope for getting additional customers.

additional revenue. However, in order to set it apart from the Starbucks proper, SBX would require separate signage, and (if possible) a large retaining wall.

PRICING

In exchange for the convenience, SBX coffee would carry a 25% premium over regular Starbucks coffee (e.g., a $2.00 coffee at the Starbucks counter would cost $2.50 at the SBX counter). This is in keeping with Starbucks' policy of marking up coffee drinks that require additional labor (e.g., Starbucks' iced coffee is currently 15% more than hot coffee, due to the additional effort of adding the ice).

Each SBX franchise would be independently owned and operated by my company, SBX, Inc., which would license the Starbucks logo and other merchandising elements, in exchange for 92% of the profits [**Exhibit 2**]. (An additional 3% would go into community programs, such as

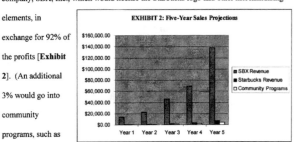

EXHIBIT 2: Five-Year Sales Projections

donations to other local coffee shops, for helping to keep the coffee scene alive.)

SUMMARY

Serving a familiar product at much higher profit margins: the idea is Starbucks to its core. I look forward to discussing this innovative proposal with you as soon as possible.

Even though this idea is their savior, it wasn't easy to get Starbucks to listen to me. First they sent me back a lengthy disclosure agreement, in which I had to agree to waive "any potential claims against Starbucks or any of its subsidiaries with respect to the Idea." Consulting my Lawyer-to-English dictionary, that translates as, "Starbucks can steal your idea at any time. Good luck suing us, cockwad."

I knew Starbucks would eventually use my idea, even though they didn't respond to my proposal, despite repeated follow-ups. But I didn't give up easily. What they needed, I thought, was a proof-of-concept. So I decided to do it. *I would set up a Starbucks inside a Starbucks.*

Starblogs

I've brought along the laptop to document this historic business venture, in real time. I'll be blogging this chapter as it happens, so you get the rich, slow-roasted flavor of this defining moment in American business history.

1:00 p.m. I've brought along Moses (friend, not the prophet) to videotape today's activities for the companion

Web site. Moe and I are shooting an intro outside the Starbucks. It is thirteen degrees outside, with winds of ninety miles per hour. My business proposal just flew out of my hands and underneath an oncoming bus. This does not bode well for our plan.

1:35 p.m. Inside the Starbucks, where the line is twelve customers deep. If ever there was a time for our idea, it is now.

1:37 p.m. The assistant manager just saw the camera and asked Moe to quit filming. Lowering the camera, Moe apologized. He then, of course, continued filming.

1:45 p.m. I just finished standing in line. All I wanted to buy was a pound of coffee and a slice of lemon loaf. The woman at the register moved with the speed and grace of a tranquilized circus elephant. She did not know how to scan in the gift cards, and customers piled up behind me like Mexican immigrants waiting to be paid an honest day's wages for harvesting coffee beans. It took *forever*, i.e., several minutes.

The elderly woman beside me finally said, "You've been here a long time."

"Right," I said. "What Starbucks really needs is an express line. A STARBUCKS EXPRESS LINE." I stared pointedly at one of the baristas, who could not hear me over the *SCCCHHHHHHHHSSSSSSHHHHH* of her milk steamer.

1:50 p.m. We will need electricity for our Starbucks Express franchise, but the only available outlet is located behind the comfortable chairs. Every Starbucks has two comfortable chairs, which are required by law to be filled with someone other than you. Today, the chairs are occupied by two young women who are sipping cappuccinos and yakking about boys. Moe and I haul our three bags of equipment over to a nearby table, where we sit down on a couple of spartan wooden stools. I stare at the women pointedly.

1:55 p.m. The wait is interminable. Bored, Moe buys a cup of green tea. This is a good choice because, frankly, I don't think Starbucks coffee tastes that good. But coffee, like beer, is a personal thing. I respect your right to throw away perfectly good money on overly bitter coffee. Hey, Budweiser is the world's best-selling beer, even though it tastes like hobo urine strained through a moccasin.

2:00 p.m. Just as it appears the women are about to finish up, one of them pulls out a paper and starts reading. The other one busies herself by chewing some gum.

2:05 p.m. Finally they leave. Moe and I move in, dragging over our satchels of equipment. The setup is perfect: We are tucked into the corner, with a large retaining wall separating us from the counter area. We are closest to the door, so we will have first dibs on any customers that enter the store.

2:10 p.m. I have put on a green apron and affixed my Starbucks Express nametag, which I printed up at Kinko's earlier this morning. We now have an extension cord running from the electrical outlet, to which we have hooked up a coffeemaker, cappuccino maker, the videocamera, and my laptop. If customers are allowed to plug in computers, I figure we can plug in anything we want. Otherwise, I believe we can sue on grounds of appliance discrimination.

2:13 p.m. I am now brewing a pot of hot coffee, using the Starbucks beans they generously ground for me a few minutes ago, and filtered water I brought from home. I also have the cappuccino machine heating up. Moe goes to the condiment bar to fetch some milk. A Starbucks within a Starbucks! The dream is coming true.

2:15 p.m. Let me describe the setup, so that historians will be able to recreate the first Starbucks Express franchise for their textbooks. Moe and I are facing each other in large overstuffed chairs, with our "homebrew" coffee station between us. We are not supposed to be filming inside the

Starbucks, so Moe is trying to hide the camera under his coat. He looks totally suspicious, like he is concealing a tommygun.

But it is for the good of humanity that we are filming this historic moment: Imagine if someone had thought to videotape the caveman that learned to forge humanity's first crude tool! The Big Bang is just a theory—why? *Nobody caught it on film.* The coffee is almost finished, and I can't wait to start serving our first customers.

2:20 p.m. Coffee's done. I pour myself a cup. Perfect strength. I personally sample each cup before I serve it, which is another way that Starbucks Express will distinguish itself from the competition. Employees will be fully wired at all times, ready to take on an army of customers. Those who don't drink caffeine will be eligible for employer-subsidized crystal meth.

2:22 p.m. Manager comes over, looking surprised. He asks us to stop filming. Moe agrees to stop filming, lowering the camera and continuing to film. I will only take brief notes from this point forward, and fill in the details later.

2:23 p.m. The manager asks why we're using the Starbucks logo.

"Not the Starbucks logo," I correct him, "the Starbucks **Express** logo."

"I need you to leave the store." He points at the door. "NOW."

Fortunately, my cappuccino machine has heated up, and I turn on the steam, which adds to the chaos immensely. *SCCCHHHHHHHHHSSSSSSHHHHH!* If you ever need to create a diversion during a difficult conversation, I recommend having a cappuccino maker nearby. Marital arguments, real estate negotiations, getting lectured by your parents about drugs: A blast of hot steam immediately distracts from uncomfortable topics.

CCCHHHHHHHSSSSSHCHCHHHSSCCCSSHHH whines the cappuccino machine.

"Can you get me a pitcher?" I ask the manager urgently, as my small cup of milk begins to overflow with froth. "I need something to hold this, so scalding milk doesn't go all over the place."

He looks exasperated. "Well, *why did you turn it on in the first place?*"

"I haven't done a lot of this. That's kind of the problem." I shoot him a pleading glance, and aim the nozzle of steam so that frothy milk blows onto my counterfeit apron.

"I'll get the pitcher," he agrees, "but then you have to leave."

He leaves to get the pitcher. Excellent.

2:25 p.m: As soon as he leaves, I shut off the steam and walk around the Starbucks, offering to top off customers' cups. "Top off?" I offer. "Warm it up?" It's always annoyed me that you can get free refills anywhere else in the country, but you have to pay for them at Starbucks. C'mon. If fucking Waffle House can top off your coffee, so can Starbucks.

"Foamer top off?" I ask a young man, offering to spoon out a dollop of frothy milk. But alas, the customers have just witnessed the scene between me and the manager, and he has instilled in their hearts a distrust for the Starbucks Express brand. No one accepts my "top 'er off" offer.

2:27 p.m: The manager returns with the pitcher, and is not happy to see me giving his customers better service than the existing Starbucks regime. "You need to leave NOW," he orders.

"We're just serving Starbucks coffee," I explain.

"LEAVE," he says, pointing at the door.

The assistant manager, a woman in her forties, has arrived for reinforcement. She puts her hand over Moe's camera, which is secreted in his lap. From my vantage point, it looks like she is granting him a sexual favor.

I try explaining the concept behind SBX to the manager, but everyone is talking over each other now. "Same coffee, faster service..."

"We're not the ones you need to submit this idea to," the manager rudely interrupts.

"Well, I sent in a business plan to Starbucks, but they didn't respond. Look, we're brewing Starbucks coffee, steaming Starbucks milk, serving it in a Starbucks. What's the problem here?"

The manager asks the barista behind the counter to call the police. If she does this as well as she rings up gift cards, I figure we've got at least another hour or two. Which is good, because packing is going to take a *long* time, with all our equipment and me taking notes on the laptop.

2:30 p.m: Two minutes later, the cops show up. I'm going to shut down the laptop now.

I Smell Bacon

We packed up the rest of our stuff—the cappuccino machine was still sizzling hot, causing multiple burns on our hands and arms—while two Boston policemen and all the store employees watched over us. This was a fine how-do-you-do. They laughed at Lee Iacocca, too, but that was mostly because he had a large scrotum. Not many people know that about the legendary businessman. The thing looked like an elephant's knuckle.

Moe and I dragged our three bags of equipment outside the door, escorted by the cops. Moe promptly dropped the glass espresso carafe, which shattered on the concrete.

"Oh boy," I said. "Sorry. We'll clean this up. Really sorry."

"What were you guys trying to do?" one of the police officers asked us.

Shattering the carafe was brilliant timing, as it added further confusion to the scene. "We were just brewing some Starbucks coffee," I said, distracted by the Starbucks customers trying to step around the broken glass.

"Why?" asked the cop. "Just curious." His partner, a steely-eyed white-haired officer, glared at us (good cop/bad cop).

I explained our Starbucks Express concept to the policeman. "It's a great idea, isn't it?" I asked him. "Same coffee, faster service?"

The police officer, whose profession requires standing in many lengthy coffee lines, agreed it was an excellent idea. He was clearly on our side. "Okay," he said, turning to leave.

"Hey, can I get a picture with you?" I asked, now that I knew he wasn't going to arrest us.

He laughed. "Well, I don't think that's a good idea." He and his partner walked back toward the cruiser. As we fumbled to get the lens cap off the camera, the cops got into their car and drove away. Probably to a Dunkin' Donuts.

Starbucks Coffee Company
PO Box 34067
Seattle, WA 98124-1067
206/447-1575

December 30, 2005

John Hargrave
SBX, Inc.
P.O. Box 990586
Boston, MA 02199

Subject: Product Sample or Idea

Dear John,

Thank you for your interest in Starbucks Coffee Company. We appreciate you wanting to share your materials with us. However, at this time, we are not interested in pursuing this opportunity with you because it does not align with our current needs.

Furthermore, because your materials included the use of our proprietary markings without Starbucks written authorization to do so, we request that you refrain from any reproductions, use or sale of the sample items or any similar items. To avoid any potential confusion or inadvertent infringement, we ask that you destroy any molds, models, blocks, stamps, silk screens, electronic data or other items used to reproduce Starbucks proprietary markings on these materials.

Thank you again for your interest in Starbucks.

Sincerely,

Customer Relations
Starbucks Coffee Company

Shirt-Changed

THERE ARE NO GUARANTEES IN LIFE.
That is, unless they're trying to sell us
something. Then we get "guaranteed satisfaction," "complete satisfaction," or "total satisfaction,"
backed by a "lifetime guarantee," "100% guarantee," or
"unconditional guarantee." We're promised a "lifetime
warranty" from their "quality-assured," "quality-
inspected," or "factory-certified" piece of crap, made
with their "uncompromising commitment to complete customer satisfaction."

But how often are we *really* satisfied? I didn't
think it was possible for *anything* to give 100 percent
satisfaction, with the possible exception of a hearty
bowel movement in an Applebee's parking lot. What
I wanted to find out was *just how long a company's
"100% guarantee" would last, when put to the test.*

My plan was to choose three clothing retailers
known for their outstanding guarantees and commitment to customer satisfaction. Then I would pit them
against each other in a "satisfaction deathmatch,"
ordering and returning the same basic T-shirt from
all three retailers, seeing who would crack first. My
three test subjects:

Lands' End has made a registered trademark out
of their claim. All merchandise from this famous
direct retailer is GUARANTEED. PERIOD.® Now, the
additional *period* is redundant, because there's
already a period at the end of *guaranteed*. A *third*
period would make an ellipses: GUARANTEED...
This would imply that something should follow,

like GUARANTEED... MOST OF THE TIME. Or:
GUARANTEED... UNTIL IT GROWS UNPROFITABLE
FOR US. I suspected this motto was more accurate,
even though it wasn't trademarked.

L.L.Bean, the famous clothing retailer, promises
"Our products are guaranteed to give 100% satisfaction in every way." This wording is also redundant,
since "100%" = "in every way." It's also not as charming as the original guarantee old L.L. posted on the
wall of his first store back in 1916, which read (not
a joke): I DO NOT CONSIDER A SALE COMPLETE UNTIL
GOODS ARE WORN OUT AND CUSTOMER STILL SATIS-
FIED. Unfortunately, he applied the same standards
to his sexual relations with *Mrs.* Bean, who later died
of excessive boning.

Nordstrom is known for having the highest
standard of customer service of any national retail
chain. They'll gift-wrap or ship anything for you
free of charge. Salespeople will often send their
customers personal handwritten notes. And their
"unconditional guarantee" states "if at any time, for
any reason, you're not completely satisfied with your
purchase, you may exchange it or return it." *At any
time.* Really? How about *1784?* You geniuses ready
to handle *time-travel paradoxes?* Don't make me go
all Stephen Hawking on your ass.

So: Lands' End, L.L.Bean, and Nordstrom. Whose
100 percent guarantee would run out first?

Round 1: Size Matters

I ordered a single item from all three retailers: a basic
men's T-shirt, size XL. Nordstrom's shirt was the most

expensive, and also the flimsiest: the fabric had the consistency of soggy Kleenex. The L.L.Bean and Lands' End shirts were both comparable in quality, suitable for wrestling grizzlies in the wild. As soon as I received the shirts, I returned them, enclosing the following letter:

John Hargrave
P.O. Box 990586
Boston, MA 02119

Lands' End
Lands' End Lane
Dodgeville, WI 53595

Dear Lands' End:

I recently lost some weight, and the enclosed T-shirt is a little too big for me. Can you replace it with a size medium?

A loyal customer,

John Hargrave

Round 1 was a softball. All they had to do was exchange the shirt for a different size. Lands' End and L.L.Bean made me pay the return postage, while Nordstrom generously included a postage-paid mailing label. I dropped the packages in the mail and received replacement T-shirts from all three retailers a few weeks later in size M. Now it was time to turn up the heat...*literally.*

Round 2: Sweatin' to the Oldies

I used each of the garments as a workout shirt for a full week, taking great care not to launder them. I wore a sweatshirt on top of the shirts, then sat in a sauna, so as to sweat out any impurities onto the filthy garments. After each workout, I would wring out the sopping shirt, leave it in a locker to dry, then put it on again the following day. By the end of each week, the shirts had body fluids on them that even *I* couldn't identify, and supposedly they came from *my body.*

I carefully sealed each shirt in a Ziploc freezer bag and left them to fester. The perspiration quickly fogged up the bags like a terrarium, giving birth to alien life-forms. After a few days, I peeked my nose into each bag, and it was revolting: high notes of homeless man's breath and incontinent dog, under-tones of wet socks, and a finish of bloody haddock. *Rank Spectator* would give it a "best buy," rating the odor 85 out of 100.

I returned each of the shirts to their respective retailers, along with the following note:

John Hargrave
P.O. Box 990586
Boston, MA 02199

L.L. Bean
3 Campus Drive
Freeport, ME 04034

Dear L.L. Bean:

Thank you for recently sending me a replacement shirt, but I've noticed a peculiar odor coming from this one. The tang is quite pungent, especially on hot days.

Would it be possible to send me another shirt?

Still a loyal customer,

John Hargrave

At this point, Lands' End threw in the towel. I received a check in the amount of $5.50, which

I guess is the value of the shirt, minus the value of shipping back to me. Since I had paid the shipping, I didn't understand this reasoning, but I was no longer 100 percent satisfied. Lands' End was out of the game.

Round 3: Out for Blood

Now it was a head-to-head grudge match. I ripped up the two remaining shirts, slathering them in ketchup and deli ham. Again, I enclosed the shirts in plastic bags, where the oozing ketchup gave them an eerie autopsy feel. Then I sent them back to Nordstrom and L.L.Bean, along with the same basic note:

John Hargrave
P.O. Box 990586
Boston, MA 02199

Nordstrom
7700 18th Street SW
Cedar Rapids, IA 52404

Dear Mr. Nordstrom:

Recently I lost a good deal of weight, thanks to Dr. Richard Porque's all-meat diet. You were generous enough to send me a replacement T-shirt (item #153600). I really appreciate your commitment to quality and customer satisfaction.

I wore the shirt on a recent safari expedition to Kenya, where my wife and I were the victims of an unfortunate incident: our tour bus was attacked by a wild zebra. I'm sure you think of the zebra as a mild and docile creature, as I did before the attack. You are thinking of zoo zebras, fat and lazy with their domesticated lifestyle, not wild zebras, which are ferocious in their desire for food and mating.

I was the closest to the window, so when I reached out to pet the animal, my arm and chest took the brunt of its attack. The incompetent fools who run this safari refused to pay for my medical expenses, claiming that the zebra's hostility was somehow MY fault. NOWHERE ON THE BUS DID IT STATE THAT FOOD WAS PROHIBITED! My wife and I tried registering a complaint with the local authorities, but they refused to help us, even though my zebra wounds were still open and bleeding.

I am enclosing my Nordstrom shirt, which I am hoping you will replace. I have enclosed the shirt in a plastic bag for sanitary reasons, and also because it smells like deli ham. (Obviously, I dropped my sandwich when the zebra attacked me.)

Thank you,

John Hargrave

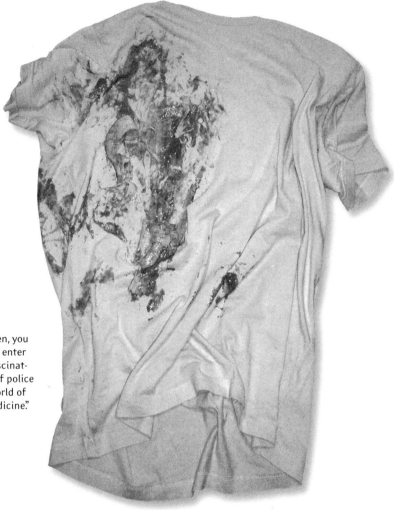

▶ "Gentlemen, you are about to enter the most fascinating sphere of police work: the world of forensic medicine."

A few days later, I received replacement shirts from both retailers. These guys were tenacious. But they had millions of customers to worry about satisfying, and I only had one: *myself.*

Round 4: Ach du Lieber

John Hargrave
P.O. Box 990586
Boston, MA 02199

L.L. Bean Returns
3 Campus Drive
Freeport, ME 04034

Dear L.L. Cool Bean:

I am still dissatisfied with this shirt, because it does not sing in German.

Oh sure, occasionally it will hum a little melody in Spanglish, but I find that annoying. As I was telling my pharmacist yesterday, my passion is the opera.

Thus, I would appreciate it if you would send me a replacement shirt, exactly like this one, but capable of singing German libretti. Preferably Wagner.

Danke schön,

John Hargrave

Finally, Nordstrom had had enough, sending me the following notice:

NORDSTROM

Order #: 25638455-0001
Item #: 1563600 SKY L

Dear Mr. Hargrave,

We have received your return and request for an exchange. Your return has been credited to your account, however we are unable to process your exchange request.

Sincerely,

Adam Seede
Contact Center Director
Nordstrom Direct

L.L.Bean, on the other hand, did send me a fourth replacement shirt, but I am sorry to report that it did not sing in German. This may seem like a minor point, but I *was* guaranteed 100 percent satisfaction. They didn't say anything about insanity.

So here are my final rankings:

Retailer	Satisfaction percentage
Lands' End	37%
Nordstrom	81%
L.L.Bean	96%

Round 5: L.L. Bribe

As I was wrapping up this chapter, I got one last letter from L.L.Bean. Wondering if they had finally developed the German-singing shirt technology, I opened the envelope to find: *another* refund check!

Yes, even after sending me a total of five shirts, L.L.Bean sent me a few extra bucks, because the T-shirt went on sale. I'm sorry, but *that* is customer service.

Retailer	Satisfaction percentage
Lands' End	37%
Nordstrom	81%
L.L.Bean	100%

I take it back. L.L.Bean has left me completely satisfied. Much as he completely satisfied *Mrs.* Bean, at least until she passed away from excessive porking. 😊

L.L.Bean

Dear Customer,

Your refund check is attached. Any portion of your payment made with Coupon Dollars will be added to any coupon dollars in your L.L.Bean Visa account. If we can be of further assistance please call our Customer Service Department at 1-800-341-4341. If you are calling from outside the United States or Canada, please select the appropriate number from the list below. We look forward to serving you again in the future.

Sincerely,
L.L.Bean Customer Service

	International Customer Service	
	Telephone	*FAX*
United Kingdom	0800-891-297	1-207-552-4080
Other Countries	1-207-552-6879	1-207-552-4080

OVERPAYMENT
THIS REFUND IS FOR AN OVERPAYMENT OR BECAUSE MERCHANDISE ON YOUR RECENT ORDER WAS ON SALE.

ORDER NUMBER   005102683306 000

MERCHANDISE VALUE	.00
TAX	.00
POSTAGE	.00
TOTAL AMOUNT	2.44

Guaranteed. You have Our Word.™

7336911

L.L.Bean *Freeport, Maine 04033*

Pay to the Order of: ************** TWO DOLLARS AND 44 CENTS ************

JOHN HARGRAVE $*****2.44

Fight the Power (Company)

I WOULDN'T BE DOING MY JOB if I didn't prank at least one utility company in this book. Telephone, cellphone, cable, gas, and oil: they gouge us with hidden fees, lock us into restrictive contracts, then give us terrible customer service when something goes wrong. Cable companies can send us an entire movie in seconds, but we still have to block out a four-hour window for one of their goddamn workers to come over to the house.

My own pet peeve is my electric company, NSTAR. I'll start with the bill:

Electricity Used			Cost of Electricity			
Rate A1-Residential Non-Heating			**Delivery Services**			
Meter 1718214			Customer Charge			6.43
Aug 29, 2005 Actual Read		6070	Distribution	.03912 X	667 KWH	26.09
Jul 30, 2005 Actual Read	-	5403	Transition *	.01645 X	667 KWH	10.97
30 Day Billed Use		667	Transmission	.00566 X	667 KWH	3.78
			Renewable Energy	.00050 X	667 KWH	0.33
1718214 KWH			Energy Conservation	.00250 X	667 KWH	1.67
07/30	547					
07/02	639		Delivery Services Total			49.27
05/31	499					
05/04	440		**Supplier Services**			
04/04	699		Generation Charge			
03/04	737		Basic Svc Fixed	.07694 X	667 KWH	51.32
02/01	734					
01/02	792		**Total Cost of Electricity**			**100.59**
12/02	684					
11/02	858					
10/02	756		*PART OF WHAT WE COLLECT IN THE TRANSITION*			
09/02	530		*CHARGE IS OWNED BY EACH OF BEC FUNDING LLC*			
08/03	712		*AND BEC FUNDING II LLC*			

It makes no fucking sense. "Transition Charge"? "BEC Funding II"? And for the love of sweet God, *why I am I paying an "Energy Conservation Charge"?* Only a ruthless monopoly would be able to charge me for conserving their energy. I'm paying *more* to use *less*. Sure, that makes sense…on the Planet of Retarded Chimps.

Rather than just blindly paying the bill, as I usually do, I called up their support line, where

I tried to get the surly customer service rep to explain some of this to me. She wasn't able to shed light on anything, which is distressing, since shedding light is their business.

"If you have problems with any of this, you should call the Department of Telecommunications and Energy," she said, testily.

"Right," I said, putting that on my to-do list right underneath ORAL SEX WITH A HOMELESS WOMAN.

"The DTE is our regulating body. They tell us what we can and can't charge."

"How is electricity made?" I asked, trying to steer her back to basics.

"In power plants," she replied.

"I know *that*," I said. "But how? Are magnets involved?"

"Sir, I don't know," she said. "I'm not a scientist."

"So you're billing me for a product that you don't understand, using billing terms that you can't explain, and unwilling to make changes without government intervention?"

There was a long pause. "Can I help you with anything else today?"

I took that as a yes.

It's Payback Time

If they were going to get creative with the way they billed me, I was going to get creative with the way I paid my bill. Using electricity, I ordered a bunch of computer-printable checks online. Then I wrote a quick random number generator, printing out *hundreds* of checks, ranging from a few cents to

several dollars. In the "memo" field, I made sure each
check contained a different insult: NSTAR IS MY
BITCH; NSTAR LICKS WOMBAT SCROTUM; NSTAR IS
NOT MY FAVORITE COMPANY; and so forth.

It was perfectly legal, and perfectly irritating.

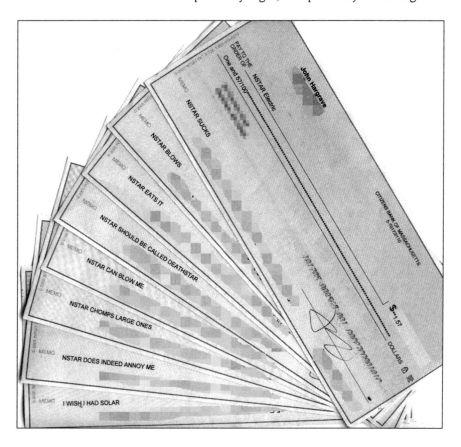

I had always wondered how obnoxious I could get
with my utility payments before they'd start to
complain, but what were they going to do, shut off
my service? They can't: *they're a monopoly!* I didn't
have a choice, and neither did they. Monopolies rule.

And so does Monopoly, especially if you own all the railroads.

A month later, I got my bank statement in the mail. It was stuffed in this *huge* office envelope, five times the size of my regular bank statement.

Salivating profusely, I opened the envelope to find it overflowing with canceled checks. *NSTAR had cashed every one of my annoying, insulting checks.*

Prankin' 2: Electric Boogaloo

I was drunk with power, so to speak, when I called VISA and asked them to add another person to my credit card account. I told them I had a Korean rock star living with me, and asked if they would mind issuing him a card, since I had recently entrusted him with all my finances.

"We'll be happy to add an additional person to your account," said the customer "care" "professional." Clackety-clack on the keyboard. "What name should we put on the card?"

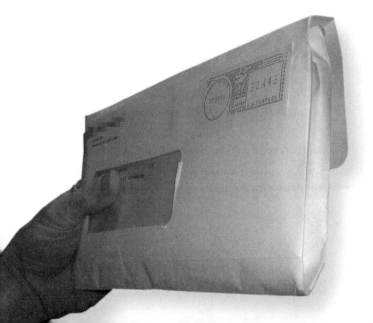

"His name is FUK YU NSTAR."

This didn't even faze him. "Could you spell that please?"

"Sure."

After we had clarified the spelling of my new Asian financial planner/solo guitarist, he repeated it back to me. "So we will send out a card to FUK YU NSTAR." He pronounced it "Fook You."

"I'm thrilled," I said. "And fook you, too."

"I'm sorry?"

"I said, Fuk Yu will be thrilled, too."

A few days later I received my utility-insulting card in the mail. Thanks, VISA!

As I like to say, if you can't beat 'em, then at least beat 'em up a little bit. If you've got to pay utility bills, try paying them with a credit card that insults them. I can't explain how rewarding it is. If you think cash back rewards are good, try a swearing credit card. Even more rewarding was the phone call to pay my bill, because I think I got the same customer service rep who wouldn't answer my questions in the first place. But then, they all sound alike.

> **CUSTOMER SERVICE REP:** How would you like to pay for that?
>
> **JOHN HARGRAVE:** Credit card.
>
> **CSR:** Okay, can I have the name on the credit card?
>
> **JH:** It's kind of long. Let me spell it for you.
>
> **CSR:** Go ahead.

JH: The first name is F-U-K.

CSR: Okay.

JH: The second one is Y-U.

CSR: Mmm-hmm.

JH: The third one is N-S-T-A-R.

CSR: *(flurry of typing, then a pause)* Is that really the name on the card?

JH: That should be the name on *everyone's* card.

It was so rewarding, my friends. They may be the power company, but for a few glorious moments, I felt like the power was all mine.

Three's Company

Comedy comes in threes, so I couldn't stop there. I used electricity to scan the credit card into my computer, then e-mailed the digital photo to Kinko's, where I asked them to print and mount it as large as they could. They had it waiting for me the next morning: a massive, 56-by-36-inch blowup of my FUK YU NSTAR credit card. It was like the wacky oversized checks they give to sweepstakes winners, except this one would be personally hand-delivered to NSTAR's chief executive officer, Tom May.

Rain fell in gray, drizzly sheets as I drove up the winding road to NSTAR's sprawling corporate campus. Perched atop a massive hill, it reminded me of a medieval fortress, only with better lighting. I drove up to the front gates of the castle, i.e., the reception lobby, carrying my enormous package, which I had thoughtfully gift wrapped.

An elderly security guard greeted me. He reminded me of the Quaker Oats guy. "What can I do for you?" he asked.

"Hi, I have a package here. It's for..." I pretended to check the label that I had printed up earlier that morning. "Tom May."

"Tom May?" he asked, surprised. "The CEO?"

"It says Tom May," I shrugged.

"Tom May," he mused, stroking his chin. "I've never had to deliver a package to him." He made a few phone calls, but didn't get anywhere. "Why don't you just drop it off, and I'll make sure it gets to him."

"Sounds good," I said, producing a clipboard with a fake signature sheet. "I just need you to sign for it."

"No problem," he said, giving John Hargrave his John Hancock.

"Post-9/11 security regulations also require me to get visual proof that I delivered the package to this address," I said, producing a digital camera. If you want to get away with anything, just mention 9/11. At least, that's what the CIA told me.

"Sure," he said, taking the camera awkwardly.

I spotted a large NSTAR sign behind the security desk. "Let's get a shot in front of that," I said, casually walking into his restricted security area.

"Yeah, that'll be great," he agreed, snapping my picture (see next page).

Thanking him for giving me something to write about, I drove away from the NSTAR fortress, chuckling over my modern-day Trojan horse. I felt electric.

▲ Apologies for the glare, but that place had too much lighting.

May Day

A week later, I called Tom May's office to make sure he had received my gift. I was connected to his receptionist, who sounded skittish. "Who is this?" she asked quietly, her voice trembling.

"Oh, this is John," I said. "I just wanted to make sure Tom got my package."

"Let me connect you with someone who can help you," she whispered fearfully, then abruptly transferred me to NSTAR security.

I think I got the same security guy who accepted the package in the first place. But then again, they all sound alike. "Who is this?" he asked, his tone more incredulous than angry.

"John Hargrave," I replied. "Did Tom get my gift?"

"It's down here with me now," replied the Oatmeal Guy.

"What are you going to do with it?"

"What do you mean, *what are we going to do with it?*"

"I was wondering if you could hang it on the wall. A little morale booster for the employees."

A pause. "Is there something I can help you with, sir?"

"Actually, yes. I have some questions about my bill, and I've been looking for someone who can answer them."

"I see. Tell you what," he offered, "let me take your number, and I'll have someone call you back."

"Sure." I gave him my cellphone number.

"And what do you want us to do with this giant credit card?"

"Raffle it off at the company party," I suggested.

We hung up, and I figured that was the last I would hear from anyone. But the next day, I got a call from Tim, my personal NSTAR customer service representative. Tim could not have been more pleasant and cordial, patiently enduring dozens of questions about my bill. I learned how electricity is made (magnets *are* involved), and how much it would cost on my bill if I electrocuted someone (almost nothing). After the interrogation was complete, Tim made the critical mistake of giving me his personal extension. Jackpot!

Now any time I have questions about my bill, I just give Tim a call. That's how I found out, just before this book went to press, that NSTAR is introducing *a simplified electric bill to all its customers.* Can you believe it? I took on the utility company, and won. Next time you're frustrated with your local monopoly, try my solution: *a massive, swearing credit card.* Apparently, that's all it takes. I've got my own NSTAR rep on call, and they're simplifying the bill. It's brilliant.

I thought fighting the power company was a big accomplishment. But then I came to my next target, a group so insidious and vile that it required an entire section of my book. ☕

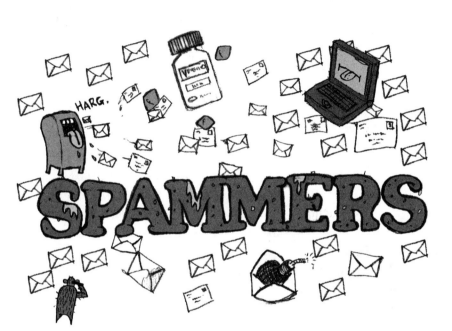

Good Morning, Vietspam

SPAMMERS CLOG OUR INBOXES with over 100 billion pieces of unsolicited e-mail *every day*,[1] trying to convince us to buy products that we don't want, often through illegal offshore companies. They're responsible for more than $21 billion in lost productivity each year,[2] not to mention ripping off millions of innocent consumers, like me, who buy their crap. They send pornography to the mailboxes of children, and Cialis advertisements to the mailboxes of nuns. With all that hanging on their conscience, you may wonder if they can sleep well at night. But I can tell you with some authority that they do.

Dolf DeRoos, the New Zealand-born entrepreneur who had been spamming me with invitations to his get-rich-quick real estate seminars, was sleeping soundly in his hotel room in La Jolla, California. He needed his rest, since he was a featured speaker at the Tony Robbins Wealth Mastery Seminar later that morning, where Dolf would be convincing hundreds of convention attendees and suckers to "never work another day of your life unless you choose to."

It was 4:00 in the morning when the phone rang in his hotel room. It took him a while to find the phone, but he eventually answered with the quiet terror of someone being roused unexpectedly from stage 4 REM sleep.

"Hello?" he whispered into the phone, groggy and disoriented.

1. "Got 2 Extra Hours for Your E-Mail?," *New York Times*, November 11, 2005. Also see "Spam Costs Are Rising at Work," *Washington Post*, June 7, 2004.

2. "Spam Costs Billions," *Information Week*, February 3, 2005.

On the other end, I was awake and refreshed, having enjoyed a good night's sleep and the luxury of being three hours ahead of Dolf's time zone.

"Good morning, Dolf!" I responded cheerily. "My name's John. I keep getting this series of unsolicited e-mails from you. The subject is, WILLING TO SELL MY REAL ESTATE WEALTH-BUILDING SECRET. Here's what the e-mails say."

And then I read him, word for word, the entire e-mail that he had been sending me relentlessly, incessantly, mercilessly, for the past few months.

It was a long message, especially since I insisted on reading out the 263-character unsubscribe link at

DOLF DE ROOS

Build real estate wealth – *practically overnight!*

AUTHOR, SPEAKER AND ENTREPRENEUR

World's Leading Real Estate Expert Silences His Critics With Impossible Task

"In ten years," challenged Dolf de Roos, "I will increase my net worth ten-fold." And he did indeed achieve his goal...
...5 years early!!

"I AM SHARING MY REAL ESTATE SECRETS FOR THE FIRST TIME!"

Now Dolf de Roos's new program is available for a limited time only. This is a LIMITED OFFER that gives you the keys to OWNING, BUYING, and RENTING your own real estate empire!

"I Started Out With Just One Property, A House Like Yours, and Showed My Critics Why My Real Estate Investment System Is Like A Cash-Generating Machine!"

Why are Other Investor's Afraid of Dolf de Roos?

Dolf de Roos's new investment program is the only certified real-estate invest-the bottom, letter for letter. Altogether, it took about five minutes to read all that random junk to Dolf, since I recited each page of the e-mail at a slow, measured pace. I didn't rush myself; I wanted to savor the moment.

God bless him, he stayed with me through the entire thing. I thought for sure he'd hang up and go back to sleep, but this man's dedication was remarkable. But I already knew that, because he had been sending me this same e-mail for months, never varying the message, even though I'd never expressed any interest in real estate seminars, and despite me actively trying to get off his list. Give this guy a copy of *The Watchtower* and a free Saturday afternoon, and he'd make an excellent Jehovah's Witness.

Get Rich Quick or Die Tryin'

A few weeks earlier, in a fit of frustration at seeing his annoying face pop up repeatedly in my Inbox, I Googled Dolf's name. I thought perhaps I could talk to him personally, tell him I wasn't interested in his get-rich-quick schemes. Google returned an entertaining, point-by-point analysis of Dolf's book *Real Estate Riches: How yo Become Rich Using Your Banker's Money* by John T. Reed, an author of twenty real estate investment books and self-described "real estate B.S. artist detector." Reed explains:

> [Dolf] has a Ph.D. in electrical engineering, but manages to sound like a college dropout from a non-selective liberal arts program.

Reed has an MBA from Harvard, so I trust him on this one. Continuing:

He constantly spouts "facts" that are merely conventional
wisdom and, after cautioning against comparing apples
and oranges, proceeds to do just that repeatedly.[3]

Reed goes on like this for 9,000 more words
(or nearly as long as a single e-mail from Dolf),
systematically destroying his real estate advice as
"nonsense," "a pack of lies," and "the opposite of
the truth." In fact, my only criticism of Reed is that he
runs out of synonyms for "dishonesty."

But Dolf *is* honest, or at least that's what he tells
us. In his single message, which I received 43,100
times,[4] he describes his rise to success. His big *a-ha!*
moment came when he realized that "almost without
exception, the rich had integrity." I assume the
exceptions would be Michael Jackson, Bernie Ebbers,
Kenneth Lay, Saddam Hussein, O.J. Simpson, Idi Amin,
Pol Pot, Mao Tse-Tung, Al Capone, Joseph Stalin, and
Genghis Khan. And possibly Dolf de Roos, because of
all the crap he e-mailed me.

Stalk This Book

It was pretty easy to track down Dolf's office number,
since it's listed prominently on his Web site. Posing
as a half-witted real estate investor, I called the
office, where his receptionist Gina answered the
phone. Gina told me that Dolf was doing a few out-
of-town speaking engagements, but he'd be back on
Monday. I asked if I could have his cellphone number.
Gina was reluctant to give that out, even when I
explained that the Koknokker deal was about to fall
apart. I asked for his e-mail, but she wouldn't give
me that, either.

3. John T. Reed's analysis
of Dolf de Roos' book
Real Estate Riches,
www.johntreed.com/
DeRoos.html

4. Give or take 43,000.

"What's with the shroud of secrecy around Dolf?" I asked Gina.

"You don't know how many people call here and want to talk to him personally," she responded.

"I'll bet I do," I said, but only to myself.

"He just doesn't have time to answer everyone's questions."

"Or listen to everyone's complaints," I said, in my brain.

I thanked her for her time, said I'd call back when he was in the office.

Fortunately, Dolf had listed his speaking itinerary on his Web site. I found out that he'd be a guest lecturer at the Tony Robbins Wealth Mastery Seminar on Friday, which costs $3,745.00 to attend, making me wonder if people are actually paying to watch Tony Robbins master *his* wealth. From there, it was a simple matter to find that the convention was being held at the Hyatt Regency La Jolla. Figuring that Dolf would be staying at the same hotel, I called the Hyatt and asked if Dolf de Roos had checked in. "Just a moment," said the polite young man at the front desk. "No sir, he hasn't arrived yet."

"And he'll be there through Sunday?" I asked, counting on the Hyatt's exceptional customer service.

"Let's see." I heard him typing on his computer. "No sir, he'll be checking out Saturday."

"Thanks," I said. "I'll make sure to call him tomorrow morning, then."

JOHN HARGRAVE: So that's how the e-mail reads, Dolf. But here's the problem: none of your unsubscribe methods actually work.

DOLF DE ROOS: Well, thanks for going through all that detail. Do you know what time it is?

JH: Hmm. That depends. What time zone are you in?

DDR: Where are you calling from?

JH: Oh, somewhere else.

DDR: Somewhere else. Are you at the event here?

JH: I'm calling on behalf of all the people who are getting your unsolicited e-mails, and we have a few requests. First of all, can we get *one* method of unsubscribing? There are four different unsubscribe methods listed on this e-mail. And second, can we get an unsubscribe method that actually *works*? Third, can we switch up the e-mails a little bit? Just a new photo, or something?

DDR: I'll manually take you off the list.

JH: I appreciate that. But I'm calling on behalf of everyone getting your e-mail.

DDR: Fine. Just give me your e-mail address and I'll unsubscribe you.

JH: But Dolf, *everyone* receiving your e-mail has the same problems. So can you work with your spam company to find a way to solve these issues?

DDR: Well firstly, that's not my company. And by law, they have to provide multiple ways to unsubscribe, because not everyone can write, or phone, or whatever.

JH: Right. And by law, aren't they supposed to actually unsubscribe you if you request it?

DDR: *(pause)* I've got to tell you, calling at 4 a.m. is rude.

JH: Right. It's also kind of rude to send the same e-mail to me dozens...

DDR: Yeah. I get it. *(angrily)* I've got the message loud and clear. Now, how many times do you want to ask me the same question?

JH: Until something gets done about it.

DDR: You've gone through this ridiculous effort of reading out every detail, every character on that e-mail. You've made your point loud and clear.

JH: Super.

DDR: I'm just keeping you on the line so we can trace the call.

JH: Sounds good.

DDR: Are you at this event? How else would you know I'm here?

JH: So what we need to do, Dolf...

DDR: Are you at the event? *Are you at the event?* You're not talking *with* me, you're talking *at* me. You are the epitome of rudeness.

JH: I find that insult rather ironic.

DDR: Well, I'm sure you do. You just don't understand what you're doing, do you?

JH: I'm trying to cut down on the amount of spam I receive?

DDR: Do you have a whitelist/blacklist system?

JH: Should I *need* to have a whitelist/blacklist system?

DDR: Oh, John. That's not even your real name. Listen: if you hassle me again, I'm going to find out where the call is coming from. I think I'll do that right now.

JH: Okay.

DDR: Are you calling internally? Are you calling internally?

JH: Dolf, I think that...

DDR: Okay, that's it. Good-bye.

And then he hung up on me. On the bright side, though, he probably had a hard time getting back to sleep.

How to Make Spammers Pay

I was walking on air the rest of the day. It was fun, tracking down spammers one by one, but it was time consuming. Who has the patience? Eventually, however, I found a better way. I wrote a series of prank articles for my Web site where I actually *ordered products* from spammers—pills, creams, and sexual aids—then reported on the real-life results when I ingested, smeared, or probed myself with their products.

These stories, which you'll read in the following chapters, got passed heavily around the Internet, because everyone hates a spammer—but secretly, everyone is curious about those herbal remedies and anal beads. After a while, my "Viagra" prank got so popular that it started showing up in the top ten search results on Google for the word "Viagra." On the Monopoly board of the Internet, this is like owning Park Place. (Boardwalk is "sex.")

So now I have a lucrative side business: selling advertising space to spammers in the very articles that ridicule them. Hey, it keeps them off the streets, and out of your mailbox. Besides, it's the only way to truly give payback to the spammers: making the spammers pay *you* back. ☺

THE V1@GRA PRANK

OKAY, OKAY, *I'LL BUY THE VIAGRA!*

Sweet Lord. How many e-mails do the Viagra people have to send me? "73% off VIAGRA!" they scream at me. "We've slashed prices because of the competition!!" which is exactly the kind of thing you want to hear coming from your pharmacist. "dan Theresa amanda Butthead nothing abgrossm steph quebec Doobie!" the e-mails triumphantly conclude, bypassing my spam filter. "sparky jesus1 groin infection!"

I get a hundred of these e-mails a day. Clearly, the online Viagra people know something about my penis that I don't.

So my reasoning went like this: maybe if I bought some of their precious Viagra, they would shut the hell up. As a bonus, I would actually *own some Viagra*, which I could use to surprise my wife on Valentine's Day. "Oh, darling!" she would exclaim. "Twelve hours of painful, nonstop intercourse? You shouldn't have!"

So I did it. I took the bait. I spent a day surfing the Viagra sites, and I was shocked by what I found. I had expected unethical, quasi-legal Web sites dispensing dangerously inaccurate medical advice. Instead, I found unethical, quasi-legal Web sites dispensing dangerously inaccurate medical advice *from people dressed up to look like doctors.*

Here's Dr. Alex Broers from the renowned medical journal s95forcheapmeds.nepzzz.com, who claims "This product is 100% SAFE tested in medical labs, and personally by me." Which means that Dr. Broers is impotent. Ha ha! "I happen to know this drug will work," went the second (and more revealing) part of Dr. Broers's endorsement, "because I myself have a limp, sagging penis." You'll notice they don't mention what kind of doctor he is. That's because he is a doctor of *love*.

100% APPROVED by all doctors

"This product is 100% SAFE tested in medical labs, and personally by me."

Dr. Alex Broers

Site after site I visited. Sites with trustworthy, dependable names like PillStore, PlanetPills, and KwikMed. A little-known fact is that *every* Viagra site offers the lowest prices on Viagra. And all lowest prices are "guaranteed."

In the end, I went with AmeriMedRx.com, which offered me the cheapest deal on Viagra (guaranteed), and two-day shipping to boot. I entered my credit card information, but then hit a roadblock. It seems you need to provide *actual medical information* in order to receive your Viagra. So I filled out the form as honestly as I could (see next page).

I could only hope that Dr. Alex Broers would be the one to review my application. He's the love doctor. He would understand.

AmeriMed the Bonerful

So I ordered some Viagra via the AmeriMed Web site, a "discreet, safe, and confidential" online pharmacy where you can "SUPER SAVE" on everything from painkillers to herpes medication.

I couldn't believe I actually had to *prove that I needed Viagra* before they'd send it to me. In fact,

General Patient Information

Patient First Name:	John
Patient Last Name:	Hargrave
Enter patient height:	5'7"
Enter patient weight:	165 lbs
Enter patient gender:	Male
Enter patient birthdate in mm/dd/yyyy format	04-April 01 1969

Please list all medications you are currently taking:

Theo-Dur, Alupent, Azmacort, Prednisone, Ibuprofen, Tylenol, Aspirin, Caffeine, Nicotine, Alcohol, Nitrous Oxide (not since high school), The Apprentice (addicted to it!), Birth Control Pills

Please list all medications that you plan to take while on this program:

See above.

Please list all allergies(include medications for any allergies):

Animals: Cats, dogs, horses, llamas, ferrets, Star Jones, many other barnyard animals. Trees: birch, beech, maple, oak, elm, the larch, the mighty scotch pine. Music: Linkin Park, Metallica,

Please list any surgeries:

Ass surgery (several years ago).

Please list any medical conditions for which you are currently being treated:

Asthma, hang nails.

(Required) Please explain the specific reason for ordering this medication. The physician must know the exact nature of the medical problem in order to prescribe this medication:

I want to make sweet, sweet love all night long.

Any additional information you'd like to share?

I once masturbated into a grapefruit.

I didn't think anyone was even reading the applications, so I filled out the form with wacky, albeit truthful, answers. A few days later, I received my "discreet, safe, and confidential" response.

Hey, this really *was* just like dealing with a real doctor! I received the same careful, thoughtful

explanation that I usually receive
from my own physician:
Still, I wanted a little
more information on why
my Viagra prescription was
being turned down, so I
called AmeriMed customer
service and gave them my
tracking number.

> **Message From Doctor**
> **Posted On 1/24/2004 4:00:50 PM**
> Dear John,
>
> We are unable to prescribe the medication you requested.
>
> Sincerely,
>
> AmeriMedRx Physician Services
> http://www.amerimedrx.com

AMERIMED: Thank you for calling AmeriMed. I'm Evelyn,
how can I help you?

JOHN HARGRAVE: Hi, I recently put in an order for a
prescription, and I was denied. The response you guys
sent me was actually rather rude.

AM: All right...what were you ordering?

JH: Viagra.

AM: Okay, let's see. *(pause)* It looks like it was denied because the doctor couldn't find the medical necessity, and
probably because of all the excess medica ti ons you're taki ng.

JH: Such as?

AM: Ah...do you smoke marijuana?

JH: Only in the shower.

AM: Prednisone, Azmacort, Alupent...do you have asthma?

JH: Only since I started smoking marijuana.

AM: Well, [Viagra] is one medication he would prefer...
he would prefer you see a doctor. It's for your benefit,
it's not an insult, it's simply that he feels that for your
health, you should see a local doctor.

JH: But your Web site says that AmeriMed was founded
to help me avoid "an embarrassing conversation with
my personal physician."

AM: Uh huh, but that's if it's approved...this physician is
not going to approve it.

JH: Is there another physician we could ask?

AM: No, we are very strict in our regulations, and we have to ask that you go see a local doctor.

JH: Look, Evelyn. I need a longer erection in my penis. Can you help me with this?

AM: I wish that I could help you, but I can't. I suggest you see a local doctor.

JH: Don't you understand that I have a *condition*? I am not well!

AM: Sir, I...

JH: I can sometimes only make love for one hour. Do you know how embarrassing that is? I mean, you're a woman. You know what I'm talking about here, don't you?

AM: I do understand, however again, I can't help you. You're going to have to see your local doctor.

JH: I don't believe this. Evelyn, listen to me: I can only sustain an erection for one hour, two hours tops.

AM: I realize that, and I don't mean to be insensitive. Again, I'm...this isn't meant as an insult to you personally. We just can't help you, unless you can get a prescription from your local doctor.

JH: Would you deny medication to a dying child?

AM: I don't...

JH: Well, my penis is like a dying child.

AM: *(growing increasingly agitated)* Sir, I cannot continue this conversation.

JH: How about you guys send me the Viagra, bill me an extra fifty dollars, and we'll call it even.

AM: I cannot do that. You're asking me to not only compromise my licensing, but...

JH: Oh, you guys are *licensed*?

AM: *(clearly offended)* Yes.

JH: Oh! Oh...oh. Oh. Well, that's a different story.

AM: You're asking me to compromise my licensing, and we simply cannot do this.

JH: Look, Evelyn. Would *you* be willing to personally fill the prescription for me, and maybe I can pay you for your services?

AM: Mr. Hargrave, I cannot continue this conversation. I have other calls to attend to.

JH: Could we meet up in an alley somewhere?

AM: All right, I'm going to take this call rather offensively. I'm letting you know that this is an offensive conversation, and I am going to hang up.

JH: Evelyn, Evelyn. Before you go. Listen.

AM: Yes.

JH: Think you can score me some Oxycontin?

AM: *(hangs up)*

So apparently, these places are a little touchy about that kind of thing. But the question remained: *What would I have to do to score some V-Bone?*

The Viagra Arrives

The secret to ordering drugs online, I discovered, is that you have to *lie*.

Can you believe that? You have to *lie* in order to get the Viagra. See, when their online form asks why you're ordering the drug, instead of writing:

I want to make love like a mighty steed.

You're supposed to say:

Male sexual function problems (erection problems)

My Viagra arrived a few days later, filled by a Spanish pharmacy in Miami. "No detailed information is available about this drug," said the packing slip—which was disturbing, since the official Viagra site has a 1,700-word fact sheet on the dangers of the drug, including the terrifying specter of "permanent damage to the penis." As I found out later, the permanent damage to the penis can occur because of *excessive sex*, but I'm getting ahead of myself.

"Consult your pharmacist if you have questions," the packing slip continued. Now, do they mean my *regular* pharmacist, or the shady Cuban pharmacist who sold me an FDA-regulated drug over the Internet? Somebody clear this up for me.

With shipping, it ran me $100 for three tablets, but that was a small price to pay for what I was about to do with it. You see, I was most intrigued by this claim on the Viagra Web site:

> You will not get an erection just by taking this medicine. VIAGRA helps a man with erectile dysfunction get an erection only when he is sexually excited.

There was only one way to test this outlandish claim: I would take Viagra at the one place I knew I wouldn't get sexually excited, and then I'd see what happened.

I would take Viagra in church.

Sunday, Randy Sunday

There we were, a normal American family going to church: Mom, Dad, and our young child. Except unbeknownst to those around us, Dad was hopped up on Viagra.

To be fair, I didn't take the Viagra *in* church. I took the Viagra *before* church, since the official Web site advises, "Take VIAGRA about one hour before you plan to have sex." This is great for those of us who plan our sex on a schedule. I have Microsoft Outlook configured to pop up a reminder when I've got a sex appointment in fifteen minutes. Sometimes my wife has to plan two, three months ahead to get on my sex calendar.

So the three of us made our way into the sanctuary, and sat in the back row. I had no idea what was going to happen, and since the Viagra literature also warns of "permanent damage to the penis," among other side effects, I wanted to have an escape route planned. If I felt permanent penis damage coming on, at least I'd be able to pull someone aside for some quick prayer, and maybe the laying on of hands.

After the organ prelude (heh), the service started. I sat quietly, listening to the choir, closely watching my lap for any popup ads. Let's just say that I was "Spocking it," i.e., exercising mind control to keep it down, a technique I perfected during ninth grade gym class. Still, when it came time for the children's sermon,

▲ I had to use the digital camera on my PDA, lest I draw attention to myself.

I had a partially inflated balloon animal on my hands. Smirking, my wife asked me if I wanted to take the toddler down to the front of the sanctuary with the other kids. "Honey, that kind of thing is frowned upon here," I whispered. "This is a *Protestant* church."

Following the children's sermon, my wife and son went to play in the kids' room, and I was left alone with my increasingly turgid thoughts. I flipped through my pew Bible to follow along with the Old Testament reading, and what page should I open to but the exceedingly horny Song of Songs:

> Your navel is a rounded goblet
> that never lacks blended wine.
> Your waist is a mound of wheat
> encircled by lilies.
>
> Your breasts are like two fawns,
> like twin fawns of a gazelle.
>
> —Song of Songs 7:2-3

Not wanting to read, but unable to look away,
I scanned down to the next steamy passage:

> I said, "I will climb the palm tree;
> I will take hold of its fruit."
> May your breasts be like clusters of grapes on the vine,
> the fragrance of your breath like apples,
> and your mouth like the best wine.
>
> —Song of Songs 7:8-9

In my pants stirred our twenty-eighth President, Woodrow Wilson.

▲ *"Those who are able,* please stand." Needless to say, I didn't.

I tried to listen to the sermon, but I could not focus. My head felt very hot, as if blood were rushing to my face. So did my marriage tackle, which was slowly engorging over the thought of those hot, wet Bible verses. And it didn't help that the young woman a few rows in front of me was wearing tight jeans. *Curse these modern churches and their liberal dress codes!*

Fortunately, I had brought along my overcoat, which I strategically placed across my lap as I tried to finish out the rest of the service. Man, I never realized how much standing you do in church. Sit, stand. Sit, stand. It's like a friggin' aerobics routine. Fortunately, the church bulletin had a footnote: *"Those who are able,* please stand."

In summary, I think the Viagra people should update their claim: "VIAGRA helps a man with erectile dysfunction get an erection only when he is sexually excited." They should add, "...but *anything* will get him sexually excited, including the Holy Word of God."

So there you have it. If it's true that "Christians aren't perfect, just forgiven," then I must be the best Christian in the world. After church, I met up with my wife, who looked at my puffy, reddened face and said, "You're swollen."

"You don't know the half of it," I said.

Later, however, she would not only know the half of it, but the *four* and a half of it.

What Viagra Feels Like

So my little experiment of taking Viagra in church resulted in a rush of blood to the old man, as I predicted. *After* the service, however, my wife and I had the entire afternoon free. And it's a good thing.

Let me clear up one thing: Viagra does not help you last longer. If you can only fish for three or four minutes before spilling the chowder, Viagra will not help you there. And, quite frankly, that's where I need the most help. I've had sneezes that have lasted longer than my lovemaking.

But it's the recovery, my friends, that really works. There is no down time. Rebooting (or should I say "rebootying") is instantaneous. You're the Insatiable Loggerman. It's like the Energizer Bunny, if, instead of banging that drum, he was banging the crap out of his lover. That's what the drum represents, you know. That rabbit is as gay as a French horn.

Anyway, partway into the seventeenth or eighteenth time, I suddenly realized that *my wife hadn't taken a drug.* She was this way naturally. Do you see what I'm, ah, *driving* at here? Suddenly I was made aware of how little I had been doing all these years to satisfy my wife! Viagra SUCKS!

"You know, honey," I said several hours later, after we had finished hosing down the walls and laundering the bedsheets, "we've still got two pills left."

She looked crestfallen. *"Only two?!"* she cried.

In conclusion, I must urge the men out there: stay away from Viagra. It is a Pandora's box of truth. Despite how much you may want to get into Pandora's box, Viagra will force you to gaze at the hideous reality: *men are lousy lovers.* ☺

Hot Rod

I RECENTLY RECEIVED AN E-MAIL from a woman named Lela Jenna, where she made fun of the size of my penis. Even though my penis has never met Ms. Jenna, she still had the audacity to write this:

John Hargrave

From: Lela Jenna
To: John Hargrave
Sent: Monday, April 26 11:32 PM
Subject: Ur Diicky Is So Smaall chief vibratile freeloader

The world most--effecctive male enhance-ment pill

Increase the length of your DICCKY by 2-5 full inches

Thicken ur DICCKY and make it much fuller & harder

CLICK HERE TO ORD.ER NOWW!

At first, I was hurt. "What's wrong with the size of my DICCKY?" I thought to myself. "No woman has ever made fun of my length, nor my girth."

"At least, *not to your face*," added my ruthlessly cruel self-esteem.

Just as few women are happy with their breasts, I think most guys are unhappy with their penises, which is why they beat them so often. And we wouldn't be receiving up to forty "penis enlarge-ment" e-mails a day if there weren't so many guys buying these solutions. So I decided to try a little experiment: *I would take the penis pills and report what happened.*

I spent many hours browsing Web sites for the best penis enlargement product, and came to the con-clusion that we are a nation of men with minuscule organs. The average penis size, I found out, is between 5.5 and 6 inches—but apparently women want lovers who need to drape their penises over a hook at night, lest they get all tangled up in penis as they sleep.

"How long do you continue to take VIMAX PILLS?" asks the Web site for Vimax, one of the 25,000 penis pills on the market. The surprising answer: "Our recommendation is when you get to 8 inches stop taking VIMAX PILLS but the choice is up to you." But what if you don't stop at 8 inches? I could just imagine my penis growing to 44 or 45 inches in size, long enough to get the leaves out of my gutters in the springtime. That would be awesome.

But wait, there's more! In addition to "mind-blowing orgasms" and "improved sexual stamina," some pills can also "triple the amount of semen you produce." This is from prosolutionspills.com, which promises, and I quote, "It will flow out all over your girlfriend drowning her in your semen. The power of your ejaculation will improve so when your orgasm is 'shoots out.'" [sic] Call me a romantic, but I would never want to drown a lover in my semen. Sure, we might go swimming in the pool I had generously filled with man-gravy, but we would exercise safety and caution. There would be no horseplay.

Regardless, I needed a *real* guarantee. I didn't want gains of "up to" "3+ inches," in "as little as" "several weeks." I wanted a *hard and fast* claim, if you'll pardon the expression. Either the penis pills delivered, or they didn't. Finally, while doing a Google search for "penis enlargement" (which currently returns 1.3 million results—try it yourself), I found an ad that promised "2, 3, even 5 inches in sixty days or less—GUARANTEED!"

Bingo! I would gain 2 inches or more within sixty days. It was guaranteed. Excitedly, I ordered the pills. Imagine the look on Lela Jenna's face, after I had packed on an additional 2, 3, or even 5 inches. I'm telling you, the woman never should have made fun of my DICCKY.

I Wish I Had Oscar Meyer's Wiener

But did I really *need* a longer penis? I was faithful to my wife, and she hadn't complained so far. Then it started to nag at me, and I had to get out a ruler... *just in case.* I had to figure out where I stood on the bell curve of penises (which, to be really accurate, would need to be curved slightly upward).

So: *what is the average penis size?* The famous *Kinsey Sex Report,* considered by many to be the authority on such matters, says the average Snausage "is between 5 and 7 inches when erect." A more recent study by Lifestyles Condom Company—and I figure they've seen more penises than the Kinsey people— puts the average at **5.877 inches.** They obtained this figure by sending a team of nurses to Cancun during spring break, and having them measure the erections of hundreds of partying college students (sadly, I'm not making this up).

But what about *width?* In 2001, the University of Texas Pan-American put out a research paper entitled "Penis Size: Survey of Female Perceptions of Sexual Satisfaction." They surveyed fifty sexually active female undergraduates (making it the sexiest research paper ever) on whether *length* or *width* was more important to sexual satisfaction. My favorite line of thearticle is, "None reported they did not know," making me sad that I did not go to the University of Texas Pan-American. A surprising 90 percent (or forty-five out of the fifty co-ed sluts interviewed) reported that *width is more important.*

So maybe the ultimate penis shape, I thought, is a *tuna can:* 1 inch long and 5 inches wide. Somehow I don't think so. You never hear women moaning, "Oh, give it to me *wide. Give me several inches more in diameter.*"

It turns out that you measure width by going *around* your penis. I discovered that this is difficult, unless you have one of those cloth tape measures that dressmakers use—but if you own one of those things, you're probably not the kind of guy worrying about his penis size. At any rate, I tried to use my Craftsman tape measure, because I thought some of its testosterone would rub off on me. Unfortunately, I lost my grip on it, and the tape measure snapped shut, seizing a patch of sensitive skin in its iron jaws.

After I finished screaming, I finally ended up using an ordinary ruler, and here are my measurements:

Length	5.875 inches
Width	4.125 inches

Do you see why I need these penis pills? I am 0.002 inches smaller than the national average, which is humiliating. *Curse my parents and their recessive penis gene!*

On the bright side, I found an easy way to gain an extra half-inch: just *push the ruler into your abdomen*. Using this trick, I am now over six inches, or *well above* the average penis length.

But let's be honest: I'm one foreskin shy of the national average. I was kind of bummed out about this, until I saw a picture of Michelangelo's *David* on one of the penis enlargement Web sites. After all, David is the idealized male figure. You don't get more perfect than Dave. I spent several minutes today examining myself in a mirror next to a picture of David. I estimated that, if David were normal human size, his flaccid penis would be approximately 2.5 inches long. I RULE! He may be ideal, but I'm packing more veal.

▲ I will admit he has better abs.

The Penis Pills Arrive

As soon as I received my penis pills in the mail, I opened the bottle to find that the safety seal was broken. I thought this was kind of gross. I mean, if you're going to sell a non-regulated, quasi-legal medication, the least you can do is *glue down the safety seal.* On the other hand, it did give an element of added danger to the experiment. I dumped out my Magna-RX pills on the counter, inspecting them carefully for used hypodermic needles, or anthrax.

Then I started to get nervous. A lethal dose of penis pills would be one of the worst ways to die, because you know they would *have* to mention it in the obituary. Fearfully, I checked the ingredients label to see just what I would be eating over the next sixty days.

"Horny goat weed" was near the top of the list. "Horny" and "weed" don't bother me, but "goat"? Could we please find a sexier animal? (I've always been partial to egrets.) I did a Google search on "goat sexuality" and discovered several Web sites that I will hopefully one day be able to forget with the aid of costly hypnosis. After I scrubbed my eyes with Ajax, I eventually found an illustration of the average goat penis (pictured at left).

AHHHHH! What the hell is that long thing? *Is it a tongue?* Will my penis grow a tongue? I was pretty weirded out by this drawing, but gradually the idea *grew on me* (no pun intended). Sure, it looks disturbing, but there's no doubt that a goat penis would be infinitely more pleasurable *for her.* Check that thing out! I can't believe that more ladies aren't getting it on with goats. Apart from the bleating, the smell, and the chewing of tin cans, I'll bet they'd make excellent lovers.

But the most disturbing thing was yet to come. There were several enclosures with the penis pills, including a sheet of instructions. Imagine my shock and horror when I read instruction 3:

> **Penis Expansion Exercise:** Here is a simple exercise that you should do for approximately five minutes daily. Using your hand, grasp the head of your penis with very little pressure (your penis should be in a flaccid or soft state) and pull slowly and gently. This should not be painful or you are most likely pulling too hard.

First, if tugging your penis for five minutes a day really worked, then I think every man on the planet would be the size of a military flagpole. Teenagers, especially, would be able to jump rope with their own penises.

Second, they never said I would have to tug my penis for five minutes a day. This is more time than I was planning to spend on my penis. Couldn't I hire someone to do this for me? I asked my wife if I could delegate this task, but she wasn't wild about that idea. And unfortunately my vacuum cleaner was broken.

So the next morning, I gathered up my courage. I popped my first non-FDA-approved penis pill, and spent five minutes in the shower doing my "exercise." And I have to say, it's the first exercise I've ever done that ended in orgasm. Beats Pilates.

Week 1 Results

First of all, the penis pills smell weird, like a combination of old man's vest and Barbara Walters's workout bra. But more disturbing, my urine has started to take on this same smell, especially in the morning. It's a little bit nasty, but I continue to press on in the name of science. You never heard Marie Curie complaining about getting poisoned by massive exposure to radiation, at least until she was about to die. Then she bitched non-stop.

Second, this ridiculous "exercise regimen," which basically involves stretching your penis out for five minutes, is not as fun as it sounds. Now, if I could hire a personal trainer—preferably from the U.S. Women's Olympic Volleyball Team—then the exercise would not be quite so boring. I have better things to do with those five minutes, such as sleeping, but

I continue to follow the prescribed regimen. I have learned to save time by stretching my penis while shaving, or while on the poo-pot.

Third, and possibly most disturbing, is that I have become increasingly sexed-up. I noted earlier that the penis pills contain an ingredient called "horny goat weed," and I think I have fallen under its spell of horniness. Several nights ago, for instance, I had a dream in which my grandmother was performing oral sex on me. Considering that my grandmother has been dead for nearly eight years, I think you'll agree that this is pretty disgusting. I mean, why couldn't it have been my *maternal* grandmother? She's hot.

So, here's how things measure up at the end of Week 1:

	Length	Width
Original	5.875	4.125
Current	5.875	4.875
Increase	0%	18%

Well, what do you know? I haven't grown longer, but I've grown *wider*. Just like Marlon Brando. In fact, I'm going to start referring to him as "Li'l Brando." Li'l Brando, and his two sons, Sonny and Fredo.

Look out, ladies. I am going to be the widest man on the planet. I'll be like a chunk of deli salami.

Week 4 Results

One thing all these penis enlargement Web sites talk about is feeling more self-confident "in the locker room," and on that point they're right. I now make it a point to unspool the garden hose whenever I go to the gym. I'm *that* guy, the one who stands naked on the scale for up to fifteen minutes at a time. Sometimes I will sneak up behind someone seated on a bench, whip it out, and *thwack!* On the head, like a boomerang. They never know what hit them. It's like being bludgeoned by a ham.

For demonstration purposes, I have cut a piece of kielbasa into roughly my own length and width:

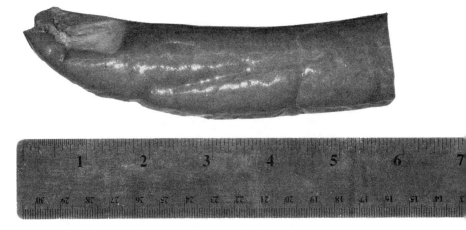

Imagine getting whacked on the head with that hunka meat! *WHOCK!* If it gets long enough, I can do some martial arts with it, like a soft, heavy pair of nunchucks.

But have I *really* grown in the past four weeks? Last night, it was time for my halfway-point measurement, and here are the *hard facts*:

	Length	Width
Original	5.875	4.125
Current	5.75	4.04
Increase	-2%	-2%

AHHHHHHHHHHHH!!! I'M SHRINKING! THESE PENIS PILLS ARE MAKING ME LOSE MY LENGTH, MY GIRTH! AAACCCHHH DU LIEBER! Sure, it's only 2 percent *now*, but in another month I could be the size of a cocktail mushroom! It could look like a little turtle poking its head out the shell!

Any male whose brain was not hopped up on horny goat weed would stop the penis pills at once—but I am determined to press on, for the benefit of humanity. Even if I end up shriveling to the size of a finger quiche, I will continue the sixty-day treatment.

Week 7 Results

One week to go. I am now receiving daily e-mails from my readers asking about the status of my penis. I haven't had this much interest in my unit since I became an altar boy in fifth grade.

Believe me, though, nobody is more interested in my penis than I am. Except possibly my testicles. Those guys are attached at the vas deferens, I swear. But what worried me was the *shrinking* from my last measurement. I was pretty nervous to whip out my ruler...worried that it would be the *only* thing I'd be whipping out, as my shrunken penis would resemble an earthworm wearing a ski hat.

So you can imagine my surprise and delight at these measurements:

	Length	Width
Original	5.875	4.125
Current	6.000	5.250
Increase	2%	27%

Sweet Mother of God! I am not shrinking—in fact, I'm growing ever *wider*. I'm like a turnip, or an overgrown radish. I always thought the phrase "pink torpedo" was just a euphemism, not a literal description of the shape.

To illustrate my added girth, I have wrapped several slices of bacon around the kielbasa:

I think you'll agree, I'm getting a whole lot meatier. And if I get hungry, I can throw my penis on the grill, which is a bonus.

▲ So. Very. Aroungry.

Final Results

Well, I did it. I finished the bottle. Sixty days spent taking the "Magna-RX" penis pills, which promised not only to add inches to my manhood, but to make me a better lover—something my wife has been asking me to do for years.

I went into this experiment a disbeliever. I thought I would see absolutely no difference, but I have to say that the penis pills *really do work*, though the results are not as dramatic as they claim. The penis pills put me in a constant state of semi-arousal, though, and let's face it: if you're the kind of guy who's taking penis pills, you probably don't need any help getting sexed up. I'm hornier than John Philip Sousa.

So without any further ado, the final measurements:

	Length	Width
Original	5.875	4.125
Current	6.000	5.250
Increase	2%	27%

▼ Displayed as a bar chart.

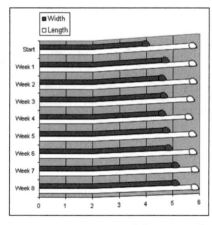

Now, I was happy with those results. My *wife* seemed happy. I was far short of the 2-inch minimum growth they promised—I gained less than a quarter-inch in length, and just over an inch in width—but who cares? I was now "above average" in penis size, and isn't that the important thing in life? If there are other, more important things in life, please let me know. And don't give me any of that crap about "poetry" or "love." I'll take a bigger schlong over a fucking haiku any day of the week.

So thus ends my experiment. Looking in the mirror nowadays, I often quote the final scene of *Boogie Nights*. "I am a star," I say, looking at my extra tenth of an inch. "I'm a star, I'm a star, I'm a star. I am a big, bright, shining star."

Chick Juice

icarumba!

FOR THOUSANDS OF YEARS, horny philosophers have wondered whether there exists in nature a true *aphrodisiac,* some food or substance that will arouse desire in the opposite sex. More recently, horny *scientists* have sought to create a chemical compound that will do the same thing, thus increasing their probability of getting a date. And even more recently, horny *spammers* have flooded my inbox with products that will "Enhance H.E.R. Seexx mood" and "M@ke ur g1rl_flend WANT U!!"

I felt the world needed to know whether these aphrodisiacs really work. I wanted something that would arouse desire and passion in my lover without the costly dates and time-consuming poetry. And I am the perfect test subject, since I have never once aroused sexual desire in any female. Thus, I undertook my most noble experiment yet: *testing various aphrodisiacs, and reporting on their effectiveness.*

Now, any educated person will tell you that aphrodisiacs don't exist. Fortunately, I'm not that educated. Not like Dr. Winnifred Cutler, who has a Ph.D. in biology from Penn, did postdoctoral behavioral endocrinology research at Stanford, and now sells a patented "horny formula" called Athena Pheromone 10X.

"In 1986, with colleagues at the University of Pennsylvania," explains Dr. Cutler on her Web site, "I discovered that sexually active young men produce pheromones." To me, that sounds like Dr. Cutler made this discovery while banging the undergrads. And who knows? Maybe she was wearing her own pheromone formula, which has been *proven* to attract the opposite sex, at least according to the "double-blind, placebo-controlled scientific study" continually mentioned on the Athena Pheromone 10X site. I tried to track down a copy of this study, but I was unable to locate a reprint of the peer-reviewed *Pheromones: Do They Juice Up the Chicks?*

So the body secretes pheromones naturally, but you can buy a small bottle of them from Dr. Cutler for $99.95. I made the purchase, and my vial of pheromones arrived in the mail a few days later, along with a small funnel for pouring the pheromones into my cologne. It didn't seem fair to mix the pheromones into colognes, although it does rhyme. I wanted my pheromones like my women: hot and stinky.

Feeling like a wolf marking his territory, I dabbed raw pheromone extract behind each ear, then around my neck. It had kind of a musky alcohol smell, like Mr. Clean's urine. Then I sat back, and waited for the tidal wave of sex.

After fifteen minutes of celibacy, I gave my wife a few hugs, letting her get a nice whiff of my hornmones. She didn't know about my experiment, and it seemed to have no discernible effect on her. In fact, I think we got into an argument over pie crust.

Undaunted, I went about my weekend errands, watching women carefully as they entered my whiff zone. I was waiting for them to leap atop me like ravenous dogs on a slice of fresh bacon, but all I saw was the same apathetic expression that I've seen since puberty.

Maybe I just needed to get closer. So I made it
a point to get on a crowded subway car, where I was
sure to be in close quarters with a female. And indeed
I was: an elderly Chinese woman sat down next to me
with a grocery bag full of cabbage. I watched her out
of the corner of my eye, to see if she might be moist
for me. With growing nausea, I realized that she was
enthusiastically picking her nose. She rolled something between her thumb and forefinger. We both lost
track of where it went, but I'm guessing in the cabbage. Never once, by the way, did she ask me on a date.

Maybe I needed more women. Fortunately, my
three-year-old had been invited to a birthday party
later in the day, and I eagerly offered to take him,
since I knew there would be tons of mothers, possibly
a few grandmothers, and the stray aunt. A loose nanny
or two. And indeed there were—it was the *mother*lode,
so to speak—but not one of them seemed interested in
me. I had to resort to hanging around the ice cream
table with the eight-year-old cousins, but they weren't
interested either, even when I tried striking up a conversation about mutual funds.

So my initial aphrodisiac experiment was not
exactly successful, but I wasn't ready to give up just
yet. It was time to turn up the juice.

Pepé Le Pew

Next I tried the patented Love-Scent, which contains
three different pheromones, mixed into a fragrant
goo. I thought this would be an improvement, since
the previous stuff made me smell a little bit like
a ferret.

They also give away FREE SAMPLES! on the Love-Scent site, so that's a bonus. But when I went to the FREE SAMPLES! page, it turned out they were actually charging ONE CENT per sample. Check it:

FREE SAMPLES! Category

Displaying 1 to 2 (of 2 products)

FREE Alter Ego, Scent of Eros, Edge and Chikara samples (MEN)

FREE samples of Alter Ego, Scent of Eros, Edge and Chikara pheromone gel for men.

$0.01

Now, I'm no economist, but last time I checked, the penny was still valid currency. If "free" now equals "one cent," then I'd like a billion frees, please. Still, the samples were $99.99 cheaper than the previous aphrodisiac I ordered, so I decided to give them a shot. They had a version of Love-Scent for men, and a version for women, so I grudgingly shelled out the two cents.

The packets came a few days later, with names like "Scent of Eros" and "The Edge." Unlike the Athena Pheromone 10X, which you're supposed to pour into your favorite aftershave, this stuff IS aftershave, and not the expensive kind. It smells a little bit like what Fabio might wear, if Fabio began to menstruate.

The instructions advised "try applying the entire packet to as much of your upper body as you can cover," but a tiny dab on my neck and wrists was as much as I could bear. I smelled like I had been raped by a Muppet.

On my morning subway commute, I moved in close to females, letting them smell my sickly reek. In the elevator at work, I squeezed in beside women, quietly monitoring their reactions. I noticed the occasional twitching of nostrils, the odd surprised sneeze, but nothing more. Women seemed as interested in me as they always have, which is not very.

It didn't matter, because there was only one woman I was interested in, and that was my wife. "Do you notice something different about my smell?" I asked Jade when I got home that evening.

She thought for a moment. "Yeah, your poop has been especially stinky," she said. "Do me a favor, burn a match."

"Come here, you romantic," I said. "Give me a hug."

"ECCCHH!" Jade nearly gagged. "What are you wearing?"

"Just the 'mones, baby."

"You smell like the New Delhi airport," she said, recoiling.

Maybe the aphrodisiac doesn't work on *all* women, I thought. Perhaps I needed to play the odds by getting myself in a room with lots of females at once. Then it hit me: *yoga.*

Everyone knows that guys never do yoga. They should call it *ho*ga. I went down to my local gym and signed up for the evening class. Before it began, I went into the locker room and just *slathered* myself in Love-Scent. I used up the rest of my sample packets, glopping it on my arms and face.

I walked into the yoga room, smelling like a Care Bear exploded in a patchouli factory. There were half a dozen middle-aged women in the class, and I could tell right away they were going to kick my ass: they all had their own mats, and they all looked strong. Most were dressed in leotards or formal yoga attire, and I had on an old T-shirt and ratty shorts. These were the yoga pros. They were progas. I had on a toga.

We started off with some simple poses. We did the "pillow pose," where you lay down with your head resting on your arms, like a pillow. Or in my case, *a pillow that had been shat upon by Strawberry Shortcake.* Man, I stank. I stank at yoga, and I stank, period.

Have you done yoga? There's a lot of bending and thrusting, with your legs spread wide and your ass in the air. It's kind of dirty. In this sexually charged atmosphere, with all these women in their sexual prime, and my 300-yard shockwave of pheromones, anything could happen.

And it did: I farted.

I swear, I don't know how they hold it in. You're tensing, you're relaxing. You're tensing, you're relaxing. I was trying to do that pose where you stretch your legs outward while balancing on your asscheeks. I was falling backward, trying to catch myself, and a low-flying duck slipped out. "AFLAC!" It was humiliating. The yoga instructor did a sharp intake of breath, kind of trying not to laugh, or maybe to gasp for air.

"Keep breathing," she intoned calmly, though I think breathing was the last thing anyone wanted to do. Between the aphrodisiac and the frappuccino, the room had taken on a new scent we might call Fruity Doodie. It was one of the most humiliating experiments I've done, and by now you should understand that's saying a lot.

So the day was a failure, but we can't really blame the Love-Scent for this one. Which is good, because I thought it would be wrong to demand my money back. But that's just my two cents.

Hard Science

Next, my research turned up the world's first true, honest-to-goodness aphrodisiac: a new drug called PT-141.

Currently in development by a New Jersey pharmaceutical company, PT-141 could be considered for FDA approval within the next year. Like Viagra and Cialis, it is being marketed as a treatment for sexual disorders, but unlike those drugs, it works on both men *and* women. "Approximately 50 million women suffer from female sexual dysfunction," claims the PT-141 Web site, though that's an estimate surely put together by a man. And probably not a very attractive one.

In an effort to see if I could score some beta-release PT-141 for my aphrodisiac test, I gave a call to Palatin Technologies, the company behind this lusty new drug. After a few calls, I eventually got through to a real live scientist.

PALATIN TECHNOLOGIES: This is Scott.

JOHN HARGRAVE: Hi, Scott. I was reading about your new PT-141 drug on the Internet.

PT: Mmm-hmm.

JH: Uh...can you send me some?

PT: No, it's not commercialized, the only thing I can have you considered for is our upcoming clinical trials. If you'd like, I can take down your personal information, and have our clinical director call you back.

JH: Yeah. That would be great. Could I get some by next weekend?

PT: No, this will not be for several months. You do need to be diagnosed with a sexual dysfunction...

JH: Would "not getting much sex" be considered a dysfunction?

PT: No, you need to have some kind of psychogenic dysfunction.

JH: What if I'm *sad* that I'm not getting much sex?

PT: Now, are you on other treatments, for instance, Viagra or Cialis?

JH: Sure. I've tried those before. I got them from a pharmacy in Miami.

PT: It's not a complicated process to see if you qualify. As I said, if you give me your contact information, we can have our clinical director give you a call.

JH: How about I just send you a hundred dollars, and you send me a sample of the PT-141?

PT: No, it's not allowed. This is not an approved product.

JH: A thousand dollars? You've probably got one laying there on your desk. Just drop it in a FedEx envelope.

PT: It's not a money issue. We're a public company; we adhere to all laws and regulations. We cannot do that, sir.

JH: PT-141 is a nasal spray, correct?

PT: That's right.

JH: Do you have plans to introduce it in a liquid that could be mixed into a drink?

PT: No, sir. Would you like to leave your name and number so we can get back to you?

JH: Sure. Just one more question: can you OD on this stuff?

PT: No. It will not hurt you.

JH: What if you took the whole thing at once? Man, that would be a fantastic way to go.

PT: We've never had anyone do that. The way we send them out is in single doses.

JH: Okay. $10,544. That's all I have in my savings account. $10,544 for just one tester.

PT: It's not a cash issue. I'm an executive officer of a public company. Just so you're aware, we don't even have access to the drug.

JH: Oh, come on, Scott. I'm sure you have a closet full of samples just down the hall.

PT: Absolutely not. It's produced in outside labs, by independent companies and suppliers.

JH: *(sigh)* Can I make some myself? I have a chemistry set down in my basement.

PT: Again, we do not create the drug ourselves...

JH: I've got the test tubes and the beakers, I'm ready to go. Just tell me what to mix.

PT: Is there anything else I can do for you?

JH: Do I need flour?

PT: If you'll excuse me, I have a meeting I need to attend to.

JH: Sure. Just one more question: in your tests, you said that one of the side effects for women is "headache."

PT: Yes, it was a very slight percentage, I think on the order of one to two percent. It was not a severe headache, not like a migraine.

JH: Are you sure they weren't just trying to get out of it?

PT: Yes. These were individuals diagnosed with sexual dysfunctions.

JH: I mean, I thought a "headache" is what the drug is supposed to cure, if you get my meaning.

PT: Yes I do, sir. I have a two-thirty meeting, so I'm going to need to go now.

JH: You know, I've been trying all these other aphrodisiacs, and none of them are working very well. I bought this stuff called Athena 10X. Have you heard of it?

PT: No, I haven't.

JH: I have it sitting on my medicine shelf, and this morning I accidentally thought it was eyedrops, and I put some pheromones in my eye.

PT: It sounds like you'll need to call your doctor about that. I have to go now.

JH: Will my eye get horny, Scott?

PT: Good-bye. *(hangs up)*

Fine. I didn't need their fancy newfangled aphrodisiac. I was going to kick up the sex drive *old school.*

Pretty Fly for a White Guy

It was time to try the granddaddy of aphrodisiacs: Spanish fly, a clear liquid made from the dried remains of a bug known as the "blister beetle." The sales pitch on one Spanish fly Web site explains that it "irritates the urogenital tract and produces an itching sensation in sensitive membranes, a feeling that allegedly increases a woman's desire for intercourse." Woo-boy! Sign me up for a night of burning noonie!

Even though the Web site assured me that Spanish fly was "completely safe when used as directed," other sites warned that it is "highly toxic, especially when ingested, and poisonous doses can lead to severe illness and even death." So: either it makes you horny, or it kills you. This was enough to make me think twice, but I bravely ordered my Spanish fly, which was shipped from Australia and arrived in an unmarked brown bottle.

But how would I get my wife to try the 'fly? Well, many foods allegedly have aphrodisiac powers: chocolate, anchovies, asparagus, and especially oysters. I decided to fix my wife a meal consisting of every possible turn-on food, and then *I would sneak the Spanish fly into the oysters.* See? My plan was brilliant. It could not fail. Unless I accidentally killed her.

On Saturday night, I told her I was going to make a special dinner for the two of us. We put the three-year-old to bed, and I prepared this candlelight spread, a sumptuous feast for the eyes as well as the genitals:

◄ Scallops are aphrodisiacs because they are round and fleshy, like breasts or buttocks.

◄ Asparagus is reputed to be an aphrodisiac, because it looks like a penis. If you can find white asparagus at the store, I swear it looks just like you're eating a dildo.

▶ Chili peppers flush the cheeks. They also make men cry, and chicks dig that.

▶ Anchovies have dozens of tiny bones that are impossible to remove. This is an aphrodisiac because it prepares you for a long night of bone-eating.

I brought out the foods one at a time, and Jade was delighted...until she saw the oysters. Then she figured out what was going on. "If you think I'm gonna put that slimy shit in my mouth," she said, smiling, "you're high."

"Oh, come on," I urged her as I sat down. "They're delicious. Put a little *cock*tail sauce on one [here I showed her the proper technique], and down the

◀ Oysters are aphrodisiacs, of course, because they resemble a cooleyhopper. I bought half a dozen, and carefully measured out the Spanish fly onto three of them.

◀ Not amused.

hatch." Then I realized: *I had forgotten which oysters had the Spanish fly.* I had put the drops on three of the oysters, and now I couldn't remember which ones! This was bad. Oyster Roulette.

She eyed the oysters warily. "These are fresh?"

"Shucked them myself," I said, though I left out the part about trying to pry open the shells with a screwdriver, accidentally gouging my index finger, bleeding on one of the oysters, and rinsing it off. By now, I had lost track of the bleedy oyster as well.

"Do I chew it?" she asked, tentatively loading one up with horseradish.

"No. Under no circumstances should you chew," I said. "Just hold your breath and swallow."

"This really *is* like sex," she said, kicking it back. And then I realized why watching a woman eat an oyster is so incredibly sexy: it's the closest most of us will ever get to seeing live lesbian action.

The meal had its ups and downs. The "up" was felt about ten minutes after the oyster, when someone's erection loudly banged the underside of the table, like the Ghost of Christmas Past. Guessing that I had eaten the Spanish fly, I began to worry about the supposed side effects of coma and death. Then I realized that Spanish fly is an aphrodisiac simply because you fear *that you might soon be dead.* You know how people going down in a plane often go down *on each other*? Same concept. Crashing planes, burning buildings, enormous meteors hurtling toward earth: all aphrodisiacs.

We finished up the meal without incident, or intercourse, and then it was time for dessert.

In the end, I don't know if it was the oysters, the Spanish fly, or the threat of me telling millions of readers if I *didn't* get sex, but I have to say that it worked. *The experiment really worked.* We climbed Mount Pork-o-lay-la, and neither of us, as far as I know, had burning noonie.

◄ **Chocolate** has been considered an aphrodisiac for centuries, and I thought an enormous chocolate rabbit could only help get the point across. **Pistachio pudding** is not an aphrodisiac, but I thought it would make a nice setting for the sprinkling of **green M&M's**, long recognized by teenagers for their magical properties.

Conclusion

Here's what I learned: there is no shortage of creams and potions out there that will supposedly put your love life in overdrive. But what most of us need is a cream called SELF-CONFIDENCE. This would be a salve, with the consistency of Vaseline, that we could smear on our face and neck to help us through the fear of rejection. Then we could boldly approach potential lovers and confidently ask them for a date. Unfortunately, our faces would be covered with a shiny layer of unctious goo, and they would turn and flee. But at least we wouldn't take it so *personally*.

Of all the aphrodisiacs I tried, the only one that worked for me was the "aphrodisiac dinner," and here's why: *you're thinking about sex the entire meal.* You're putting lots of genital-looking things in your mouths; you both know what's going on. It's subtle, but it's obvious. It's very exciting. You've got to try it. But maybe that's just the Spanish fly talking.

My aphrodisiac experiment made me realize something: *romance is a lot of hard work.* Isn't there anything for the lazy lover, the guy or gal who just wants to get up and get down? Fortunately, there is. It's called masturbation.

Remember: Your hand will never reject you. Your hand is a total slut. 😛

Going Postal

Junk mail. It should be called "shit mail." (SPAM = Shit Posing As Mail.) The industry term for this useless paper is "direct mail," so called because it goes *directly* into your trash can. But that's not really true, is it? There's all the time you have to spend sorting through it, just in case you miss an electric bill or L.L.Bean rebate check buried in the vaginal folds of the 112-page supermarket circular.

In order to trick us into opening it, they now create junk mail that *looks* important, making it less likely that we'll notice the stuff that really *is* important. We didn't ask for this crap, but *we're* the ones who have to sort it out, throw it away, tie it in bags, haul it to the dump, and pray that a wandering member of the Russian mob doesn't use it to steal our identity.

It's not *our* crap, it's *theirs*. So one day it occurred to me: *why not send their junk mail back to them in those postage-paid envelopes they include with their useless offers?*

Looking on the Internet, I found this trick had been tried by thousands of frustrated junk mail recipients before me. However, there was an awful lot of misinformation surrounding the proper use of postage-paid envelopes, or *"revengelopes,"* as I began to call them. I meticulously scoured hundreds of U.S. postal regulations, then conducted lengthy phone interviews with chief U.S. postal regulators, who reluctantly gave me the answers I was looking for.

So here it is: the truth about revengelopes. This is worth the price of the book right here.

1. You can stuff nearly anything you want into postage-paid envelopes, and legally send them back to junk mailers, at their expense. The junk mail company pays a flat rate for each piece of mail they receive back (60 cents per piece at the time of this writing), plus any additional postage for weight over one ounce. The post office gets paid; the junk mailer gets screwed. Win/win. Now the caveats.

2. You *cannot* mail anything that falls under the USPS definition of "illegal or hazardous materials." This includes fecal matter, which must be enclosed in authorized containers and properly labeled, which I think you'll agree takes the fun out of mailing poo.

3. Also: it's got to fit inside the envelope. You can't tape an envelope to a brick and drop it in a mailbox. There is an obscure postal regulation that allows mail carriers to treat this as a "nonmailable item." If you include a return address, they'll deliver the brick back to you; otherwise, they'll throw it away.

Since everything had to fit inside the envelope, this made an interesting challenge: how much junk could I send back to the junk mail companies? *How heavy could I get one of these envelopes?*

Experiment 1: Steel Chains

When I received an invitation to sign up for the Harvard Alumni Association MasterCard, I quickly filled out the application, stuffing it back into the envelope with a heavy steel chain. I thought the chain conveyed strength and dignity, like Harvard. At least, before Harvard started offering cheesy-ass credit cards to its alumni.

How to know if the junk mail company actually received my revengelope was a bit of a pickle. USPS regulations don't allow postal employees to add any

extras like "Delivery Confirmation" or "Signature
Confirmation" to postage-paid envelopes. I mulled
over this problem for weeks, until the obvious solution finally occurred to me: *I'd send them a credit
card application with my prank package!* Then, when
I received my new credit card in the mail a few weeks
later, I'd know they had paid for the envelope.
I would charge them to send me charge
cards. These were going to be the
heaviest, most *expensive*
credit card applications
in history.

It was tough,
but I managed to
get the envelope
closed. I encased
the envelope in
tape, noting the
hilarious warning
on the back: WARNING:
TAMPERING WITH THIS ENVELOPE OR ITS CONTENTS
MAY RESULT IN LEGAL ACTION. I love this warning,
because it's the kind of insanity that only a lawyer
could dream up. They also had a CUSTOMER LOCATOR
CODE printed on the envelope, which is supposed to
scare you into thinking, WE KNOW EXACTLY WHO
YOU ARE. Great! Then *stop sending me shit.*

I was pleased to find that my envelope weighed
in at a whopping **1 pound, 9 ounces**. And a few weeks
later, I got my new Harvard Alumni MasterCard in
the mail, letting me know that my envelope had been
received, paid for, and processed:

It was a pretty good start. But I knew I could do more. Weigh, *weigh* more.

Experiment 2: Lead

Like Lindsay Lohan, I became obsessed with weight. This was a problem so difficult that it required science. *Heavy* science.

Density, you will recall, is a measure of mass per unit of volume. What I needed was a material or substance of extremely high density that could easily fit into a standard business envelope. The highest density known is that of a neutron star, but the shipping charges on one of those things is astronomical. The most dense naturally occurring substance on earth is *iridium*, at 22,650 kg/m³, or in layman's terms, "really fuckin' heavy." It also costs more than *solid* gold, which weighs in at 19,300 kg/m³. I think you'll agree that sending gold bars to junk mail companies would defeat the point.

The easiest heavy material to get my hands on was *lead*, at a density of 11,340 kg/m³, or eleven times heavier than water. If there's still a local hardware store in your town, then they probably stock *lead flashing*, which is used in roofing projects, and can be easily molded into any shape you desire. The hardware guy, a wiry fellow in his forties, picked up an enormous roll of it, grunting heavily, then dropped it on the counter. *THUNK.*

"Wow," I said. "That looks heavy."

"Try to lift it," he challenged me.

"D'OHHHH!" I groaned, trying to hoist the damned thing off the counter. It was very awkward from a standing position. This was embarrassing, since guys must be able to lift *anything* in front of other guys. I strained to pick it up, veins popping from my neck. *"Shitballs!"* I grunted, accidentally crapping my pants.

"Heavy, ain't it?"

"I think I just blew out a testicle."

He chuckled. "You all right?"

"That's the heaviest thing I've lifted since I was trapped beneath one of Scarlett Johansson's breasts."

"How much you need, then?"

"Oh, a couple of feet," I said. "Just enough to fit inside this." I pulled out a prepaid envelope for a Visa Platinum credit card.

"Right," he said, winking at me. He pulled out a pair of metal shears and cut off a long piece. "Tell you what," he said. "This stuff is cheap. Just take it. No charge."

"Thanks!" I said, folding the lead into the envelope, along with my application. When you're getting back at the junk mailers, everyone wants to help.

My lead-filled revengelope weighed **1 pound 14 ounces**, and I received my new Visa card in the mail a few weeks later. This was great. My only regret was that I couldn't afford actual *platinum* to enclose with my Visa Platinum card application, because that would have delivered an additional layer of heavy irony, or at least an additional layer of heavy iron.

I knew lead was the way to go: it was heavy and cheap. But how could I get it *even heavier*?

Experiment 3: Solid Bar of Lead

I had to order it from a specialty supplier, which makes it impractical for most of us. But once I had an actual bar of lead in my hands, I knew it was the right choice. The thing was just unbelievably heavy. There's a reason that one of the weapons in Clue was a lead pipe, not a *copper* or *iron* pipe, which are lighter and thus far less effective for killing. Smack Colonel Mustard on the head with a titanium pipe, and you just make him mad. Of course, the lead gradually seeps into your bloodstream, and makes you forget your name and birthday, but at least that bastard Mustard is dead. That fucker raped my giraffe.

Rather than sending off another credit card application, I used a postage-paid envelope sent to me by Senator Harry Reid. Normally I don't donate to political campaigns, but Senator Reid's junk mail letter guaranteed that any gift I sent him would be TRIPLED. Wow! How does this work, Senator Reid? Fortunately, he provides an easy-to-understand diagram:

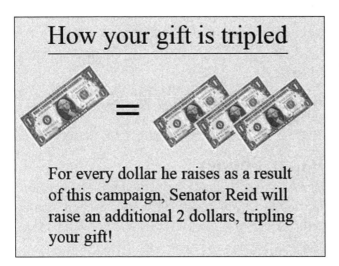

How your gift is tripled

For every dollar he raises as a result of this campaign, Senator Reid will raise an additional 2 dollars, tripling your gift!

So let's see: For every dollar contributed, Senator Reid will raise two more dollars. But doesn't he have to triple all *those* dollars, as well? Something tells me Senator Reid isn't so good at math. And in that respect, he'll probably fit right into our political system.

So I wrote Senator Reid a check for 3.33333333333333333..., which, when tripled, would equal an even $10.00. And in the spirit of the campaign, I decided to triple his *postage* as well, by sending my tax-deductible contribution of a lead bar.

The bar was so heavy that it tore through the flimsy paper envelope, so I had to tape the envelope *around* the bar, making it more of a lead wrapper than a proper envelope. Still, the lead-stuffed revengelope weighed in at an astonishing **5.2 pounds**. And was delivered successfully, as you can see from my canceled check:

The bank rounded down, by the way. ▼

Paper Pooper

Screwing over spammers with their own paper was fun, but I really just wanted to get rid of the mail altogether. I went back to the Internet to find out if this was possible, and you know what? It's getting pretty hard to believe anything you read on the Web. I swear, it's like they'll let *anyone* write stuff there nowadays. For instance, I found this bit of advice on one well-respected reference site:

> Try filling out United States Postal Service Form 1500, "Application for Listing and/or Prohibitory Order." This form is intended to stop someone from sending "pandering advertisements" which you feel is "erotically arousing or sexually provocative." However, the law is very specific that the definition of arousing or provocative is "determined by the addressee in his sole discretion." The guy at the desk might be confused...but they really do have to take it, and will![1]

1. MetaFilter's URL: photos.metafilter.com/mefi/45358

I found the form in question, which is meant to be used if you've received unsolicited pornography through the U.S. Mail. Frankly, I wish they'd create a form that would score me *more* unsolicited porn. *That's* junk mail I wouldn't mind receiving, rather than the J. Crew catalog, which is what I decided to complain about:

If anyone hassled me, I was going to explain that I was a recovering sex addict, and the J. Crew spring swimsuit collection was a tremendous temptation for me, particularly the tankinis. I made up similar stories for the Dell catalog and a local Century 21 flyer.

My first mistake, I think, besides agreeing to write this book, was to take the forms to my local post office branch, the place where I regularly send out all my prank mailings. Now, I have tremendous respect for the United States Post Office, I really do. Name me one other form of communication delivery that works as reliably and cheaply. My cellphone company charges me a hundred bucks a month to provide a shitty connection that drops out every time someone turns on a microwave oven.

The guys at my local branch knew me by name. Unfortunately, they thought this name was "Freak Boy." For months, they had been processing my ridiculous letters to Starbucks and Lands' End, answering my idiotic questions, and they were losing their patience with me. The P.O. was P.O.'d. Now I was handing them a set of obscure USPS forms, asking them to prevent Michael Dell from sending me any more sexually suggestive computer catalogs.

The guy at the desk *was* confused, as the Internet predicted. So far, so good. He called over his manager, a middle-aged Korean woman who peered at the forms over her spectacles. A few curious postal workers surrounded her. This was turning into a scene.

"What is this?" she asked.

"It's PS Form 1500," I said. "I find these pamphlets sexually suggestive, and wish to be protected from further mailings."

"What's wrong with *this*?" she said, thumbing through the Century 21 brochure. Behind me, a long line of customers was forming, everyone straining to hear our conversation. I should have done this in an out-of-state post office.

"I'm a recovering sex addict," I told her, quietly but firmly. "The word *condominium* reminds me

of the word *condom*, and that reminds me of sex."
I looked at her pointedly. "*Unprotected* sex. The best
kind."

Tom, the middle-aged postal employee with the
arm tattoos (I know them all by name as well), told
the manager, "Ah, he just wants to stop getting junk
mail. Hang on, we'll give you an address you can
write to get your name removed."

"No," I insisted. "I really find these mailings
sexually suggestive, and the Internet told me you
guys have to accept this form."

"I can't take this," said the manager, a little too
loudly, handing them back to me. "That's not what
this form is supposed to be used for. This is for
pornography."

"This IS pornography!" I said, stabbing my finger
at a charming storybook split-level for $368,000.

"Here you go," said Tom, who had returned with
the following address scribbled on a piece of paper:

DMA Mail Preference Service
Post Office Box 603
Carmel, New York 10512-0643

The manager gave me back my forms, and I had
no choice but to slink away, unable to convince anyone of my real estate lies. I felt like Dolf de Roos.

Getting Off the Junk

I went home and sent a postcard to the address above,
asking to have my name removed from junk mail
lists. It took a few months, but eventually my junk
mail slowed to a trickle, then practically disappeared.

So we end this section with a crucial victory against the forces of darkness: the junk mail removal address listed *really does work*. Still no cure for spam, but at least there's a way to get off the junk.

Now, if only there was a cure for *stupidity*, I wouldn't have been forced to write this next section. ☺

The Celebrity Sincerity Test

 I'M SICK OF CELEBRITIES parading around their important social causes. Have you noticed that they're always *trendy* causes? How about some non-trendy causes for a change? Did you know they have seeing eye monkeys, for instance? This is true: "service monkeys," as they are called, are trained to fetch objects for quadriplegics and help them with everyday tasks, like playing the lute. Actually, we don't know if they can play the lute, because *no celebrity has ever endorsed the cause of seeing eye monkeys.*

AIDS is trendy, which is ironic: a disease transmitted by unsafe sex is a *safe* political cause. But what about, for instance, genital warts? "Hi, I'm Cher. Up to 50 percent of sexually active men and women suffer from genital warts. I've had them since 1971. My labia look like two oysters smothered in gravel." See, you'd never hear that.

I suppose the stars would argue that they're raising awareness of these important, politically correct causes. Listen up: there's a reason you're called ENTERTAINERS! You're supposed to *entertain*, not *bring us down!* Do we not know that 19 million people have AIDS?[1] Besides, when was the last time you gave money to a charity because a star raised your awareness? If that worked, nonprofits would be falling over themselves to line up celebrities. Consider: *Sally Struthers is no longer the spokeswoman for Christian Children's Fund.* True, she ate the children, but still.

1. I don't know how many people actually have AIDS. (Too busy to look it up.)

I'm not saying I doubt the stars' sincerity. Wait a tic. Yes, I am! I *am* saying that. Who's to say that Jerry Lewis doesn't do his telethon each year, not to help the suffering of sick and disabled children, but because it's *twenty-three hours more TV time than he's going to get otherwise?* I'm sorry to be cynical here, but...wait a lamb's shake. No, I'm not! I'm *not* sorry to be cynical! I'm not sorry at all!

When You Wish Upon a Star

Here's what I wanted to know: *which stars are the most sincere about their chosen causes?* More importantly, *which stars are the* least *sincere?* To find out, I posed as a twelve-year-old girl with a terminal illness.

Making up a disease, I sent ten different celebrities this handwritten letter, personalized for each star with a drawing.

The only thing scarier than the drawing of Oprah is the fact that I *was actually trying to draw Oprah well.* I have the artistic ability of an attorney, or possibly a "monkey with promise." My fourth grade art teacher once gave us an assignment to sketch an elephant from memory. The brutally mangled creature I produced was so revolting to her that

Dear Oprah:

My name is Jane Hargrave. I am 12 years old. I am in the hospital because I have intelritis, which is a disease of the pancreas. At first when the doctors told me I was sad. But then they told me more than 25% of kids survive for more than 3 years, and I have faith in God I will survive!

I am writing because I am also trying to help people. I read you are involved with helping kids learn, and so am I! Even tho I am stuck in the hospital I am trying to raise money for Oprahs Angel Network (my uncle is helping me).

I love to draw, and made a few drawings of you which I am trying to sell to nurses and doctors here I will send any money to your angel network is that OK? I am sending you the best one I have made so far.

If your not too busy you can call me at ███-██-███ (my dad's phone). I would also love an autographed photo to hang by my hospital bed. It would make me feel good to look at it.

Your biggest fan,
Jane Hargrave

Oprah Winfrey
"Angel"

she had to look away. "Where's the TAIL?" she screamed. "Where's the TRUNK?" I had actually *forgotten* to draw a trunk, and had drawn a petite nose instead. Anyway, it's that kind of gentle nurturing of my artistic talent that has led to this sorry state of affairs. On the other hand, my terrifying celebrity illustrations somehow seemed fitting for a dying twelve-year-old girl.

Which socially minded celebrities would respond to this poor girl? In my mind, if you're a bleeding heart celebrity, there's no excuse for not answering this letter. *Only a monster would ignore a dying child.*

People Magazine's Ten Most Annoying Celebrities

Developing my list of celebrity targets was more difficult than I expected. Many of the usual suspects (Michael Moore, Susan Sarandon, Sean Penn) are not actually affiliated with any particular organization, and good for them. Merely having strong political views did not qualify a celebrity for my prank. Charlton Heston, for instance, could hardly be described as "bleeding-heart," unless you mean the blood spurting from the shotgun hole through his victim's aorta.

Sting was an obvious first choice. This twatwaffle has been whining about the rain forest for years. I visited the rain forest, and guess what? *Still rainy.* Nobody's chopped it down, because Costa Rica is making a fortune on ecotourism, with or without his nasally twang. Don't stand so, don't stand so, don't stand so close to me.

Bono was next. Everyone knows that Bono is not only going directly to Heaven, but once there, will actively campaign on behalf of all the sinners in Hell. Bono will spend long walks in the garden with God Himself, who will be pleasantly amused that Bono has taken time out of his busy schedule to speak with Him, even though God only knows U2's music from the young interns that work the Pearly Gates. Still, Bono will speak with surprising authority on the plight of Hell's residents, and God will be so impressed with the depth of his knowledge on the issue that He will eventually pass a bill to allow a limited number of Hell's residents into Heaven for the first time, where they will promptly rape and murder all the angels.

Madonna was third on the list, because she supports the American Foundation for AIDS Research. This surprised me, since I thought she had renounced everything American, including her accent *and* her ability to sell records in this country. By the way, what is it with one-named celebrities and social causes? Is the number of names inversely proportional to their inflated sense of self-worth? (It goes the other way as well: David Lee Roth is one of the *least* charitable people I know.)

Angelina Jolie, as you may know, campaigns for the 2 million victims of Lip Inflation Puffiness Syndrome. Whether their swollen kissers are caused by heredity, or a doctor sneezing while performing a collagen injection, this nonprofit seeks to protect the rights of those with grotesquely oversized flappers. Other honorary members of the foundation include Steven Tyler, Julia Roberts, and the late Don Knotts.

The truth is that Ms. Jolie is actually a devoted humanitarian, and an official Goodwill Ambassador for the United Nations High Commissioner for Refugees. This is great, because instead of trying to flee in makeshift life rafts, Cambodian refugees can now use her lips as an emergency flotation device.

Rosie O'Donnell has set up her own nonprofit organization called "Rosie's For All Kids Foundation," which describes itself as "just that—*for all kids*, because every child deserves to feel safe and loved, and to have opportunities for a better future." Hey, I love kids so much that I made one. But, I mean, ALL kids? Let's be honest: some kids don't deserve to feel safe *or* loved. From my own elementary school experience, I can think of at least three or four children who deserved to be left under a highway bridge for a couple of nights. A few days spent foraging for rat meat, or bathing in gas station sinks, would have straightened them out *real* fast, and maybe they would have quit punching me. "For All Kids?" Bitch, please. Try to be a little more selective.

Pamela Anderson made it onto the list because she supports the radical animal rights group People for the Ethical Treatment of Animals. I think PETA should worry more about the ethical treatment of *humans*, since it supports groups like the restaurant-firebombing American Liberation Front. It also opposes *all* animal testing, which the *Wall Street Journal* found ironic enough to comment on:

> [Animal testing] ought to be of interest to Ms. Anderson, who suffers from Hepatitis C, a virus that puts her at high risk for liver disease and liver cancer. The American Liver Foundation believes that animal testing is essential for finding a cure, and Ms. Anderson herself served in 2002 as grand marshal for an American Liver Foundation fund-raiser. Must have left her PETA T-shirt at home that day.[2]

Oooh! Burn! I love it when the *Wall Street Journal* tries to get snarky, because it only happens about once every...well, that's the only time. That newspaper is more constipated than a pregnant woman on an all-cheese diet.

Steven Spielberg supports a variety of charitable causes including The Shoah Foundation, STAR-BRIGHT Foundation, and Dreamworks Studios. Hang on...I'm sorry. Upon further research, it turns out that Dreamworks is actually a *for*-profit corporation. I merely thought it was a charity, given its financial performance in recent years. I mean, *Baywatch*? Somebody's got to be underwriting that crap.

Ronald McDonald, although not technically a *human* celebrity, rounded out my list at number ten. As a member of the clown race, I thought that Mr. McDonald could relate to the plight of a suffering child. Clowns throughout history have been humiliated,

2. *Wall Street Journal,* July 16, 2004

laughed at, sprayed with seltzer, shot out of cannons, thrown in front of charging bulls, crammed into imaginary glass boxes, and forced to pile into tiny cars like Jews at Auschwitz. It's no wonder so many of them are sad!

Mr. McDonald has also founded his own charity, the Ronald McDonald House, which helps terminally ill children and their families. Although I don't know why they cram all the sick kids into one house, I guess that's the way clowns have learned to do things.

So here is my final list, the big celebrity ten, the ones whose sincerity would be put to the test:

CELEBRITY	TRENDY CAUSE	ORGANIZATION
Pam Anderson	Animal rights	PETA
Bono	Debt, AIDS, trade, Africa	DATA (Debt, AIDS Trade, Africa)
Angelina Jolie	Refugee protection	UNHCR (United Nations High Commissioner for Refugees)
Jerry Lewis	Muscular Dystrophy	MDA
Madonna	AIDS	amFAR (American Foundation for AIDS Research)
Ronald McDonald	Children's health	Ronald McDonald House
Rosie O'Donnell	Disadvantaged children	Rosie's For All Kids Foundation
Steven Spielberg	Israel experience	Righteous Persons Foundation
Sting	Environment	Rainforest Foundation
Oprah Winfrey	Educational programs	Oprah's Angel Network

I thought we also needed a "control," a famous person who should serve as our baseline respondent. So I added an eleventh celebrity:

CELEBRITY	TRENDY CAUSE	ORGANIZATION
Charles Manson	Evil	The Manson Family

I could only pray that Manson would come in last.

The First Letter

Each of my letters followed the same format. The twelve-year-old was a huge fan of <CELEBRITY>. Even though her pancreas was giving out, she was trying to raise money for <TRENDY CAUSE> by drawing pictures of <CELEBRITY> and selling them to the doctors and nurses. I could have just done a mail merge in Word, if I didn't have to handwrite each of the letters to make them believable.

Even though it was just a form letter, the *illustrations* really showed off my creativity.

Before sending out the letters, I established some ground rules. *Not responding* was the lowest a celebrity could go. Believe me, there is no excuse. For *ten years*, I've personally

▼ Madonna, if she had done time in a women's prison.

Madonna

See all the letters, with their disturbingly grotesque illustrations: www.prankthemonkey.com/celebrity

answered every goddamn e-mail that people have sent me via my Web site (somewhere around 35,000 e-mails). Sure, I don't have *millions* of people writing me, but that's why the stars have MONEY, so they can hire a STAFF to answer their MAIL.

Some kind of response was necessary for the stars to maintain their integrity, even if it was a form letter. A personal note would be even better, and a phone call would be the ultimate response. Remember: "Jane" wasn't asking for a personal visit, mostly because she didn't exist.

And now we come to the interactive portion of the book. Before turning the page, close your eyes and try to guess which celebrity answered first. Review the chart on page 128, and think about which celebrity you find most admirable and trustworthy. Hold that celebrity in your mind, then turn the page.

▼ Spielberg came out like the forbidden love child of Leonard Maltin and Al Roker.

Stephen Spielberg

Charles Manson

▲ The only one I was actually proud of, strangely enough, was the Manson drawing.

Ronald McDonald Responds

I didn't get the first call directly from Ron, of course. He has handlers. Sometimes you'll get a call from Grimace, who otherwise sits on his ass most of the day, eating fries and surfing porn. Mayor McCheese's people occasionally make the call, when they're not busy drafting anti-Hamburglar legislation, or trying to annex the Burger King's neighboring territory.

I got a call from Julie, who was with the Ronald McDonald House. I told her I was Jane's father, and expressed how grateful I was to have received a call back so quickly—which was true, because now I had something to write about. She told me how touched she was by Jane's letter, how she loved the drawing. I have to admit, it *was* one of my better drawings, because it's pretty easy to draw a clown. I apologize if that sounds clownist. I don't mean to imply that clowns are inferior to humans, only that they are easier to draw.

"We'd like to have Ronald make a personal phone call to your daughter!" she offered.

"That would be great," I said, realizing that I hadn't thought through this stunt at all. "I'll tell you what. How about tomorrow evening? I'm going to visit her in the ICU."

"Oh, they let you use your cellphone in the ICU?"

"Yeah." I laughed off my error. "We've gotten to know them pretty well over at St. Elizabeth's." I had no idea what I was saying. "They let us bend the rules from time to time."

"That's great," she said. "How's tomorrow evening at five thirty?"

"That would be fantastic. This will make her day."

"Talk to you then."

I spent the rest of the day trying to figure out how I was going to pull this off. I thought about enlisting the aid of an actual twelve-year-old girl, but what kind of parent would allow *that?* "Hey, I need your daughter to pretend to be a dying child, so I can make fun of good, honest people doing the Lord's work."

"Sure," they'd respond. "Do you need her to pose for pornography, too?"

In the end, I decided to play the part of my daughter myself. For some reason, this seemed like a good idea at the time. I figured that even if they suspected something, they wouldn't say anything, because *who wants to insult a terminally ill child?*

What Am I, a Clown? Do I Amuse You?

When the phone rang at 5:30 the next evening, my heart was pounding.

I was going to speak to him! The clown that had sold billions and billions of burgers around the world, possibly the most famous clown in history. Who's bigger? Bozo? Give me a fucking break. Bozo isn't fit to lick Ronald's wacky oversized shoes.

"Hello?" I answered.

"Um...hello!" said Ronald McDonald. He sounded temporarily confused, but still making every attempt to be cheery.

"Oh, hi!" I realized Ron was expecting to speak with a twelve-year-old girl. "This is John. Would you like me to put Jane on the phone?"

"Sure!" he said.

"Just one sec."

I rustled the phone, and began to speak in an absolutely *terrible* falsetto. I was trying, I really was, but I was about twenty-five years and one gender away from being able to pull off a voice like a twelve-year-old girl.

"It's Ronald McDonald!"

"Hello, Ronald!" I sounded like somebody had just kicked me in the nuts.

"Hi! I wanted to call and chat with one of my biggest fans! I just got your letter here, and I got this *beautiful* drawing you made for me. You know, I get so many drawings and letters every year, but I think this is one of the greatest, *coolest* pictures I've ever seen! I'm going to put it right on my refrigerator when I get home!"

"Thank you, Ronald!" I croaked.

"Thank *you* so much! It was a lovely, lovely picture!"

"Thank you!" I was afraid to say anything else. This was excruciating.

"I see here that you have a lot of other drawings that you've been trying to sell to the staff, and raise some money. How's that going? Are they buying them from you?"

"Yeah! I've been drawing a lot, and practicing my drawings, and one of the nurses—Florence—just bought one of my drawings for five dollars. So, I'm going to give the money to the Ronald McDonald charity."

"Well, that is wonderful. I think you're one of the coolest, most wonderful people in the world, and I'm proud to call you my friend!"

"I'm proud to call you my friend, too."

We chatted for a few minutes, with Ronald driving the conversation. I guess when you talk with sick kids all day, you learn to carry the bulk of the talking. You also learn not to question their voice, even when they sound like a pre-op transsexual. I told Ronald I loved him, and he said he loved me, too. We said goodbye.

A few days later, I received a goodie bag in the mail, stuffed with toys, plush dolls, and other surprises that normally require the purchase of a Happy Meal. On a 1-10 scale of celebrity responses, Ronald turned it up to 11: a phone call, an autographed photo, and tons of free stuff. Whatever you think about the service at McDonald's, the service at the McDonald *House* is outstanding.

I did end up making a substantial donation to the Ronald McDonald House. Otherwise, I was going to need Bono to campaign on *my* behalf in the afterlife.

Jerry Lewis Responds

The King of Comedy himself, the great **Jerry Lewis**, responded next. He promptly sent back an autographed photo, personalized appropriately for a dying child.

to Jane –
au good
wishes!
Jerry Lewis

So: Ronald McDonald and Jerry Lewis had proven their sincerity and commitment to their causes. But what about the remaining celebrities? It was time to turn up the heat.

John Hargrave
P.O. Box 990586
Boston, MA 02199

Ms. Oprah Winfrey
c/o Creative Artists Agency
9830 Wilshire Boulevard
Beverly Hills, CA 90212-1825

Dear Ms. Winfrey:

This is a difficult letter to write. My 12-year-old daughter Jane has a rare disease of the pancreas. Even though we remain hopeful and strong, her doctors are telling us she has less than three months to live.

Jane recently sent you a hand-drawn portrait, along with a request for an autographed photo or a phone call. She really worships and adores your work with Oprah's Angel Network, and is actually trying to raise money for your cause, even from her weakened condition in her hospital bed.

I realize you're incredibly busy, but if there's any way you could send her a photo, or give her a call at my cellphone (▮▮▮▮▮▮▮), it would bring her an awful lot of hope during her final days.

Thank you,

John Hargrave

The Second Letter

After a month, I sent out the follow-up letter on the left to all the nonresponsive celebrities.

I didn't have to wait long for the next celebrity to respond. A few days later, I received the familiar yellow slip in my P.O. box, indicating that I had received an item that was too large to fit into the box. I took it up to the counter clerk, who gave me the obligatory eyeroll and sigh, then went back to fetch my package. When he brought it back, my heart dropped into my shoes as I saw the return address, scribbled in disturbing handwriting: MANSON.

I stared at it for a few seconds, unbelieving.

"This is a package from Charles Manson," I told
the postal worker.

"*The* Charles Manson?" he asked.

I picked it up. It was very heavy, and it rattled.

"I'm scared," I said.

"Well, if I don't see you again, I'll know what
happened!" he said, chuckling. He seemed fairly
cheery about the possibility of not seeing me again.

"Yeah." Charlie apparently had someone handling
his mail for him, because his MANSON return address
had another return address sticker pasted over it.
The front of the package read, "JOHN'S DAUGHTER"
and "DO NOT OPEN TILL CHRISTMAS"

I brought it back to the office, where I nervously
set it down on the desk. I was too frightened to open
it. *What was inside?* A human hand? A monkey cock?
I needed a bomb-sniffing dog, or an intern, to open
it for me. I continued to stare at the package on the
commute home, expecting it to leak something toxic.
I was blown away (poor choice of words) that *Charles
Manson* responded before 80 percent of the celebrities. I could just hear their excuses: "Oh sure, he's
got *time* to respond. He's in *jail*! What *else* does he
have to do?" Well, apparently he doesn't have time
to get involved with a charity that he never follows
up on. That's one thing.

Also: Manson is said to receive 60,000 pieces of
mail a year, more than any other prisoner in the U.S.
prison system.[3] And the dude is now in his *seventies*.
He's not only busy, he's *old*. If Manson could respond,
Sting could respond. So shut your celebrity cornhole,
and get a secretary.

3. www.reference.com/
browse/wiki/
Charles_Manson

Still, it was the DO NOT OPEN TILL CHRISTMAS that really got me. Sure! I'll open a package from the embodiment of ultimate evil on Christmas morn, with the whole family gathered 'round! "Hey everybody, it's the bloody shiv that Manson used to slay a fellow inmate! Merry Christmas!"

Then I thought: *hey, why* not *wait for Christmas?* It was still weeks away, but we were planning to host all the relatives, and I thought it would make for some interesting afternoon entertainment. Besides, Manson likes family get-togethers.

Bono Responds

U2 fans, as well as those who think they went downhill after *The Joshua Tree*, will be pleased to know that the next response was from **Bono**, or at least Bono's agency, which shipped a large package from Ireland, containing several band photographs, a U2 T-shirt, and a handwritten note apologizing that Bono could not autograph the photo, as he was on tour.

And thus, Bono's canonization in the order of saints is complete.

St. Bono, future generations will call him, *the patron saint of sunglasses.*

U2

The Third Letter

In late December, I sent out my final plea to the remaining celebs.

To drive the point home, I actually doused the letter in my own tears (saline solution). I enclosed a five-dollar bill with each letter, and sent them early enough to make sure they arrived by Christmas. This was the ultimate test: would celebrities take money from a dead girl, *on Christmas?*

John Hargrave
P.O. Box 990586
Boston, MA 02199

Ms. Oprah Winfrey
c/o Creative Artists Agency
9830 Wilshire Boulevard
Beverly Hills, CA 90212-1825

Dear Ms. Winfrey:

I wrote you a few months ago, asking if you would please call or write my 12-year-old daughter Jane, who was diagnosed with a rare disease of the pancreas. She was drawing sketches of you in an attempt to raise money for your charity Oprah's Angel Network.

You never responded, and now it's too late. Jane passed away last Monday.

Words cannot begin to describe the grief and loss that floods my heart and consumes my every waking moment. This letter is covered in my tears, because I have lost my baby girl. She was a beautiful and radiant human being: smart, amazing, with a heart full of love for your cause.

Even though I have always had strong religious beliefs (Presbyterian), I now feel that either God does not exist, or has made my family the victim of a cruel joke. It is unbearable, this crushing feeling of despair, this overwhelming sense of hopelessness. I find myself praying that God will take my entire family, so that we can once again be with my beautiful daughter, our friend.

I am sorry to bother you with my problems. You are a busy person, and have more important matters to look after. I just wanted you to know that one of the doctors at the ICU where Jane spent the last months of her life actually bought a sketch of you, one of the sketches that Jane sent you to be autographed.

As Jane wanted this money to go to Oprah's Angel Network, I am sending the proceeds to you now, in hopes that it will help the disadvantaged and needy. This is what Jane would have wanted.

Sincerely,

John Hargrave

Rosie O'Donnell Responds

Just before the holidays, I received the letter below in my mailbox.

This was a nice response, though I didn't quite buy the "moving offices" excuse, since I sent all three letters to the same P.O. box. Still, the letter was generous and appropriate. Rosie moved from the "naughty" to "nice" list, and just in the nick of time. The *St.* Nick of time.

John Hargrave
P.O. Box 990586
Boston, MA 02199

Dear Mr. Hargrave,

On behalf of Rosie and the Foundation, we are deeply sorry for the loss of your daughter. Our thoughts and hearts are with you and your family.

In the process of moving offices, we did not receive Jane's sketches. If we had, we would have facilitated a call with Rosie. We are very sorry to have missed that opportunity.

Thank you for the $5 cash donation Jane raised from the sale of her sketches. We greatly appreciate her creative and diligent efforts to help other children. Her donation will be added to our Project Katrina Initiative, from which 100% of the donations received will go directly to hurricane relief for children. Our Project Katrina Initiative provides emergency short-term relief to displaced children and supports organizations in Louisiana, Mississippi, and Alabama that provide childcare, early childhood education, and after-school programs.

We extend our heartfelt condolences to you during this difficult time. May you find some comfort in knowing that Jane's generosity, determination, and kindness will bring light to the lives of children in need.

With greatest sympathy,

Sandra L. Cobden
Executive Director

* As required by law, we also acknowledge that your monetary contribution is without goods or services provided in return. Rosie's For All Kids Foundation is a non-profit organization classified as 501(c)3 by the Internal Revenue Service. Your contribution to the Foundation is tax-deductible to the extent permitted by law.

P.O. BOX 225, ALLENDALE, NEW JERSEY 07401   PH (201) 934-5567   FAX (201) 760-9665

A Manson Family Christmas

It took incredible discipline, incredible patience and fortitude, to wait until Christmas to open the Manson package. For weeks, it sat under the tree, quiet and threatening. I was both curious and terrified, but I obeyed the instructions: DO NOT OPEN TILL CHRISTMAS. We all know what happened *last time* someone obeyed Manson's instructions, but I was hoping this would have a happier ending. Still, just to be safe, I moved the package out to the garage on Christmas Eve.

Finally, the big day arrived. I sat through the normal Christmas routine, full of nervous energy.

"All right," I announced to the family around noon. "It's time."

"Where you going?" asked my father, who had not yet heard the story.

"Oh, just opening a gift from Charles Manson," I said nonchalantly as I headed out to the garage.

My heart was throbbing as I took the package out into the street. My brother videotaped the moment, while other relatives watched from 25 yards away, which I hoped would be outside the blast zone. I didn't have a proper hard hat, so I wore my bicycle helmet and safety goggles as I began slowly cutting open the package. Heavily fortified with many layers of packing tape, it took me several minutes to open.

"Look out for the car!" my mother shouted.

I got out of the way just as a car whizzed by. It would be ironic if the package was completely safe, but I was run over by a speeding vehicle.

As my neighbors began flocking to their windows to see what was going on, I resumed the cutting. With each swipe of the knife, I was afraid that a swarm of violent insects would shoot out of the package and consume my face.

"Maybe it's a human pancreas," my brother suggested helpfully. "You know, for little Jane Hargrave."

Finally, I sawed through all the tape. I took a deep breath, gripping the two halves of the box top. Then, with a dramatic flourish, I opened the package to find...

MACARONI.

Yes, Charles Manson had sent me a box full of macaroni. Apparently, he was not only America's most notorious criminal, but also an amateur Italian chef. But...wait! No! *The macaroni was only the packing material!* There was something inside!

Slowly, I brushed away the pasta to find three small wooden keepsake boxes. One was labeled LOVE, one had decorative beading on top, and one featured a large hand-painted pink heart.

"This is how Pandora must have felt," I muttered as I lifted up the boxes. "Should I unleash every plague and pestilence known to mankind?" I asked the human race. "Or should I leave the boxes sealed?"

Summoning all of my courage, I opened the first box. It was empty except for Manson's hand-carved signature.

Watch the Manson package being opened on Christmas:
www.prankthemonkey.com/celebrity

The other boxes were the same. Manson had sent the most thoughtful gift of all: *three handcrafted keepsake boxes for the dying twelve-year-old girl.* They call Manson crazy, but to me the craziest thing was that he sent a more charitable gift than any of the other charity-obsessed stars.

Celebrity Sincerity: The Results

After months of waiting patiently for additional responses, I finally gave up on the remaining celebs. Here are the final results, from least to most sincere:

CELEBRITY	RESPONSE	SINCERE?
Oprah Winfrey	No response	Insincere
Sting	No response	Insincere
Steven Spielberg	No response	Insincere
Madonna	No response	Insincere
Angelina Jolie	No response	Insincere
Pam Anderson	No response	Insincere
Rosie O'Donnell	Letter	Sincere
Bono	Letter, photos, T-shirt	Quite sincere
Jerry Lewis	Autographed photo	Very sincere
Ronald McDonald	Phone call, gifts	Extremely sincere
Charles Manson	Handcrafted gift boxes	Wicked sincere

Dear Charles:

Thank you!!

jewelry box ↓

Your kindness means

So much to me

← me

THANK YOU

Thank you so much for the hand-made jewelry boxes you sent me for Christmas. I have great news: my entolritis is completely cured! It was very scary for a few days... my heartbeat went down so low they thought I was dead. But thanks to support and prayers from people like you, I am completely in remission and will be starting school again next week. You have given me faith in famous people again!

From my family to yours,
Jane Hargrave

I Kissed Bill Gates

 WE WERE SQUEEZED INTO an overflow room at the Las Vegas Hilton, straining to make out a grainy TV image of Microsoft CEO Bill Gates. His keynote speech was broadcasting live from a large amphitheater down the hall, but my crew and I had arrived too late to get inside the packed auditorium. Geeks were drawn to Gates like Peter Jackson to a ham festival. Some loved him, most hated him, but everyone secretly worshipped him. Even here in the conference room, people were shoulder to shoulder, straining to catch a glimpse of the World's Richest Man, as he told about a dazzling new future with Microsoft.

In time, I would learn that Bill Gates promised this future *every* year—but as far as I could see, Microsoft products continued to suck harder than ever. I still couldn't figure out how to change the default font in Word. The search function in Outlook was still a piece of shit. Microsoft products were getting almost as cumbersome and poorly designed as Macs. I had a lot of questions for Mr. Gates to answer: why do you continually stuff features I don't use into more expensive versions of the same crappy software? Why do you always release Microsoft products before they're ready? And: how much can you bench-press?

Were these questions for Bill Gates? I thought they were. He was the most powerful executive at Microsoft, arguably the most powerful man in the world, and the ultimate responsibility for all these crappy Microsoft products had to rest with someone.

The buck, I thought, should stop with Bill. He had a lot of explaining to do.

"We've got to interview this guy," I told Al, my fellow troublemaker, who would many years later draw the illustrations for this book. "We've got to interview Gates."

"Good luck," said Al, his eyes glued to the screen.

Gates was untouchable. You had to be fucking *Time* to get near him, or at least fucking a *Time* editor. It was unlikely the Microsoft people were ever going to give us a legitimate interview, especially since we were dressed up as giant silver robots.

Pushing the Reporting Envelope

I wasn't exactly a traditional reporter. I covered "the lighter side of technology" for Ziff-Davis, a large media company that flew me out to Las Vegas each year to file humorous commentary on COMDEX, the world's largest technology orgy. My comedy crew and I developed our own style of "ambush interview," where we would run up to a celebrity, dressed in a ridiculous costume, and begin asking a string of bizarre and colorful questions. Most of the time we were drunk. Our ridiculous stunts were literally a riot: like the time we threw hundreds of dollars of money into an angry mob of computer geeks on the convention floor. Or the time we challenged gangsta rapper Ice-T to a fight. Our irreverent technology reports were eagerly, or perhaps inadvertently, read by millions of people each year.

We knew an interview with Bill Gates would blast our ratings through the mothereffing *roof*. We had questions prepared, and we were determined to track him down by any means necessary. By a strange twist of fate, we would have our first opportunity that night, when all of us would attend the same party at the Las Vegas Harley-Davidson Cafe. Because when you think "Harley-Davidson," you naturally think of a giant party of nerds.

Party Like It's Approximately 1999

Dweebs doing drugs, drinking, and dancing: the party that night, surprisingly, was a riot scene. Instead of fat, bearded bikers, the Harley-Davidson club was overrun with fat, bearded UNIX administrators. The music was pumped up to bowel-liquifying levels, and you couldn't cut through the crowd with a greased wiener. This was no place to be wearing a silver robot costume, especially one made out of non-breathable, polyurethane-coated PVC. The alcohol, lack of hydration, and inadequate costume ventilation quickly got to me, and I felt faint. I forced my way to the bar and asked for a glass of water, where I sat, breathing heavily, until the dark swimmy spots in my head started to fade.

Al came over to the bar and told me that Michael Dell, CEO of Dell Computer Corporation, was in the hizzy. That was a must-have interview, so we pushed our way through the crowd, trying desperately to shout directions to each other over the noise and chaos. We were in the middle of the dance floor, looking around, when we heard the crowd begin to cheer over the thunderous music, like a family of weasels being thrown into a screaming jet engine. At first, I assumed that everyone wanted the robot guys to dance, so I began *doing* the robot. Then I saw him, up on the stage: *Bill Gates.*

Let me describe the scene. We were packed to the point of suffocation down on the dance floor, but there was *another* group of people dancing up on stage, the VIP dance floor. Bill Gates was actually *dancing*, a series of awkward, spastic gyrations that resembled a chicken on methamphetamine. Trying desperately to groove with him was this amazing knockout supermodel—who was not, it should be pointed out, his wife. At 6 foot 2, she hovered over the geeky CEO with long tanned legs and enormous, Vegas-size breasts. The thing I remember most clearly about that moment is that amusingly, neither of them could dance.

"Let's go!" I screamed to my cohorts, and began furiously clawing my way to the stage. As I looked around for a stage entrance, I was stopped by a bouncer with a tree stump neck and redwood arms.

"Where are you going?!" he roared over the music, clearly prejudiced against robots.

"I have to get up on stage!" I shouted. "I'm with Ziff-Davis!" I flashed him my cheesy badge that we had made at Kinko's that morning for five cents.

"Why?"

"They told me to get up there!" I hollered. "I have to make a speech!"

He looked troubled. "All right," he finally relented, and let me pass. I scrambled up on stage, only to see Bill Gates striding off the opposite side.

With an interview so close, I couldn't let him get away. I took chase after the famous software mogul. What happened over the next ninety seconds was the kind of thing you only see in movies.

HARGRAVE motions at crew, still on the dance floor, to catch BILL GATES.

CREW pushes their way through the crowd, chasing GATES.

GATES, led by a small entourage, makes his way to side of club. Like Jesus, people are screaming to shake his hand, to touch the hem of his garment.

HARGRAVE is now along wall, fighting the mob to get to GATES.

Quick pan across to CREW, heading him off from the opposite side.

At the last moment, GATES is whisked down a side hallway, and out of sight. HARGRAVE and CREW meet up at the same doorway moments later, slamming through the swinging door. They see GATES being pushed into an elevator by his security people, who quickly follow him in, looking worriedly over their shoulder at the silver robots bearing down upon them.

As the elevator doors begin to close, HARGRAVE leaps forward, trying to grab it. Like the final scene in 12 Monkeys, we see a slow-motion shot of HARGRAVE flying through the air, a tape recorder in his outstretched hand, as the door closes just inches beyond his grasp.

*Just before he hits the ground, POV shot inside the elevator, where GATES is surrounded by his handlers, who are trying desperately to protect him. In the middle of all this, GATES continues dancing spasmodically, completely oblivious to what is happening. Eerily, however, **there is no music playing.***

To this day, I still wonder why Gates was continuing to dance. I mean, I've been to some wild parties, but when flying robots come after me, I stop dancing and flush the hallucinogens down the toilet.

One Year Later

The following year, we found ourselves back in Vegas, back at the same industry party, covering the same crap. The only thing different was our costumes, which were even more outrageous. We looked like the Village People threw up on us, in alphabetical order: biker, construction worker, cowboy, Indian, policeman, soldier. You could see a little of each of those styles, and several others. It was bizarre, even for Vegas.

Andrew, one of my crew members, who would one day shoot the back cover photo for this book, came over to the bar. "Bill Gates is over there," he said nonchalantly, sipping a drink.

I did a spit take, spraying Sam Adams on Andrew's giant inflatable pink hat. "You're shitting me," I said.

"Dude, look for yourself."

I looked over and saw Bill Gates standing on the upper level of the club, chatting casually with a small throng of fans.

"We're going in," I said to my crew. The four of us cut our way across the crowd, through the cacophonous music, up the stairs, until there we saw our prey: the one, the only, BFG.

People were crowded around him, three deep. *Everyone* wanted to talk with the titan of technology, probably to complain about Windows Media Player. Fortunately, none of those people were dressed like Elton John's proctologist. Within moments, my ridiculous costume, plus a fair amount of shoving, got me standing right next to the sultan of software, Mr. Bill Gates.

Picture this: Billy G. and his homies, surrounded by a bunch of idiots in fruity costumes. The business-man talking to Bill was pitching some lame-ass business idea to him, while Bill nodded politely, looking somewhat concerned as he saw us approach-ing. There were no handlers in sight; Bill was unpro-tected, completely exposed to the common man. This would turn out to be his biggest mistake.

I waited patiently for the idiot to finish, then began what I believe is the most important interview in the history of modern media. Ladies and gentlemen, my Bill Gates exclusive:

JOHN HARGRAVE: Should the browser wars be fought with guns?

BILL GATES: I'm…uh, I'm not really here to answer ques-tions.

JH: When human cloning becomes affordable, how many clones of yourself will you have made?

BG: (smiling) I'm just not here to answer questions.

JH: Tell me about the first girl you ever kissed.

BG: (smiling) Hmm.

JH: How much can you bench press?

BG: (slightly exasperated) I'm sorry…who are you with?

JH: How do I turn off the Autocorrect feature in Word?

BG: (eyeing my Kinko's badge) You're with Ziff-Davis?

JH: Boxers or briefs?

BG: (looking around helplessly)

Wow! Hard-hitting questions! I should be working for *60 Minutes*. I was like Lesley Stahl, only with a larger penis. Maybe I would end up with enough juicy material to turn my exclusive interview into a full-length book, or at least a chapter in this one.

Gates looked around for support, but the crowd was just chuckling. You have to understand that at the time, he really was the most hated figure in technology. The U.S. Department of Justice was fighting Microsoft for abusing its Windows monopoly; smaller technology companies were being forced out of business. Microsoft, not Google, was the Evil Empire. No one was eager to rush to Bill's aid.

"You know what?" This was the money question, the one that would get him to cry. "I just really love your products, and I want to give you a hug." I held open my arms and moved toward him. "Will you hug me?"

Like a cornered animal, his eyes darted back and forth, searching for an escape route. He was backed against a railing, with the crowd pressing against him from all sides. And then, with my giant fluorescent hat and freshly glittered face, I drew Bill Gates into a warm embrace.

Gates clenched his fist tightly, wedging it between our bellies to keep us from getting too close. (Intimacy issues.) I was so close to him that he had no choice but to halfheartedly place his hand on my shoulder. Imagine coming up the stairs at that point, expecting to catch a glimpse of Bill Gates, and then finding him hugging a homosexual pirate. I was like the flamboyant son he never had.

I nestled my head into his chest, so close that I could smell his sweater. Slowly, I began to grind my pelvis into his leg. He didn't like that at all, which I can understand. Dry humping is never very comfortable. It's really an activity for teenagers and Catholics, not two grown men.

I held the hug for a long time. It was uncomfortable, but I wanted to make sure the crew was getting it on film. And then, for my grand finale, just before I released him from our lovelock, I bent down and gently kissed his nipple.

Two Nipples for a Dime

As I've told this story over the years, I've had a few people accuse me of exaggerating my accomplishment. "You didn't *really* kiss his nipple," they say. "He had on a sweater."

First of all, I explain, the phrase "kissing one's ass" doesn't mean that the ass has to be naked. For one, that would be unsanitary. Also: impractical. Ass-kissers would never inconvenience their subjects by asking them to remove their pants.

Second, I point out that *no one* has ever kissed Bill Gates's bare nipple, except for Steve Ballmer, and that was way back in college. Harvard was a lot more free-spirited in those days.

It is, quite simply, the richest nipple in the world. Even if it has to split everything fifty/fifty with the other nipple, that still makes it worth $23.3 billion dollars.[1] That's richer than Warren Buffett's nipples ($22 billion apiece). Richard Branson's nipples look like the flattened silver dollars of a crack whore at a

1. Source: *Forbes* annual ranking of the world's richest people. Broken down on a per-nipple basis.

measly $1.6 billion each. And poor Martha Stewart can barely scrape together $1 billion dollars with both her tired, aging nipples combined.

My gesture of love and friendship toward Bill Gates was very different from the gesture I made toward another celebrity a few years later. But when you've pranked the King of Capitalism, there's only one person more famous: the King of Pop. ☺

The Making of Michael Jackson's Thriller

▲ This is Michael Jackson's credit card.

▲ Note the question mark.

AS WE'VE LEARNED, IT'S EASY to get a credit card in Michael Jackson's name—or any other celebrity, for that matter. Just get a legitimate card in your *own* name, then call your credit card company and ask to add an "additional cardmember." With your new credit card, you can create all manner of mischief. Like, for instance, *staging a public appearance of Michael Jackson in Boston when he was living in Bahrain.* Which is exactly what I did.

The first step was to make reservations for Mr. Jackson at every expensive hotel in Boston: the Ritz-Carlton, the Four Seasons, and Boston's most elegant hotel, the Fairmont Copley Plaza. Posing as Mr. Jackson's assistant, I booked their most expensive suites, grilling hotel managers and security staff about how they would ensure Mr. Jackson's privacy. I asked for platters of cold cuts to be waiting when he arrived. "*Plenty of ham*," I demanded. "Mr. Jackson is fond of ham."

This stunt was going to cost me a fortune, except I was planning on canceling all the hotel reservations before Saturday night even arrived. I just needed a plausible story for The Media, who were next on my hit list.

I made an anonymous call to the *Boston Herald* news desk, tipping off the editor that Michael Jackson would be arriving at the Copley Plaza hotel at 6:30 p.m. on Saturday. Calling from a filthy payphone (someone had recently dipped the receiver in a carton of chow mein), I repeated the process for every Boston newspaper and TV station. Then I went home and sent anonymous e-mails to all the Michael Jackson fan sites, who were thrilled to hear that the King of Pop might be making a royal visit to his home country.

Satisfied that the buzz was building, I turned my attention to the most challenging task of all: pulling together the players needed to pull off this caper, an *Ocean's 11*-style heist that would require over a dozen accomplices, thousands of dollars, and would ultimately make headlines across the world.

It was, quite simply, my greatest media hoax to date.

Wanna Be Startin' Somethin'

I chose my longtime collaborator Moses Blumenstiel to play the part of Michael Jackson, not because he looks anything like the famous rock star, but because he's a very funny improv comedian who I thought could pull it off. I also had to find actors to play Jackson's bodyguards, film crew, paparazzi, and fans. Then I went to Kinko's and ran off business cards for all the appropriate players, including myself.

GEORGE J. HARGRAVE
Event/Media Coordinator
ZUG, Inc.

P.O. Box 990586
Boston, MA 02199
P (781) 555-1214
F (781) 555-1215

When people get suspicious about our pranks, a business card usually reassures them: no one can believe that an ordinary practical joker would take the time to do fake business cards. (In truth, Kinko's can turn them around in an hour.)

The most difficult task was finding an actor to play Michael's "son." His real-life son, Prince, was nine years old. Because a child would be unpredictable in a high-stress environment, I needed to find the next best alternative: *a live midget.*

In Our Small Way

I swear, it is *impossible* to find a midget in this town nowadays. I called talent scouts and modeling agencies, *begging* someone to locate a midget. Where the hell are all the midget actors when you need them? They can't be that busy. Sure, there's an occasional gig as an Oompa-Loompa, maybe they need somebody for the R2-D2 costume, but I can't imagine they're out auditioning for the lead in *Death of a Salesman.* Come on. There are only so many Morning Zoo promos you can do.

After twenty or thirty phone calls, I grew so desperate that—not a joke—I called the Latina Talent Agency, on the off-chance they had a Mexican midget. I spoke with a lithe young man named Gerson, who assured me, through his thick accent, that they had what I needed.

"Yes," he purred, "we have a small man."

"How small?" I asked. Using medical charts, I had calculated Prince's approximate height.

"He is very small," he assured me. "A very short man."

"I need a *midget*," I explained. "If I just needed a short guy, I'd use myself. Do you know what a midget is?" I hated sounding like a jerk, but I wasn't sure he knew what the word meant.

"Yes, yes, a midget," he repeated. "Like Tattoo."

"Yes! 'The plane.'"

Gerson laughed. "Yes, the plane. *Si.* You will like this man I have for you," he insisted. "He is twenty-three years old, but he looks very young."

"Great," I said. "What's his name?"

"His name is Hugo."

Tabloid Junkie

Everyone arrived at the studio on Saturday afternoon to begin filming our documentary. I was delighted to see that Hugo was *perfect* for the part: a small man of perhaps four and a half feet, he looked like a teenager. Since Hugo would have a blanket over his head throughout the caper (just like Michael Jackson's children), Gerson came along to serve as his "guide." This would turn out to be incredibly good fortune.

I ran our crew of stunt actors through the plan. At precisely 6:30 p.m., Michael Jackson would make his grand entrance through the front doors of the Fairmont Copley Plaza, Boston's flashiest hotel. Amidst the cacophony of the film crew, screaming fans, and paparazzi, Michael and his posse would make their way into a waiting limousine. They would then drive to a nearby fashion mall, where Jackson would vomit all over the window of a Victoria's Secret.

The vomit was key. Michael Jackson shopping in a mall was an interesting story, but Michael Jackson *puking* in a mall was irresistible. The next day, every tabloid around the world would have the story spattered across their pages.

Collecting the vomit, however, was not an easy task. It was a *queasy* task. I wasn't going to gather up a *stranger's* vomit (that's just gross), so several nights earlier I had eaten an entire pizza, then followed it with Syrup of Ipecac, the vomit-inducing liquid that's given to people who have accidentally ingested poison. The only thing that tastes more vile than Syrup of Ipecac, I discovered, is Syrup of Ipecac *on the way back up.* I spent the next hour hurling up meaty chunks of goo, extremely unhappy about the way my life was turning out.

I stored the bag of vomit in the vegetable drawer of my refrigerator until the day of the prank, so it was well-preserved—in fact, it still smelled like pizza. And a few hours later, I would be wearing most of it on my shoes, suit, and glasses.

Thriller

There we were, a dozen professional pranksters getting ready to pull off the media hoax of the century. We synchronized our watches, and I dispatched the stunt crew to their starting positions. Moses and Hugo, who would play Michael Jackson and his nine-year-old son, went to the basement of the hotel to get in costume. The fans took their places in Copley Square, holding up WE ♥ YOU MICHAEL signs and gathering a crowd. The film crew and I snuck into the hotel lobby to quietly shoot interior footage.

And we then had a happy surprise: later in the evening, *R&B legend Gladys Knight would be performing at that very hotel.* It was another incredibly lucky coincidence: the Motown diva would be playing this black-tie gala dinner, a twentieth-anniversary fundraising event for an inner-city charity. Dozens of well-dressed African Americans were already checking into registration.

I saw a sign reading MEDIA CHECK-IN, and confidently strode up to the table. Fully in character now, I gave the young white woman a smile. "Michael Jackson will be at the hotel tonight," I said. "We're wondering if it would be possible to have him attend the show."

"*The* Michael Jackson?" she stammered.

"Yes, a Michael Jackson," I said quickly, as if I were sick of this question. "Maybe it would be possible for Mr. Jackson to meet up with Ms. Knight after the show?" I had changed into my suit, and had on my cellphone headset, so I looked like the real deal.

"Well, I'll, ah...I'll be happy to take your number and have someone get in touch."

"Great," I said, giving her the number of my stunt cellphone. "Give me a call."

Butterflies

Finally, we were ready. Down in the hotel basement, we got the cameras rolling, then slowly brought out our players. One of the greatest challenges of my life was keeping a straight face while looking at Moses. It was just preposterous. With gauze wrapped around his head, and his mismatched shirt and scarf, he looked like he had come straight out of the burn unit. In 1974.

Hugo, our little person, came out next. He and Gerson had been patiently waiting in a toilet stall for the last hour, a blanket over Hugo's head. Hugo had moved to the big city to break into acting, and I found out later this was his first gig. I wonder if he thinks all acting jobs are like that: *first you sit in the toilet with a stranger for an hour, then you walk around with a blanket on your head.*

We were the world's most bizarre entourage, which was perfect: exactly what you'd expect from Wacko Jacko. We crammed into the hotel elevators, and even though I had drilled everyone to stay in character, I started cracking up as soon as the doors closed. I couldn't help it: this was nuts. Our hearts were exploding.

And then the elevator doors opened, and all eyes were upon us. Showtime.

Greatest Show on Earth

For the fans gathered outside Boston's wealthiest hotel on that cold Saturday evening, it was a once-in-a-lifetime opportunity to see a rare public appearance of the world's most famous pop star. Tourists and curious onlookers were drawn into the scene, making them both victims and participants of the prank. The rumor spread through the crowd like herpes in a CPR class: *Michael Jackson is coming.*

A black stretch limousine pulled up to the entrance, and a wave of cheering and screaming began to ripple through the public square. The

gold-encrusted doors of the hotel opened to reveal a
full film crew, their bright, hot camera lights illumi-
nating a strange creature whose head was completely
wrapped in gauze, his mouth covered in a dust mask.
He looked not so much like *Michael Jackson* as *the*
Elephant Man with sunglasses.

I have to admit, the
chaos was scarier than I had
expected. We piled into the
limo as fans and paparazzi

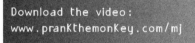
Download the video:
www.prankthemonkey.com/mj

banged on the windows and hollered his name. It was
a heady stew of anarchy and barely contained rage.
The limo driver, who thought he was escorting the
real Michael Jackson, kept his cool, but his eyes
betrayed fear. POP! POP! went camera flashbulbs,
with *fake* press and *real* press right up in our face,
and impossible to distinguish.

The limo took us to Copley Place, an upscale
shopping galleria just a block away, with fans and
photographers following after us. With the help
of "bodyguards" and confused security officers, we
escorted MJ to fancy fashion stores, drawing stares
and crowds everywhere we went. Once inside, we
worked with the store's uniformed security guards
to keep our celebrity safe. Using the credit card we
had ordered in his name, Michael bought a glove.

Heading toward the nearby Victoria's Secret,
Michael started to complain of stomach pain. We
slowly made our way to the huge plate-glass display
outside the famous lingerie store. The mannequins
were dressed in thongs and garters, their erect nipples barely covered by lacy bras. It was, quite frankly,

the sluttiest shop window I've ever seen. Victoria's Secret is starting to look like a fucking Amsterdam whorehouse.

While Moe made the appropriate noises (it sounded like a small dog choking on a ball of yarn), I squeezed the bag of upchuck, firing a horrible *vomit explosion* onto the window. It was Hollywood-level puke pyrotechnics; I was the Jerry Bruckheimer of barf. The Victoria's Secret mannequin whores stared passively at the partially digested pizza as it dripped down the glass in long, filthy streaks. What a bunch of dummies.

Then we got the fuck out of there.

As we hurried away, I realized one flaw in our logic: *Michael Jackson had just thrown up through two layers of Ace Bandage and a surgical mask.* We could only hope that people would be too confused to notice.

We had almost reached the mall property line when two uniformed security guards cut us off. Worse, their uniforms were *suits*, which is always a bad sign. Rent-a-cops are generally harmless, but the suits are bad news. They demanded that we turn off the cameras and relinquish the tape. "You did not have permission to be filming here!" they hissed at us.

"I don't know what to tell you," I said, walking around them. "What's done is done, guys."

They blocked me again, and we continued to argue. My cellphone rang. Knowing that it would provide a much-needed distraction, and since my headset was already in my ear, I slid a slippery hand into my pocket and pressed the button.

"Hi, honey!" my wife said cheerily on the other side.

"Wanted to let you know that the Barney show just let out." She had taken our three-year-old to see Barney.

I looked at my group devolving into chaos, the menacing security guards hemming us in from all sides. I wiped a finger, still shiny from vomit, across my forehead. "Worst. Timing. Ever," I said to my wife.

"Okay, then!" She hung up.

It was time to take charge. "I can't believe you're treating the great Michael Jackson in this way," I said, ushering our camera crew out the door. "I'm very disappointed." Perhaps they didn't have a legal leg to stand on, or perhaps they were just relieved to see us go, but they didn't stop us as we walked past them, out into the waiting limousine.

As we rode back to the studio, the stink of vomit reeking up the limousine, I reflected on the evening. Our test run had revealed only one problem: *Moses looked nothing like Michael Jackson.* Moses is a tall white male. Michael Jackson is a small white *freak.*

After weeks of methodical planning, it was time to improvise. "Gerson," I said, "how would you like to play Michael Jackson?"

"*Si,*" he responded.

Back in the studio, we went to work on creating Michael 2.0. I knew right away that Gerson was the one. Once he put on the hat and the mask, I have to tell you: *the dude looked like Michael Jackson.*

With our new Michael, we would fool the world. Or at least the organizers of the Gladys Knight gala, who would completely fall for our ruse. Within hours, we would be sneaking our fake Michael Jackson into the $10,000-a-plate charity event, where we would be treated like the celebrities that we were not.

▶ We also decided to let Hugo spend some time without the blanket on his head. Poor guy hadn't seen daylight in two hours.

Don't Stop 'Til You Get Enough

I went over to the hotel to meet the event coordinator, a Caucasian man about my own age, well-dressed, black goatee. He introduced himself.

"George Hargrave," I said, shaking his hand. "As we discussed, Mr. Jackson would love to come see the show."

He paused for several seconds, looking me straight in the eyes. "Michael Jackson is coming?" he asked skeptically.

"Well, if you'll have him," I said. He was suspicious, so I talked quickly, redirecting the conversation. "We have a limo for the evening, of course, and I was wondering if you have a back door Mr. Jackson could come in?" (This was probably not the first time a man was asked if he had a back door Mr. Jackson could come in.)

The event producer sized me up once more. "We do have a service entrance," he said slowly. "It leads up to a private balcony area that we could section off for your party."

"That would be excellent," I said, quietly relieved. "There will probably be eight to ten of us."

"Okay. Would you like to come backstage with me?" he asked, leading the way into the ornate concert ballroom.

I followed him, nervous as hell. That was a close call, but I thought I had sold it. He wanted to believe. We all want to believe. That is why people fall for these pranks: *who doesn't want to meet Michael Jackson?*

We walked up to the balcony, looking down into an ornate ballroom. The place was *packed.* The mayor of Boston was there, along with every prominent African American in the city. I couldn't believe our luck: *Michael Jackson was about to appear before a huge audience of wealthy R&B fans.*

"We could close off this balcony for you," said the coordinator, pointing to a large curtain that could be pulled down to give us private seating.

"That would be excellent," I said. We agreed on a seating arrangement for Michael's bodyguards, then walked down the stairwell to an unmarked metal door that led outside. "His limo could park out here. He'd come in this service entrance, then walk down this hallway to the balcony."

He pointed up the hallway, where several guards in suits watched us from their permanent security station. We'd have to walk directly past them.

"Fine," I said, quietly soiling my pants. "This will be just fine."

▲ Puttin' on the Ritz crackers.

Whatever Happens

I went back to the studio and loaded the crew into the limo again. Man, Gerson looked good as Michael Jackson. If you do a side-by-side comparison, you might be able to tell it's not him, but if you were *expecting* to see Michael Jackson, *it was him.*

Our previous run had been meticulously planned, but this time we were flying by the seat of our pants. As we drove up to the Fairmont Copley Plaza hotel, my mind was racing. My heart was racing. The two organs were side-by-side in the final lap of the Daytona 500, with my liver and spleen cheering from the sidelines. I looked over at Gerson, who was wearing khakis and an Ace Hardware dust mask.

I looked down at my suit and shoes, still spattered with vomit. There was no way we were going to pull this off.

"Okay, team," I said. "Big smiles. We're going to pull this off."

I got out of the limo and ushered the team through the service entrance. I pretended to be talking on my headset as we whisked past the security guards. Hotel employees were lined up in the service hallway, especially younger women, wanting to catch a glimpse of Michael Jackson.

The event producer and the hotel manager were waiting to escort us up the stairs to Mr. Jackson's private balcony. I looked back. The crew was still following behind, Moses filming with his hidden camera. The concert had started, and the music grew almost deafeningly loud as we approached the balcony seating area. It was dark and noisy, which was perfect. It was like a strip club with a $10,000 cover.

"CAN WE GET YOU ANYTHING?" asked the hotel manager as the gang took their seats at our private table.

"A BOWL OF NUTS," I said, without hesitation. I figured this was the perfect request, since Michael Jackson *is* nuts.

They disappeared, and a few minutes later, a waitress came back up with an *enormous* pile of gourmet nuts in an expensive silver bowl.

▼ I swear, being a celebrity is the easiest motherfucking job in the world.

Dangerous

The show was fantastic. I tried to allow myself a few minutes to enjoy it, but my mind was flying. I was playing elaborate mental games of speed chess, trying to weigh our next move. The good news was that Gerson was perfectly playing the part of Michael Jackson, nodding his head to the music and even clapping along. Only an accomplished musician would have noticed the dead giveaway: *he was clapping on beats 1 and 3.*

The concert organizers kept coming up to the balcony to get a glimpse of the reclusive pop star, and I did my best to keep them far away from the table, yelling small talk over the music.

"SO THIS IS A CHARITY EVENT?" I asked the tall middle-aged woman in charge of fund-raising.

"YES," she said. She pointed over to Hugo. "IS THAT HIS SON?" she asked.

"I THINK IT'S BEST FOR ME NOT TO TALK ABOUT THAT," I responded, shutting her down. There was awkward silence, filled only by R&B music blasted at 200 decibels.

"COULD MR. JACKSON MAKE A DONATION?" I asked, immediately regretting the question.

"SURE!" she said, her eyes lighting up. "LET ME GET YOU A DONATION FORM." She paused uncertainly. "HOW WOULD HE LIKE TO PAY FOR THIS? YOU TELL ME."

"WELL," I said, thinking quickly, "WOULD YOU TAKE A CREDIT CARD?"

Smooth Criminal

What the hell, I said to myself a few minutes later, as Gerson forged Michael Jackson's signature to a legally binding form. *If you're going to prank a charity, you better even out the karma.*

"HE'S SORRY IT CAN'T BE MORE," I told the event organizer, handing her the donation form and Michael's credit card. "HE'S HAD SOME FINANCIAL DIFFICULTIES LATELY."

She nodded, looking down at the number. "WE APPRECIATE IT!"

"CAN WE PAY YOU FOR THE SEATS HERE?" I asked. "THE NUTS?"

"NO, NO," she said. "IT WAS OUR PLEASURE."

Gladys Knight (no Pips) played her last song, and the house lights went up. It was time to make our move. "Stand up, and walk near the balcony," I said to Gerson over thunderous applause. "It's time for your photo op."

He stood up, and over the applause for Gladys Knight, there was just this *audible gasp.* Flashbulbs

began popping toward the balcony. Celebrity news travels fast, and by this time, every person in the ballroom had heard that Michael Jackson was in the room. It was glorious.

I ran downstairs to find the event coordinator, who was talking with a late-middle-aged black man dressed in a tuxedo. "George," he greeted me, "this is Ms. Knight's manager."

"Pleased to meet you," I said, all business. "So do you think we could have Mr. Jackson meet with Ms. Knight?"

The manager, who was just like me, only representing a *real* celebrity, gave me a long glare. "Gladys Knight has *met* Michael Jackson," he growled. "She *discovered* him, when he was a little boy with the Jackson 5."

My stomach lurched. "Of course," I recovered quickly. "So would they like to meet *up*?"

"They have *met*," he repeated. "Do you understand what I am saying?"

I completely understood, unlike the event producer, who seemed to have no idea what was going on between us. "We can probably make it happen," he said brightly, clearly enthusiastic about getting a photo of the two stars together at his party.

"Tell you what," I said quickly, "let me go upstairs and see how he's feeling." On the way upstairs, I made a quick call to the driver and asked him to get the limo ready.

When I returned to the balcony, I found even more bad news: a young alcoholic reporter was seated directly across from Gerson, leaning into him threateningly.

"Excuse me, sir!" I said, adrenaline coursing through my system. "You need to leave. NOW!"

"You're not Michael Jackson," the reporter growled, looking directly into Gerson's face, a hungry lion sizing up a pregnant hyena. "If you were Michael Jackson, how'd I get this close to you?" Later, I would find out that he simply walked around the curtain, as my crew watched helplessly.

"If you do not leave RIGHT NOW," I commanded, "I am going to call the police. GET OUT." I pointed at the curtain, summoning the team that it was time to go.

"You're not Michael Jackson," he repeated, backing away. Now we had curious guests peering around the curtain. "This is NOT Michael Jackson!" he shouted.

He had a point: this was not the King of Pop. It was the King of Poop. The façade was crumbling, and we couldn't sustain the hoax much longer. Although I desperately wanted Michael to meet Gladys Knight, I had to make one of the toughest calls of my pranking career. Like a general ordering the troops to withdraw, I decided to get us out of there.

"We're going to have to go," I told the producer as we quickly hustled out the service entrance. "Mr. Jackson isn't feeling up to meeting Gladys tonight."

"You sure?" he asked, looking at me with renewed skepticism. The prank was coming apart, I could feel it. I just needed to get everyone out of there safely.

"I'm sure," I said, backing toward the entrance where the limo awaited. There was a small raised lip to the service door, and I tripped over it with a loud BANG, staggering backward.

"HEY!" shouted the producer as I tripped. "Come here."

I resisted the urge to turn and run. Out of the corner of my eye, I saw Hugo getting into the limousine. We were so close.

"Yes?" I asked.

"Do you have a card?"

GEORGE J. HARGRAVE
Event/Media Coordinator
ZUG, Inc.

P.O. Box 990586
Boston, MA 02199
P (781) 995-1234
F (781) 995-1235

"Yes," I said, opening my wallet and pulling out the fake card I had produced at Kinko's. "Yes, I do."

As he stood there examining it, I quickly got in the limo and asked the driver to take us away: somewhere, anywhere but here.

"Where you want to go?" asked the driver, who I'm pretty sure had figured out he wasn't driving around Michael Jackson.

I let out a long sigh of relief. "How far of a drive is Bahrain?"

Invincible

We awoke the next morning to a media frenzy. Every news station in Boston picked up the story; it even made the front page of the *Boston Herald.* From there, the story was syndicated to media outlets around the globe. Most reporters saw through the disguise, but the story was still irresistible: an unknown gang of pranksters made their way into a black-tie fund-raiser, got the VIP treatment, and then left with only an anonymous donation.

The donation was the detail that made the story great. Sure, we successfully got in and out of the concert without dropping character. Sure, we covered our tracks so well that even the world media couldn't track us down. But getting out when we did, leaving behind only the anonymous donation—*that* was the added touch of class.

Imagine the security guard going home that night to his wife and children: "You guys will *never guess* who came into the hotel tonight!" Imagine the waitress, her head spinning as she carefully arranges that bowl of nuts. Imagine being at that concert, an R&B legend in front of you and a pop legend watching from above.

It was only one night, but for everyone who was there, it was the greatest night of our lives.

Hurley-Whirler

ELIZABETH HURLEY WAS MAKING a mall appearance.

That's unfair. Gary Coleman makes a "mall appearance." When Liz Hurley does it, it's a "charity luncheon." *Survivor* castaways do mall appearances. Liz Hurley does "signings."

The occasion of Liz Hurley's visit was a nationwide tour to promote breast cancer. She was traveling with Evelyn Lauder, a senior executive of the Estée Lauder Corporation and creator of the famous "pink ribbon," which personally I feel should have been saved for *vagina* cancer, but what do I know. They dedicated the brown ribbon to colon cancer, they should have saved pink for cooter cancer. Sadly, I'm not in charge of these things, and so the world is awash in madness.

Lauder and Hurley (great name for a pair of cops) were generously giving their time and money to tour the country, promoting breast cancer. Still, I felt they needed to give *more*. Since cancer *takes* everything—your health, dignity, ultimately your life—I thought they should *give* everything. And "everything," in the case of these two women, is a lot.

Hurley is rich, even by Hollywood standards: she's worth an estimated 17 million pounds, which is ironic, since she only weighs 125 of them. But that's pocket change next to Evelyn Lauder, whose family owns over $6 billion of Estée Lauder stock,' not to mention several warehouses of leftover Hydrating Facial Scrub.

Despite (and thanks to) their wealth, both women are active philanthropists: they've raised over $70 million for breast cancer research. Still, it remains the second leading cause of death in American women.[2] That's a lot of sick tits.

Yes. They needed to give more. My idea was that I would draw up the last will and testament for both women, put a sheet of carbon paper on top of the documents, then stand in line to get their autographs. When they signed my autograph book, they'd actually be *signing their own wills,* transferring all their worldly goods to my godmother, Pat. She'd know what to do with all that money.

Cancer: It Eats at You

Everything I know about cancer I learned from Pat, who has battled the disease for the past seven years. It started with a cyst the size of a canteloupe, and went downhill from there. She's been injected with so much chemotherapy that they installed a drug port into her chest to keep her veins from collapsing. Currently, she takes forty-three pills a day: pain drugs, nausea drugs, anti-depressant drugs, anti-stress drugs, drugs to counteract the effects of other drugs, and the occasional recreational drug. And she gets to enjoy our world-class American medical "care," like the doctor who initially misdiagnosed her with bowel problems, even though she had Stage 4 ovarian cancer. "Whoops!" the doctor said later. "Sorry, my bad."[3]

I watched her lose her health and her hair, while she hung on to her humor and her hope. To me, it's

1. Source: Estée Lauder Companies.

2. Source: American Cancer Society.

3. I'm paraphrasing.

her hopefulness that's just incredibly inspiring, since there's still no cure for cancer, and probably never will be. To paraphrase one of the great philosophers of our time:

> They ain't curing cancer, 'cause there ain't no money in the cure; the money's in the *medicine*.
>
> What they will do with cancer is the same thing they do with everything else: they will figure out a way for you to *live with it*.
>
> Get you to the next stop, so they can get more of your money.[4]

My thinking was, why raise all that money just to give it back to big pharmaceutical companies? Why not give it to the people who really need it: the patients who have to *deal with* the big pharmaceutical companies?

If I could ease the suffering of just one cancer victim, it would all be worthwhile. I couldn't take away the pain, but I could at least make her more comfortable. *Several billion dollars* more comfortable.

Where There's a Will, There's a Way

Drafting up the wills was the easy part. You can download sample wills online, and I just filled in the blanks. Upon the death of either Elizabeth Hurley or Evelyn Lauder, I would become the sole executor of their estates, i.e., the guy who hands out the money. All of their assets, however, would be transferred directly to my godmother: everything from Liz Hurley's mansions to Lauder's nuclear bunker stocked with exfoliating creme. From there,

4. Chris Rock, *Bigger and Blacker*, 1999.

I would let Pat distribute their wealth to other cancer survivors. Or she could buy East Timor. Whatever.

I spent the next day traveling all over the city, looking for carbon paper. Staples didn't have it. OfficeMax didn't have it. I tried finding other office supply stores, but they all went out of business because of Staples and OfficeMax. Who knew it was so difficult to find a sheet of fucking carbon paper nowadays? I mean, it seems like I'm *constantly* pressing hard, because I'm making three copies. Clearly the carbon paper people are still in business, but I guess they only sell direct to bureaucracies nowadays.

Because I had foolishly waited until the day of the charity luncheon to prepare for my prank, I had to improvise. In my briefcase, I had a piece of artwork my three-year-old had recently brought home from day care. Using an X-Acto knife, I cut out a series of little windows, then artfully folded the wills behind them, making sure the signature line was positioned behind the holes in the paper. Then I sealed up the back with a Manson-size mountain of tape, forming a kind of bizarre greeting card (see next page).

I wrote ELIZABETH HURLEY and EVELYN LAUDER under the appropriate windows, to indicate where they should sign. The rest I filled in with imaginary family names: UNCLE CHUCK, COUSIN CLETUS, and so forth. One window was reserved for Boston Red Sox all-star DAVID ORTIZ. It was absolutely ridiculous, but I was under the gun.

I ran over to Saks Fifth Avenue, where Hurley and Lauder were holding their charity luncheon upstairs,

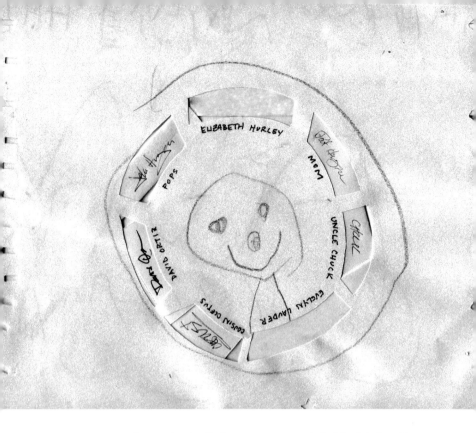

in a private dining area surrounded by high-roller donors. I got in the autograph line downstairs, along with the common folk. The fellow in front of me, in fact, was *extremely* common: easily 300 pounds, his hair was greasy and matted under a filthy baseball cap. He wore a nasty-ass jacket, covered with food stains, and was clutching a plastic grocery bag of magazines, all with Hurley's face on the cover.

He was a professional autograph collector.

I was pissed that this oaf was standing in front of me. *He was jeopardizing the mission.* The Saks people were already nervously flitting about, carefully examining every item that people wanted signed. I could just see them enforcing a no-bizarre-items policy, even though half the women in the line behind me were waiting for Lauder to sign their Purifying Mud Foam Cleanser or Anti-Cellulite Visible Contouring Serum. To me, this was weird, like asking Mr. Whipple to sign the Charmin.

From the looks of things, every employee of Saks Fifth Avenue Enterprises had decided to work today, even the two straight guys. They all milled about, wearing pink ribbons, anxiously eyeing the staircase where the two celebrities would be making their appearance. It was clear that there was not enough work for them all to do, so they continued to circulate through the line, checking and rechecking everyone's items.

"What is it?" asked a middle-aged store employee, holding my bizarre prank up to the light.

"It's an origami card," I explained. "It's for a family friend battling cancer."

"Isn't that sweet?" she said. "Look at this, Debbie." Debbie came over, and agreed that it was sweet. Both were wearing too many cosmetics. They looked whorish, like the married women of Georgia. They smelled like a Yankee Candle outlet store.

"Do you have an extra pink ribbon?" I asked, trying to distract them.

"Sure!" A few minutes later, Debbie brought over an *enormous* box full of pink ribbons.

"Thanks," I said, reaching into the box. As I pinned it onto my breast pocket, I reflected that all that pink ribbon money could have bought someone medical marijuana for a year. *And* the cheese waffles to go with it.

I Think I'm Gonna Hurl-ey

Brunch must have been filling, because they were now an hour late. In front of me, Comic Book Guy was getting impatient, looking at his watch and letting out long, smelly sighs. The Saks people were wired and jittery, looking for something, *anything*, to do while they waited. Debbie came through the line again, giving instructions. "When Ms. Hurley arrives, we're all going to applaud," she said, nodding vigorously to indicate that we should go along with this cockamamie plan.

"Why?" I asked.

"To make her feel welcome," she said, nodding even more violently.

"What about Ms. Lauder?" I asked.

"Oh, applaud her too."

A few minutes later, there was a small ripple of applause, then a collective gasp, and everyone spun around to face the back stairs. It was...yes! There she...oh, no. It was just a random person coming down the stairs. Bitch had gotten everyone so worked up that...oh! But behind her! It was...OH, MY LORD, THERE SHE IS! ELIZABETH HURLEY, THE ICON OF BEAUTY AND STYLE! A massive wave of applause rolled throughout the store. People were cheering, clambering on top of each other to catch a glimpse as she walked by. One of the male employees near me ejaculated in his shorts. I heard it go off like a soft cannon.

I looked at the autograph hound standing in front of me, who had seen this a hundred times before. He and I were the only ones not applauding; though to be fair, it might have been because he was too fat to clap his hands together. Evelyn Lauder, a dignified, stately woman, strode alongside Hurley. She was probably in her sixties, but her skin looked in its forties. Her liver spots were in their twenties. Her wrinkles were just learning to drive.

The two humanitarians took their place in front of the shoe department and made a little speech. I couldn't hear most of it, because I had 300 pounds of quivering manflesh in front of me. Ironically, I couldn't hear their speech about sweater melons, because this guy's sweater melons were blocking the sound. The one fragment I did hear was Liz Hurley saying, "Thanks to your support, breast cancer is now 97 percent curable if detected early."

"So can I give you an exam?" I asked, but quietly, so Lard Lad wouldn't think I was talking to him.

Finally, Hurley and Lauder took their place at the autograph table, and the line started moving. I watched Ignatius J. Reilly patiently display his stacks of magazines to the 14 or 15 Saks employees who wanted to once again check them over. They reluctantly let him present them all to Hurley, who didn't even wrinkle her nose at his fanboy funk. She signed them all, quickly and graciously, and he was on his way. Things were looking good.

Next, it was my turn. "What is this?" asked an impeccable Saks manager in his fifties.

"It's an origami card," Debbie told him.

"Right," I said, somehow keeping a straight face. "An origami card." A three-year-old's artwork, I realized, was far more manipulative than carbon paper.

"Okay," he said, pointing me to the table.

Evelyn Lauder was first. "This card is for a family friend who's battling cancer," I explained. "It was designed by my three-year-old, her godson."

"Isn't that wonderful," said the executive vice president of a $6.3 billion cosmetics company, peering over her reading glasses.

"If you could sign this," I continued, "it would be like *giving her everything*."

Marker in hand, she began to sign the *bottom* of the card, *not her allotted window!* Liz Hurley, sitting next to her, saved the day. "No, no," she said, pointing out the proper window.

"Oh," said Evelyn, placing her marker on the signature line of her last will and testament. And then, with one swipe of her Sharpie, Evelyn Lauder transferred her worldly assets to my godmother upon her death.

I moved down the table to Elizabeth Hurley, and found myself face-to-face with one of the world's most recognizable faces. "So is she really *that* beautiful?" several people asked me later. Hey, it's Liz Hurley. You want to see what she looks like, go rent fucking *Austin Powers*.

She looked over the card. "Are you sure you want *our* signatures on this?" she asked, pointing to the item of great sentimental value.

"Absolutely," I said. "It would be like *giving the world to her*."

And with that, she did, in fact, give the world to her.

Now I really *have* given my godmother a reason to keep fighting. All she has to do is outlive one of these two women. And between you and me, Evelyn Lauder may be older than she looks. I think she might have been wearing a touch of concealer. 🐌

LAST WILL AND TESTAMENT OF EVELYN LAUDER

THIS IS THE LAST WILL AND TESTAMENT of Evelyn Lauder, of 60 East 56th Street, in the City of New York, in the state of New York, in the Country of USA.

I HEREBY REVOKE all former Wills and other Testamentary dispositions by me at any time heretofore made and DECLARE this to be and contain my Last Will and Testament.

I NOMINATE, CONSTITUTE AND APPOINT John Hargrave, of Boston, MA, in the Country of United States, to be the sole Executor and Trustee of this my Last Will and Testament, and I herein after refer to him as my 'Trustee'.

I GIVE, DEVISE AND BEQUEATH all my estate, both real and personal, of every nature and kind and wheresoever situate, including any property over which I may have a general power of appointment, to Patricia Hodgson, of Pelham, AL, in the country of United States, if she survives me for a period of 30 days, for her own use absolutely.

IF Patricia Hodgson should predecease me, or die within a period of 30 days following my death, I GIVE, DEVISE AND BEQUEATH all my estate, both real and personal, of every nature and kind and wheresoever situate, including any property over which I may have a general power of appointment, to my Trustee to hold upon the following trusts:

a) To use his discretion in the realization of my estate, with power to my Trustee to sell, call in and convert into money any part of my estate not consisting of money at such time or times, in such manner and upon such terms, and either for cash or credit or for part cash and part credit, as my said Trustee in his uncontrolled discretion may decide upon, or to postpone such conversion of my estate or any part or parts thereof for such length of time as he may think best and I HEREBY DECLARE that my said Trustee may retain any portion of my estate in the form in which it may be at my death (notwithstanding that it may not be in the form of an investment in which Trustee is authorized to invest funds and whether or not there is a liability attached to any such portion of my estate) for such length of time as my said Trustee may in his discretion deem advisable, and my Trustee shall not be held responsible for any loss that may happen to my estate by reason of his so doing.

b) To pay out of the capital of my general estate my just debts, funeral and testamentary expenses and all succession duties and inheritance and death taxes, whether imposed by or pursuant to the law of this or any province, state, country or jurisdiction whatsoever, that may be payable in connection with an insurance on my life or any gift or benefit given by me either in my lifetime or by survivorship or by this my Will or any Codicil thereto.

IN WITNESS WHEREOF I have hereunto set my hand to this and the preceding page at Boston, Massachusetts, in the country of United States, this 6 October 2005.

Evelyn Lauder

Evelyn Lauder

LAST WILL AND TESTAMENT OF ELIZABETH HURLEY

THIS IS THE LAST WILL AND TESTAMENT of Elizabeth Hurley, Actress, of 3 Cromwell Street, in the City of London, in the Country of United Kingdom.

I HEREBY REVOKE all former Wills and other Testamentary dispositions by me at any time heretofore made and DECLARE this to be and contain my Last Will and Testament.

I NOMINATE, CONSTITUTE AND APPOINT John Hargrave, of Boston, MA, in the Country of United States, to be the sole Executor and Trustee of this my Last Will and Testament, and I herein after refer to him as my 'Trustee'.

I GIVE, DEVISE AND BEQUEATH all my estate, both real and personal, of every nature and kind and wheresoever situate, including any property over which I may have a general power of appointment, to Patricia Hodgson, of Pelham, AL, in the country of United States, if she survives me for a period of 30 days, for her own use absolutely.

IF Patricia Hodgson should predecease me, or die within a period of 30 days following my death, I GIVE, DEVISE AND BEQUEATH all my estate, both real and personal, of every nature and kind and wheresoever situate, including any property over which I may have a general power of appointment, to my Trustee to hold upon the following trusts:

a) To use his discretion in the realization of my estate, with power to my Trustee to sell, call in and convert into money any part of my estate not consisting of money at such time or times, in such manner and upon such terms, and either for cash or credit or for part cash and part credit, as my said Trustee in his uncontrolled discretion may decide upon, or to postpone such conversion of my estate or any part or parts thereof for such length of time as he may think best and I HEREBY DECLARE that my said Trustee may retain any portion of my estate in the form in which it may be at my death (notwithstanding that it may not be in the form of an investment in which Trustee is authorized to invest funds and whether or not there is a liability attached to any such portion of my estate) for such length of time as my said Trustee may in his discretion deem advisable, and my Trustee shall not be held responsible for any loss that may happen to my estate by reason of his so doing.

b) To pay out of the capital of my general estate my just debts, funeral and testamentary expenses and all succession duties and inheritance and death taxes, whether imposed by or pursuant to the law of this or any province, state, country or jurisdiction whatsoever, that may be payable in connection with an insurance on my life or any gift or benefit given by me either in my lifetime or by survivorship or by this my Will or any Codicil thereto.

IN WITNESS WHEREOF I have hereunto set my hand to this and the preceding page at Boston, Massachusetts, in the country of United States, this 6 October 2005.

_____

Elizabeth Hurley

Kutcher in the Lie

ASHTON KUTCHER IS THE MOST ANNOYING celebrity in the world.

Let's start with his movies, which critics have called "witless,"[1] "irritating,"[2] "pointless,"[3] "predictable,"[4] "uninspired,"[5] "offensive,"[6] "insufferable,"[7] "stupid,"[8] "really stupid,"[9] "impossibly stupid,"[10] "unfunny,"[11] "desperately unfunny,"[12] "gratingly unfunny,"[13] "strenuously unfunny,"[14] "achingly unfunny,"[15] "excruciatingly unfunny,"[16] and "just terrible...a witless, moronic bore."[17] And then we get to the *bad* reviews. Jack Mathews in *New York Daily News* says, "Any movie starring Ashton Kutcher requires our suspension of disbelief."[18] Peter Howell of the *Toronto Star* states: "Ashton Kutcher continues to be a punch line for which no satisfactory joke has yet been written."[19]

Even worse than his movies is his MTV show *Punk'd.* It's kind of like *Candid Camera* for morons, featuring D-list celebrities put into uncomfortable situations and filmed with hidden cameras. Kutcher's idea of a clever prank is to find the car of an obscure rap star, run over it with a monster truck, then watch his reaction. A *truly* clever prank would be to find the car of Bill Ford, CEO of Ford Motor Company, run over it with a Toyota SUV, then watch *his* reaction. Do you understand the difference? I hope by this point in the book you understand the difference. He lowers the art form. Somewhere, Allen Funt is rolling around in his grave, which is pretty remarkable, considering he isn't dead yet.

1. "Just Married," Roger Ebert, *Chicago Sun-Times.*

2. "Just Married," Claudia Puig, *USA Today.*

3. "Guess Who," A. O. Scott, *New York Times.*

4. "Guess Who," Peter L'Official, *Village Voice.*

5. "Just Married," James Berardinelli, *Reelviews.*

6. "A Lot Like Love," Allison Benedikt, *Chicago Tribune.*

7. "A Lot Like Love," Owen Gleiberman, *Entertainment Weekly.*

8. "Dude, Where's My Car?", Andy Weil, *Houston Chronicle.*

9. "Just Married," David Grove, *Film Threat.*

10. "Guess Who," Kevin Allison, *Premiere Magazine.*

11. "Guess Who," James Berardinelli, *Reelviews.*

12. "Cheaper by the Dozen," Dustin Putman, TheMovieBoy.com.

13. "Dude, Where's My Car?", Michael Rechtshaffen, *Hollywood Reporter.*

14. "Dude, Where's My Car?" Chris Hewitt, *St. Paul Pioneer Press.*

15. "A Lot Like Love," Brian Orndorf, Filmjerk.com.

16. "Cheaper By The Dozen," Terry Lawson, *Detroit Free Press.*

17. "Just Married," Frank Swietek, *One Guy's Opinion.*

18. "A Lot Like Love," Jack Mathews, *New York Daily News.*

19. "A Lot Like Love," Peter Howell, *The Toronto Star.*

Hang on. Just did some research. Allen Funt is dead after all. Apparently, his head exploded after Season 1 of *Punk'd.*

Dude, Where's My Cerebral Cortex?

I could overlook all this. What I could not ignore was Ashton Kutcher's proclamation that he could not be pranked, that *he could not be outsmarted.* I mean, c'mon. Dat boy so dumb, he think fruit punch is a gay boxer.

A few years ago, pre-TiVo, I was flipping the channels and happened to catch my first nausea-inducing episode of *Punk'd.* In this episode, Kutcher's camera crew tries to pull a practical joke on him. He figures out they're up to something, turns the tables, then ends the episode by defiantly screaming, "You cannot punk me! *You cannot punk the master!*"

Anyone who would make a claim like this on national TV is a real asshat. Look: I've been pranked many times. It's not that hard. I would never throw down such a moronic challenge, because you're just asking for every fucktard in America to track down your home phone number and hack into your voicemail system. But then I thought: Hey, what if someone really *did* hack into his voicemail system? And then I thought: Why go to all the trouble? *Why not just fake it?*

Imagine, as I did, two teenagers obtaining Kutcher's personal number. They find a way into his voicemail, record all his privately saved messages, then post them on the Internet for the world to hear. It had all the makings of a media frenzy: young,

cocky star brought down by shadowy hackers.
The loss of privacy in a digital age. The corruption
of today's youth and the deliciously ironic prank
on the man-child who was corrupting them.

In fact, the more I thought about it, the more it
seemed like an opportunity to prank not only Kutcher,
but *the entire world media*. See, I like to dream big.
Unlike Kutcher, who will settle for The Rock. I wanted
to pull one over on every celebrity-obsessed journalist,
every two-bit gossip reporter on the planet. And
Ashton Kutcher, with his "you cannot punk me"
challenge, would be at the heart of my masterpiece.

Fuck you, punk, I thought. *I'll not only prank you,
I'll do it with nothing but a cellphone and Google.*

Kutcher vs. Kutcher

First, I had to get my name legally changed to
Ashton Kutcher.

You've heard the saying "We become what we
most abhor," and I was about to provide the demonstration. I was a little bit nervous about the legal
implications of my idea because I suspected that a
double-hard cockknocker like Kutcher would probably not have a great sense of humor about being
pranked himself. So I figured that changing my name
would allow me to legally *do* or *say* anything about
Ashton Kutcher that I wanted, because I would essentially be *saying it about myself.*

I filed the appropriate paperwork at my local city
hall, requesting a court hearing to change my name
from John Myers Hargrave to Christopher Ashton
Kutcher. The fact that "Chris" is his first name, not
"Ashton," was a serendipitous detail I uncovered in

COMMONWEATH OF MASSACHUSETTS
TRIAL COURT
PROBATE & FAMILY COURT DEPARTMENT

DOCKET NO:

I, ▓▓▓▓▓ ▓▓▓▓▓▓▓ *Register of Probate for*
said ▓▓▓▓▓ *hereby certify, that at a Probate*
Court hearing held at ▓▓▓ *Massachusetts, in and for*
said County, on the __Twenty-Ninth__ *day of* <u>JUNE</u> *in the*
year Two Thousand _Five_, on application, and after due
public notice thereof, and for sufficient reason
consistent with the public 'interest, and satisfactory to
said Court, the name of

<u>JOHN MYERS HARGRAVE</u>

of ▓▓▓▓ *in said county, was changed to:*

CHRISTOPHER ASHTON KUTCHER

which name he/she should thereafter bear as his/her legal
name

In Witness Whereof, I have hereunto set my hand
and affixed the seal of the Probate & Family Court, this

<u>29TH</u> day of <u>JUNE</u>

in the year Two Thousand <u>Five</u>

REGISTER & CLERK MAGISTRATE
PROBATE & FAMILY COURT

my exhaustive research on my mark. I thought "Chris Kutcher" would seem less suspicious to the judge I'd be facing in court, especially if the judge's daughter watched a lot of MTV.

A few weeks later, I showed up for my 8:30 a.m. court appointment. The last time I had seen the inside of a courtroom was after my CVS arrest (that case was thrown out instantly, by the way), and I had forgotten how depressing they are. The judge was nearly two hours late, so I had plenty of time to watch all the people getting divorces and arguing about child custody. The woman sitting next to me sobbed uncontrollably for the better part of an hour, while her friend tried to comfort her. One guy was led into the courtroom in handcuffs. I prayed I wouldn't be leaving the same way.

Finally: here come da judge. "All rise." Bespectacled, no-nonsense guy in his sixties. Dude swaggered in like Jagger taking the stage, making it clear he wasn't going to *give no* satisfaction. I found myself hoping two things: (1) he didn't know who Ashton Kutcher was, and (2) no one on his staff had Googled my name beforehand. I had everything planned, except those two contingencies.

Around 10:30, the judge called my name. I approached the bench as he leafed through my docket. He didn't look happy. "Why are you changing your name from John Hargrave to Christopher Kutcher?" he asked me.

"Well, a number of personal reasons, your honor." I swallowed. "I became a born-again Christian." This is true–I *am* a Christian–I just didn't tell him that I became a Christian *when I was five.* I was choosing my words very carefully, so as not to perjure myself.

"I'm not proud of a lot of the things I've done," I confessed to the judge. Again: true. When I was a teenager, I once masturbated into a microwaved grapefruit. "I recognize that that's who I was, but I also feel the need to make a change, symbolically as well as literally."

"How'd you decide on this name?" he growled, although he had tuned out after "Christian."

"Well, I did some research into my family history..."

"This is approved," he said, cutting me off and signing my application. I didn't get to finish, "...Also, I want to humiliate Ashton Kutcher."

Being Ashton Kutcher

Again I tell you: being a Hollywood star is the easiest fucking profession on earth. You call anyone, *anywhere,* and they will bend over backward to help you out, because *we are a culture obsessed with celebrity.* "You'd like me to investigate monogramming your underwear with imported Thai silk? Of course, Mr. Kutcher!" "You'd like me to discreetly arrange to have the wombat removed from inside your rectum? No problem, Mr. Kutcher!"

My plan was to fill up my own voicemail box with dozens of calls to "Ashton Kutcher." I called travel agents, I called tailors, I called tap dance studios. I called L.L.Bean, because they guarantee 100 percent satisfaction, and celebrities get an extra 20 percent. I asked ridiculous questions, sent them on bizarre fact-finding missions, then told them to call back and leave a message when they had uncovered the answer. Sometimes I used my new name of Ashton Kutcher, sometimes I said I was Ashton Kutcher's assistant. It didn't matter: people would leave me detailed messages with the answer to any ridiculous question, as long as I mentioned the Ash-hole.

Of course, it helped that I had ordered a full set

of credit cards in Ashton Kutcher's name. As we've established by now, the credit card companies don't give a fuck. "Issue you a new credit card in the name of a well-known celebrity without any supporting documentation? Certainly, sir, no problem!" This is a fun little thing you should do tonight: Call up your credit card company and ask to have Ashton Kutcher added to your account. Get them to send an additional card in his name, and just start using it everywhere. It's perfectly legal, and you don't even have to go to the trouble of changing your name. Thank God for credit card companies, and to our government for doing such a crack job protecting our privacy.

I called the Bellagio Hotel in Las Vegas and made a reservation for the Penthouse Suite. This was cool: 1,356 square feet of living space, with rooms for up to twenty people. I savored the details as she described the suite to me: two and a half baths, a chauffeured limo from the airport, a VIP lounge waiting when you arrived. I put in a reservation for two nights, which would have run me $1,900 if I weren't going to cancel it in two weeks.

"Now, I need you to ensure our privacy," I said. "I'll be traveling with Demi, and possibly Bruce. And all the kids. Do you understand?"

"Yes, sir."

"We need to be protected."

"We can register you under an alias," she suggested.

"An alias." I loved this idea. "That would be excellent. Please put the name under John Myers Hargrave. And call me back when you've confirmed the reservation."

Taking Prank Phone Calls to a Whole New Level

I did an assload of research on Ashton Kutcher, one of the more painful experiences of my life. I watched as many of his movies as I could stomach, dug up old talk show appearances, and Googled him dry. Then I wrote scripts for a dozen of my friends, who called my voicemail pretending to be various people from Ashton's life: from his twin brother Michael, to his production partner Jason, to a number of anonymous starfuckers who just wanted to leave him a message because they could. I wanted *verisimilitude.* Most of the messages had to be boring, mundane stuff, with one really scandalous message that would capture the media's attention.

Recording that message proved to be the most difficult of all. I wanted a woman who would recount, *in graphic detail*, a recent sexual encounter with Ashton Kutcher. I needed someone with a really filthy mouth, a total phone whore, not just "I like kissing your pee-pee." My wife was pretty disgusted with the whole endeavor by this point, so I couldn't talk her into it. Next I thought about asking my mother. She sounds a little bit like Demi Moore, but I didn't think she could, you know, *pull it off.*

So I broke down and called a phone sex line. After I went through a central operator that took Ashton Kutcher's credit card number, I was connected with a woman who sounded remarkably like Halle Berry.

"This is Bailey," she introduced herself. "What's your name, baby?"

"My name is Ashton," I said. "Friends call me Ash."

"Hey, Ash," she said. "How you doing?"

"A little nervous."

She giggled. "Don't be. Let me tell you a little about myself."

"I'd love to hear that."

"I have long brown hair. My eyes are green, and I have big boobs. 36D."

"Those are large." I had to give her that.

"Yeah, pretty big." She giggled. "All natural."

"Hey, I have kind of an unusual request for you."

"Anything you want, baby," she said. "I'm hot and ready."

"Are you sure?" I asked. "It's weird."

"I'll break any taboo you want. Anything for you."

"I'd like to record this call."

There was a long pause. "Um…I don't think we can do that. I don't think they allow me to be recorded."

"I thought you were hot and ready, willing to break any taboo."

"Yeah. I don't think they'll let me be recorded, though. Mmm. Yeah."

"Mmm," I said disappointedly. Long pause.

"Yeah. Mmm."

"Yeah."

We were saying all the right words, but the passion just wasn't there. It was the worst phone sex ever.

Star Sixty-nine

The next night, I tried again. This time, I made my wife sit with me so she could verify everything was aboveboard. Though initially resistant, she found herself amused by my speakerphone sex conversations, as I tried to find someone who would let me record a custom phone sex message for Ashton Kutcher.

You may find this hard to believe, but a lot of the phone sex lines are not that reputable. You don't know how much you're being charged by the minute, and it's all very confusing. One sex worker answered the phone, and I was like, "Sorry, how much is this costing me?" It was the least romantic pickup line ever. I'm researching all these operators on the Web, bargain-shopping. Jade is sitting in the corner, arms folded, giving me a look like *I cannot believe you're haggling the phone sex operators, you cheap bastard.*

Finally, we hit paydirt. I found a phone sex worker who was willing to let me record some serious X-rated raunch:

Ash, I was thinking about last night earlier, and I have to tell you it made me a little wet. (*giggles*) I hope that you liked me sucking your cock, because that's my favorite thing to do. (*giggles, moan*) You really have a nice one, too. I liked squeezing your balls, and I liked stroking your shaft with my tongue. Especially the underside, because I know that drives you crazy. And oh, I just can't wait to put it in my mouth again! (*giggles*) Mmm. You are something special, Ash, I tell you. Laying on that bed, sucking your cock. I'm surprised you were able to give me such a big load after all that fucking! Your come was really tasty...you know I love to taste it. Hopefully we can recreate that again sometime. I'd really enjoy that. Maybe I'll bring a friend along next time and let her join in with us. I'd like to be eating her pussy while you're fucking me from behind. You're an amazing guy, and let's do it again soon, okay?

It was hot, and I have to admit that I got a semi. She didn't exactly sound like Halle Berry, more like

Halle Berry's hairdresser, only with a little more sinus congestion, but fuck it. We could fix it in the mix. I just needed to get the sex on tape. From there, I'd convert it to mp3, so "Ashton Kutcher's mistress" could easily be traded on file-sharing networks, where her throaty moans would ultimately be downloaded to 200 million iPods worldwide.

Round 1: The Prank Hits

Just after midnight on Monday, September 19, a mysterious Web site called AshtonHacked.com quietly winked online.

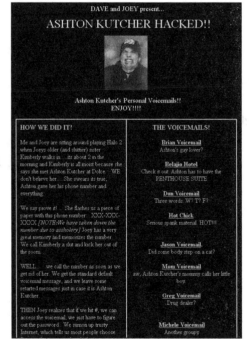

The site was "created" by two teenagers, Dave and Joey, who explained the backstory in broken Teenglish. In addition to downloadable sound files of all the phone calls, the AshtonHacked.com site contained lots of little details that only hardcore Ashton fans would catch, hidden Easter eggs, even an angry message from an irate Bruce Willis (I had hired an L.A. voice actor, Jim Meskimen, the guy who did the soundtrack to the famous "This Land Is Your Land" cartoon).

Now I just needed a way to spread the word. Fortunately, I had an ace in the hole: the great FARK.com.

FARK Me, Baby

FARK is a site that continually links to humorous and interest-  ing news stories from around the globe. Even if you've never heard of it, I can tell you from personal experience that every wacky morning DJ in the country reads this site for funny headlines each morning. Sites like FARK have become hugely influential on what gets reported by "traditional" media, even though the tagline reads, "It's not news, it's FARK." The site is meant to be an entertaining look at wacky stories, but thousands of media outlets treat it as *actual news.*

My pal Drew Curtis, who runs the site, was sick of the media stealing his headlines without giving him credit. He offered to promote my stunt if I could promise it would deliver revenge on lazy, dimwitted reporters. Assuring him that it would, I convinced him to link to AshtonHacked.com first thing on Monday morning, when all the news outlets would be looking for the week's big stories. From there, it spread like a cold sore on Courtney Love's lip.

I anxiously monitored the site all day, as well as four dummy e-mail accounts, three instant messenger profiles, two phone lines, and my *special voice-mail tree*, which served as my secret window into the success of the prank. Hidden within one of Ashton's "voicemails" was a phone number left by another anonymous girlfriend, "Michelle." People who called Michelle got a digital voicemail system that recorded their messages as sound files, then sent them to my e-mail box. By just checking my e-mail, I could see how many people had fallen for the prank so thoroughly that they had called the number, hoping to speak with "Michelle" about "Ashton Kutcher."

This was such an elaborate hoax that even *I* was starting to get confused.

Master Baiter

By mid-afternoon, the voicemail box was jammed full with messages. There were dozens of requests for interviews with morning DJs. There were vicious, horrible messages from angry teenagers. There were people who didn't believe it was real, but needed to call the number, *just in case.* I frantically tried to keep clearing the mailbox all day long, so I wouldn't miss any excitement, but it kept filling up again. When you pull a stunt like this, you have to be prepared for any reaction, including *none at all.* Sometimes, despite your best plans, nobody bites. It looked like I was going to have the opposite problem: *keeping the prank under control.*

The serious reporters tracked me down through my anonymous e-mail accounts, deluging me with interview requests. Posing as a friend of the teenagers who created the site, I spent an hour or two on the phone with the young hotshot reporter from the *Washington Post* who had recently broken a real-life story about hackers breaking into Paris Hilton's cellphone. He was on the verge of reporting the stunt as a legitimate break-in, but ultimately wanted to talk with the teenage hackers, and I wasn't able to make that happen.

Fortunately, the *New York Daily News* didn't have such high standards. The number six newspaper in

America reported the break-in as the lead story of their "Daily Dish" gossip column. "Ashton Kutcher isn't the only one who feels 'punk'd' by a Web site claiming to have obtained his private voicemails," the paper gleefully reported. "Ashtonhacked.com offers recordings allegedly pulled off Kutcher's cell phone, including one young lady (who isn't Demi Moore) graphically recounting a sex act she claimed to have performed with him the night before."

From there, the story was picked up by United Press International, one of the three primary U.S. wire services. This is like hitting the media lottery, since wire services distribute their stories to other news organizations around the world, which usually run them without further fact-checking. It's the atomic bomb of publicity. Within hours, the UPI story was being reprinted on Web sites from the United Kingdom to India, and Kutcher's handlers were getting annoyed: "Ashton's spokesperson insists everything on the site is fake," the article breathlessly reported, adding that Ashton himself thought the messages were "so lame." And I suppose he would know all about that, since last night I watched a three-hour infomercial for "Lame," and Ashton Kutcher was the host.

Round 2: The Prank Deepens

By the weekend, the Web site had *over a million pageviews*, and the server kept crashing under the load of all those people trying to download the audio files. And then something incredible happened, a once-in-a-lifetime coincidence: *Ashton Kutcher and Demi Moore got married.*

This was amazing, unplanned timing. The newlyweds had secretly sold their wedding photos to *OK!* magazine for $3 million, and in the process had locked out the other gossip rags. I got lucky. Really lucky. Gossip columnists were starving, desperate for details on the celebrity wedding of the year. I couldn't have been in a better place at a better time. Prankwise, it was the perfect storm.

Within hours of the news, I drafted an e-mail claiming I had inside information that the Ashton Kutcher wedding was fake. It was just a stunt for his MTV show, I claimed, attaching a realistic-looking e-mail from the executive producer of *Punk'd*:

- - - - - Original Message - - - - -

From: Goldberg, Jason
Sent: Friday, September 23 8:04 p.m.
Subject: FW: Update

Team:

Quick update: AshtonHacked.com got over 1 million hits in its first five days, and the dummy VM has something like 2,500 messages from fans, filling up faster than we can clean it out.

About part 2 of the stunt: preparations for the ceremony are in full swing, and its actually MORE hell than preparing a real wedding, if that's possible. Please note that the start time has been CHANGED to 8:00 p.m., due to a fuckup with the caterer, so we need everyone there NO LATER than 4:00 p.m. Players need to be fully miked and in costume by 5:45 p.m. Please remember that not everyone attending knows that this is for the show, so bring your a-game and keep your mouth shut.

The e-mail admitted that AshtonHacked.com was a prank. But that was the perfect setup, because *my* hoax made it seem like their wedding was *also* a hoax. How could anyone question that the two were related? "So you think someone just *happened* to plan this prank during the same week they got married? It was just *random coincidence?*" It was! But who would believe such a freakishly improbable thing?

I looked up every celebrity columnist and entertainment reporter I could find. Like everyone else in power, the media doesn't want to be bothered by ordinary citizens, so here's the easy way to track down reporters. Don't send a letter to the editor. That's for chumps. *Newsweek* reporters use letters to the editors to light their bongs. Instead, you look for their byline, then you guess at the e-mail address. For instance, if you find out that Jack Meoff writes for *Newsweek*, his e-mail address is probably either:

jack_meoff@newsweek.com
or
jack.meoff@newsweek.com
or
jmeoff@newsweek.com.

It only takes a couple of hours to completely blitz the American media landscape in this way, and a few reporters are sure to bite, particularly those with mild mental retardation (53 percent).

And my strategy worked: within hours I had responses from *USA Today*, the *Los Angeles Times*, *New York Post*, *US Magazine*, and many others. Two celebrities getting married is the biggest story for an entertainment reporter, and two celebrities *not* getting married when the competition says they *are* getting married is possibly the biggest story of all time—with the possible exception of Michael Jackson showing up at a Gladys Knight concert with a young boy.

I strung along the various reporters, trying to see who would run with the story first. I played them against each other: "The guy from the *L.A. Times* says he's going to run the story first, and asked me not to talk with you." This drives them nuts. Fortunately, in the world of celebrity reporting, printing it *first* is more important than printing it *correctly*. The story of Ashton and Demi's "fake wedding" hit the bottom-feeding tabloid Web sites first, then rapidly spread from there. When it appeared on the *Entertainment Weekly* Web site, I knew the story was picking up steam. By this time, Kutcher's reps sounded pretty annoyed by my shenanigans, now referring to them as "those stupid voicemails." It appeared as the lead story on E! Entertainment's Web site, then hit the *New York Post*.

And that's when I got the e-mail from *Access Hollywood.*

Keep in mind: I was still anonymous. I did a half-hour phone interview with *Access Hollywood,* the syndicated celebrity TV show, regaling them with stories about how great Ashton Kutcher was, how smart he was to be pulling this stunt over on the media, how they should all bow down to his clever-ness. (All true.) That night, Ashton Kutcher's "fake wedding" ran as the lead story on *Access Hollywood.* They did me the favor of interviewing a bunch of other celebrities on whether Ashton and Demi were really married. This was tremendously funny.

"I can't go on rumors," said Sean "Diddy" Combs, as they caught him outside a nightclub. "I haven't spoken to him."

"Oh, it's real," said Rene Russo, proving that she's smarter than her acting.

"I believe everything I read," quipped Robert Downey, Jr.

At home, I sat watching all this nonsense, laughing my ass off. I got more laughs from that seven minutes of TV than from all seven seasons of *That '70s Show.*

Round 3: The Gloves Come Off

That's about the time I got an e-mail from Ashton Kutcher's attorney (this is the *other* Ashton Kutcher, not the one writing this story). I am prevented from printing it here, but let's agree that a letter from an attorney is generally not a good thing. Rarely do lawyers come bearing good cheer. They're the Bad News Barristers.

John Myers Hargrave
P.O. Box 990586
Boston, MA 02199

Executive Counsel
MTV Networks
1515 Broadway
New York, NY 10008

Dear

I received your thoughtful cease and desist letter dated   I have no problem taking down the website in question. However, I have one request.

I think it's only fair that Mr. Kutcher admits he's been pranked. Would it be possible to have Mr. Kutcher send me some communication (e-mail, fax, or voicemail) confirming that he has, in fact, been "Punk'd"? (Although I realize that "Punk'd" is a licensed trademark of MTV Networks, I'm hoping we can make this one exception.)

Since I will be printing these letters on my website, such a gesture would show that both Mr. Kutcher and MTV have a sense of humor.

In good faith, I am removing the parody site, and hope that you can convince Mr. Kutcher to also do the right thing.

Truly yours,

John Hargrave

I confessed to the hoax, and responded with a compromise: if Ashton would be willing to admit that he had been thoroughly pranked, I would come clean with the story. In good faith, I took down the Web site while I waited for the note of surrender.

I also sent a note out to all the reporters I had duped, but surprisingly, none of them issued retractions. Apparently, reporters don't like to admit when they're wrong as much as they like to admit when someone *else* is wrong.

Finally, on Friday afternoon at 4:00, Ashton Kutcher sent me the fax I had been waiting for:

> "You got to be able to make fun of yourself.
> I mean, I think that that's like a key in, in
> life, like, like try to make fun of yourself
> better than other people can make fun
> of you...and then you win."

> —Ashton Kutcher on *The Tonight Show*

I grabbed it from the fax tray, laughing like a young gay man. I was totally impressed that Ashton Kutcher lived by the prankster's code of honor. But I had painted him into a corner: if he *didn't* respond, he would have looked humorless and hypocritical. After all, he makes a living convincing celebrities to say, "I got Punk'd." Without that admission, he's got nothing. I was pleased to see that he is, at least, a prankster of honor, even after his soul-crushing defeat at the hands of his *doppelganger.*

With my comedy broadsword, I had vanquished the world's most pompous celebrity. Now I had to think bigger. Could I prank the world's most pompous *monarchy*?

Could I prank the Queen of England? ☺

Royal Pain in the Ass

LIKE EVERYTHING IN GOVERNMENT, the process of British knighthood involves filling out a form, as I discovered when I sent the following letter.

John Hargrave
P.O. Box 990586
Boston, MA 02199
UNITED STATES

Her Majesty The Queen
Buckingham Palace
London SW1A 1AA
UNITED KINGDOM

Your Majesty:

I would like to be knighted.

Please send me the appropriate forms, manuals, etc.

I look forward to your speedy reply.

Sincerely,

Sir John Hargrave (to be)

BUCKINGHAM PALACE

The Queen has asked the Private Secretary to thank Mr. Hargrave for his letter, and to inform him that recommendations for honours are made to Her Majesty by the Prime Minister. An *Honours Nomination Form* is enclosed with this letter which may be completed and returned to:

The Ceremonial Secretariat
Cabinet Office
35 Great Smith Street
London SW1P 3BQ

Traditionally, someone *nominates* you for knighthood, thus saving you the hassle of the paperwork.
Recently, however, the process was changed so that
you can now nominate yourself. This was good news,
since the instruction sheet (yes, there is an instruction sheet for the knighting form) explains that
British honors are reserved for those who have
"made a difference to their community." It's a bit
sobering to look back on your life and realize that
you've made no difference to your community at
all, and in fact regularly pour lead paint down your
community's sewer grate because you're too lazy
to recycle it.

I realized the only way I was going to obtain the
ultimate title of honor and integrity was by *lying*.
I would have to make up an alternate history for
myself. I felt guilty about this, until I started to
research the history of the British royal family. As I
looked into the centuries of "graceless behavior, greed,
bad manners, arrogance, swinish self-indulgence,
and lurid sexual misconduct," I realized a forged background looked tame by comparison.' Hell, a lying
American would probably fit right in.

The application form turned out to be just like
a college admission essay: I had to describe every
wonderful thing I had ever done, even though I hadn't
done any of them. I breathlessly described my
contributions to humanity, which included causes
like endangered animals, global warming, multiple
sclerosis, drug addiction, and high cholesterol. It was
kind of fun to make up a nobler life for myself, to lie
about my honesty. But even more enjoyable were the

1. Michael Korda. "Family
Drama," *U.S. News & World
Report,* April 18, 2005.

letters of recommendation, which I also forged. One of my reference letters was written by a slightly batty Harvard professor; the other was from a Chinese bird doctor with the most tenuous grasp of English.

Read the full application:
www.pranKthemonKey.com/royal

My primary accomplishment, the one that would earn me the knighthood, was that I had developed a vaccine for the *bird flu*, a pretty impressive claim that I backed up by editing key entries on Wikipedia.org, the popular online encyclopedia. Since the Wikipedia is written and updated entirely by users (making it the least reliable reference source in the world), I simply edited the entries of key historical figures to make them agree with the details in my application. Then I printed out pages from the Wikipedia and attached them as proof of my claims. I guess it wasn't honorable to rewrite other people's lives to suit my own needs, but hey, that's what historians have been doing for years.

The Queen Has Spoken

A few weeks later, I got the disappointing follow-up response (shown on the next page) to my meticulously falsified application.

That stuck-up *bitch*! Those Royals are so full of themselves. "Your Highness" this and "Your Majesty" that. They think they're fucking *royalty*. Royal *douchebags*, if you ask me.

CabinetOffice

Ceremonial Secretariat	35 Great Smith Street	Telephone: 020 7276 2776
	London	Fax: 020 7276 2766
	SW1P 3BQ	E-mail: barbara.walsh@cabinet-office.x.gsi.gov.uk
		Web: www.cabinet-office.gov.uk/ceremonial

Private and Confidential
Mr John Hargrave
PO Box 990586
Boston MA
USA 02492

Your reference:
Our reference:

Dear Mr Hargrave

Thank you for returning your completed nomination form with letters of support recommending yourself for an honour.

We are currently considering your self nomination for an award. But we prefer nominations to be made by someone other than the individual concerned to ensure a measure of unbiased support and independence.

Yours sincerely
Barbara Walsh

Support Officer

I needed to get someone else to send in my application for me. I needed someone important, someone who carried some real weight. And then it hit me: who carries more weight than *The Incredible Hulk?*

You Wouldn't Like Him When He's Angry

I didn't get the *actual* Hulk. For that, you've got to book Bruce Banner, then prompt him into an insane rage. Instead, I went the easier route and just got Lou Ferrigno, the internationally famous bodybuilder who played The Incredible Hulk in the 1970s TV show. Mr. Ferrigno is one of the many celebrities available for personal greetings through the "Hollywood Is Calling" service (www.HollywoodIsCalling.com). For a reasonable fee, these celebrities will call your friend, spouse, or potential employer and leave a personal message, thank-you note, or job recommendation. It's a terrific service that comes in handy on so many occasions, like trying to impress the Queen of England.

Mr. Ferrigno called my voicemail a few days later and left the following note of recommendation:

> Hi, this is Lou Ferrigno from HollywoodIsCalling.com. I want to wish John Hargrove the best of luck and for his fantastic services, what he has saved all these, uh, separate bird species, and all of the stuff he's done to immunize bird infections, and I want to say to the U.K. that he's done a fantastic job. All the best. Bye.

Hah? Did Lou come through, or what? HULK RECOMMEND! HULK KNOW APPLICANT FOR SEVERAL YEARS! UNNNGGHHH! HULK FREQUENTLY OBSERVE CHIVALRY AND VIRTUE IN APPLICANT! *HULK RECOMMEND HIGHLY!*

I burned The Hulk's recommendation to CD, then sent it to the Queen as a new application for my knighthood. Now there was nothing left to do but wait.

And wait.

For several months.

Patience is a virtue, but fuck being virtuous.

I wanted to be a knight, *now.*

Locked in the Cabinet

I tried calling the British Cabinet Office to check
on my application, but they kept giving me the
runaround. I imagined my application locked up in
a musty basement at Buckingham Palace, possibly
next to one of the illegitimate children of Prince
Philip, who I've heard they keep in a small cage
down there.

The bureaucracy was driving me crazy. The
British probably *still have* the Holy Grail; it was
just locked in a filing cabinet by some government
clerk. I don't know why Arthur had to go on all those
quests to find it, when he just needed to fill out
Form 537-AD(b), *Petition to Request the Release of
Enchanted Chalice.*

I wanted the knighthood so badly, I could taste
it. (It tasted like pheasant.) I immersed myself in
Kitty Kelley's scandalous tell-all book, *The Royals,*
a 550-page volume of which approximately 12 are
factually correct. The book, which is outlawed in
the United Kingdom, tells of spoiled princesses
demanding "jammy dodgers," which are circular
white-bread sandwiches made with imported
raspberry jam. Damn. I wants me some of them
jammy dodgers.

To get more information on my benefit package
once I was knighted, I called the Buckingham Palace
press office. I spoke with a pleasant young woman,
who was happy to help me, but only because I told
her I was a reporter from the *New York Times.*

"I'm writing an article on the knighting process," I said. "Can you answer a few questions?"

"Certainly."

"Is it true that knights get royal discounts at participating restaurants and cinemas?"

She paused. "That's not something that I'm aware of. A knighthood is simply an honour that means the nation has acknowledged that you've made a contribution."

"So no 2-for-1 deals at Arby's, then."

"That would be up to the organisation or institution in question."

"Arby's."

"Yes."

"Good." I scribbled some notes. "Is it true that recently knighted subjects receive a complimentary croquet set?"

There was a long pause. "Um...no. When someone's given an honour such as knighthood, they're given a title, but nothing else changes. They have formal recognition from the state, and from the people, because they've made a contribution to British life. But they don't automatically get privileges."

"Okay," I said dejectedly. "No free hunting rifle and riding crop, then?"

"You might be given that by someone, but that's not something that's given by the Palace. As I've said, apart from being given the title, there's no other entitlement."

"How about complimentary crown shinings at all participating car washes?"

"Again," she said, exhibiting the tenacious politeness that defines the British, "I wouldn't know anything more about that."

"Is it true that a knight can legally walk up to any member of the British empire and give them a French kiss?"

"Right," she said slowly, "I really can't help you any more, I'm afraid."

"How about a *British* kiss?"

"Sorry?"

"That's no tongue, lips tightly pursed."

"Right. Okay, thank you for calling."

Then she hung up on me. Once again, I was cold, lonely, and knightless. It seemed to me I was living like a candle in the wind, never knowing who to cling to when the rain set in.

You follow up, you follow up, you follow up, until one day you just get fed up. Fine. If the Queen wouldn't do it, I'd do it myself. *I would legally change my name to Sir John Hargrave.*

Knighting Myself

I went down to the courthouse and filed another petition to change my name, then showed up at my court-appointed date. Unfortunately, I ended up facing the same judge who had let me change my name to Ashton Kutcher. This was going to be difficult to explain.

"You were just here a couple of months ago," he growled, though I suspected he was just reading that in my docket. How could he possibly remember me? The guy sees a thousand cases a day.

"Yes, your honor." Presentation was everything: I had dressed in an ill-fitting suit, my hair disheveled. I wanted to look good, but not *too* good. Serious, but still slightly off balance.

"Let me get this straight." He leafed angrily through my files, trying to reconstruct the story. "You were John Myers Hargrave. You changed your name to Christopher Ashton Kutcher. Now you want to be called *Sir* John Myers Hargrave."

"Yes, your honor." When standing before a judge, "Yes, your honor" is usually a safe answer to any question, unless he is asking if you just murdered your wife's lover.

"How'd you decide on this name?" he growled.

I tried using my previous trick again. "When I became a Christian, I was deeply inspired by an ancient order of chivalry called The Knights of Kutcher. I want to change back to my given name, but add the 'Sir' as a reminder of their virtues of integrity and..."

"All right," he said, cutting me off. Again, he had tuned out after "Christian." Hallelujah! Again, Jesus had saved me. I was not just born again; I was now *triple*-born.

And so my name was once again legally changed.

The proper form of address, for your future reference, is either "Sir John" or "Sir John Hargrave." You're not supposed to say "Sir Hargrave," as that shows your inexperience with nobility.

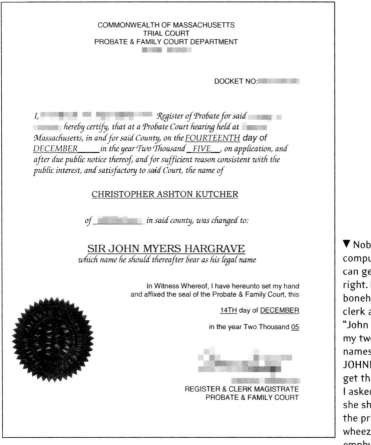

COMMONWEALTH OF MASSACHUSETTS
TRIAL COURT
PROBATE & FAMILY COURT DEPARTMENT

DOCKET NO:

I, ▓▓▓▓▓ ▓▓ ▓▓▓▓▓▓ *Register of Probate for said* ▓▓▓ ▓ ▓▓▓▓▓ *hereby certify, that at a Probate Court hearing held at* ▓▓▓ *Massachusetts, in and for said County, on the* FOURTEENTH day of DECEMBER in the year Two Thousand FIVE, *on application, and after due public notice thereof, and for sufficient reason consistent with the public interest, and satisfactory to said Court, the name of*

CHRISTOPHER ASHTON KUTCHER

of ▓▓▓▓▓ *in said county, was changed to:*

SIR JOHN MYERS HARGRAVE
which name he should thereafter bear as his legal name

In Witness Whereof, I have hereunto set my hand
and affixed the seal of the Probate & Family Court, this

14TH day of DECEMBER

in the year Two Thousand 05

REGISTER & CLERK MAGISTRATE
PROBATE & FAMILY COURT

▼ Nobody's computer system can get the name right. Here the boneheaded RMV clerk abbreviated "John Myers," my two middle names, as JOHNM. "Can we get that fixed?" I asked when she showed me the printout. She wheezed out an emphysematic, phlegmy sigh. "It's close enough."

I've got to tell you: after getting blown off by the Queen, it feels pretty good to give her a royal screw. Or at least that's what The Duke of Edinburgh tells me. "Bring a small tub of royal jelly, though," he warned me during a recent grouse hunting expedition. "At her age, they should call her 'Your *Dryness.*'"

Sir john Hargrave

Member Type:
Member Number:
Member Since:

□ Metro
□ Continuous
□ eMember

▲ Here the computer was able to print out "Sir John" as the "First Name" field, but forced the "J" lower case. These nefarious computer systems are *prejudiced against royalty*! I am going to phone the Earl of Wessex, and we shall file a petition at *once*!

Although my new title carried the expectation of chivalry and virtue, I wanted to be a royal *bastard*. So I called the government bureaucrats at the British Cabinet Office to rub their noses in it.

SIR JOHN HARGRAVE: Hey, just wanted to let you know I sent in an Honours Nomination Form last year.

BRITISH CABINET OFFICE: Right.

SJH: I was hoping to be knighted, but you didn't see fit to bestow the honour on me.

BCO: Okay.

SJH: So I had my name legally changed from John Hargrave to *Sir* John Hargrave, because I couldn't wait.

BCO: *(long pause)*

SJH: Just a heads up.

BCO: Right.

SJH: What's the official royal policy on this?

BCO: What is the official royal policy on you changing your name from John Hargrave to Sir John Hargrave?

SJH: Yes.

BCO: Well, ah, we're not exactly *in approval* of it.

SJH: But I can still refer to myself as Sir John, right? Because I've already ordered the stationery.

BCO: *(angry sigh)* Where do you live, Sir?

SJH: I live in the United States. And thank you for calling me Sir.

BCO: Right. Well, to be perfectly frank, you might have changed your name to Sir John Hargrave, but frankly that's no meaning to us whatsoever.

SJH: Why not?

BCO: Because we haven't given it to you! We haven't *given* you a knighthood, that's why.

SJH: Well, is there any practical difference?

BCO: If you came to this country and started calling yourself Sir John Hargrave when you haven't been awarded a knighthood, then you could be in breach of the law.

SJH: Why? It's my name.

BCO: Sir, to be perfectly frank, this conversation isn't really going anywhere. I don't think there's very much more we can say to you, Sir.

And with that, he abruptly hung up on me. But at least he consistently addressed me by my proper name. Lost the battle, won the war.

▲ My nameplate at work. It's fun to make everyone call me "Sir," including my boss.

Look: I may be an honorary member of the royal family, but deep down, I'm still just the same regular guy. Sure, my full name may be His Royal Highness Sir John Myers Hargrave, Prince of Boston, Earl of Cuyahoga Falls, Duke of Birmingham, Lord of Tuscaloosa, Prince and Great Steward of Memphis, Tennessee. But when I enter a room, you don't need to bow or curtsy. We can keep it informal. You can call me by my first name...Sir. 😃

Congress Is a Joke

Do politicians have a sense of humor? The common wisdom, of course, is that politicians are as funny as a groin injury. President Taft, for instance, was considered so unfunny that senators were known to gnaw off their own limbs while listening to his jokes, giving rise to the term "stump speech."

But are *all* politicians devoid of humor? To find out, I put together a historic stunt that reached the highest levels of our government: the one hundred members of the United States Senate.

The Setup

Posing as a ten-year-old boy, I sent a handwritten letter to each of our nation's U.S. senators. I discovered that getting a response from a top elected official is not an easy task, even though I used an actual ten-year-old boy to write my letter. Weeks passed, with no response.

The reason for the delay, I later discovered, was that all 100 joke letters were screened for traces of chemical residue, in accordance with Homeland Security regulations. Federal marshals wearing protective suits held the joke messages up to ultraviolet lights with long tweezers. Trained dogs sniffed hungrily over the letters, their keen noses able to detect anything—*except the scent of prank.*

Dear Senator,

My name is John Hargrave, and I am in the fifth grade at Fiske Elementary school in Wellesley, Ma. For my Social Studies class, Mrs. Rawson assingded us a goverment project. I want to be a comedian when I grow up, so I am writing every U.S. Senator and asking what there favorite joke is.

Please send the joke on the included form.

Sincerely,
John Hargrave
Age 10

Finally, the letters went through, and I pestered our nation's senators by e-mail until the responses started coming in. Yes, senators actually took time from their busy schedules to write a joke, and send it to me. Well, not to *me*, but to a lying ten-year-old kid.

The responses follow in alphabetical order.

BEN NIGHTHORSE CAMPBELL
COLORADO

United States Senate
WASHINGTON, DC 20510-0605

April 7, 2003

Mr. John Hargrave
P.O. Box 57013
Babson Park, MA 02457

Dear Mr. Hargrave

Thank you for writing and asking about my favorite joke. I represent the great state of Colorado and my favorite joke is: Why did the pig have ink all over his face? Because it came out of the pen.

Thank for your letter and good luck in all you do.

Sincerely,

Ben Nighthorse Campbell
U.S. Senator

BNC:cw

6950 EAST BELLEVIEW AVENUE	3600 JOHN F. KENNEDY PARKWAY	ASPINALL FEDERAL BUILDING	212 NORTH WAHSATCH AVENUE	500 NORTH MAIN STREET	679 EAST 2ND AVENUE
SUITE 200	SUITE 209	400 ROOD AVE., ROOM 213	SUITE 203	SUITE 648	SUITE B
GREENWOOD VILLAGE, CO 80111	FORT COLLINS, CO 80525	GRAND JUNCTION, CO 81501	COLORADO SPRINGS, CO 80903	PUEBLO, CO 81003	DURANGO, CO 81301
303/843-4100	970/206-1788	970/241-6631	719/636-9092	719/542-8667	970/585-0277

PRINTED ON RECYCLED PAPER

Senator Ben Nighthorse Campbell (R-CO)

Without a doubt, Colorado has the *coolest* senator: the only Native American in the Senate, a renowned jewelry designer, former member of the U.S. Olympic judo team, and an avid motorcycle enthusiast. Received the U.S. Capitol Police Service Award for coming to the aid of an officer struggling with a violent felon. You try to filibuster this guy, he'll fili*bust your ass.*

SENATOR JOKE FORM

Please mail back to me by <u>March 19, 2003</u>! Thank You!

My name is Senator ⸻ *Conrad* ⸻

And I represent the great state of ⸻ *North Dakota* ⸻

And my favorite joke is *Sherlock Holmes and Dr. Watson go on a camping trip. After a good dinner they retired for the night and went to sleep. Some hours later, Holmes wakes up and nudges his faithful friend. "Watson, look up at the sky and tell me what you see." "I see millions and millions of stars, Holmes," replies Watson. "And what do you deduce from that?" Watson ponders for a minute. "Well, astronomically it tells me that there are millions of galaxies and potentially billions of planets. Astrologically, I observe Saturn is in Leo. Horologically, I deduce the time is approximately a quarter past three. Meteorologically, I suspect that we will have a beautiful day tomorrow. What does it tell you, Holmes?" Holmes is silent for a moment. "WATSON, you idiot!" he says. "Someone has stolen our tent!!"*

Please return joke in my envelope, or to:
John Hargrave
P.O. Box 57013
Babson Park, MA
02457-0012

I am hoping to get all 100 senators to respond with your favorite joke!!
Please try to mail back to me by March 19! Thank you!!!

SINCERELY,

John Hargrave

(and parents)

Senator Kent Conrad (D-ND)

Conrad was one of the only senators to use the form I provided. I have to believe he had an intern do it, since the joke is pretty long and the handwriting is pretty girly. Still, you have to appreciate the time taken by someone on the Conrad staff to write out this entire joke by hand. Since Conrad represents one of the most rural states in the nation, and serves on the Senate Agriculture Committee, a joke about sleeping in a field seems appropriate.

JON S. CORZINE
NEW JERSEY

COMMITTEES:
BANKING, HOUSING, AND
URBAN AFFAIRS
BUDGET
FOREIGN RELATIONS

United States Senate

WASHINGTON, DC 20510-3004

502 SENATE HART OFFICE BUILDING
WASHINGTON, DC 20510
(202) 224-4744

ONE GATEWAY CENTER
11TH FLOOR
NEWARK, NJ 07102
(973) 645-3030

208 WHITE HORSE PIKE
SUITE 18-19
BARRINGTON, NJ 08007
(856) 757-5353

May 5, 2003

John Hargrave
PO Box 57013
Babson Park, Massachusetts 02457-0013

Dear John:

Thank you for contacting me as a part of your Social Studies project. I apologize for not responding sooner, but the United States Senate mail delivery system has been substantially delayed due to the remediation process each piece of mail must undergo. However, I appreciate the opportunity to be involved with such a unique project.

As you are not a resident of the great State of New Jersey, I thought it would be nice to take this opportunity to share a few fun and interesting facts with you about the State that I call home. New Jersey has a number of State symbols like the violet, our State flower. But did you know that New Jersey has an official dinosaur, too? The Hadrosaurus foulkii dinosaur was first discovered in Haddonfield, New Jersey. The Hadrosaurus was about two-stories tall, over 30 feet long, and an herbivore. Other State symbols include the State insect, the honeybee; the State dance, the square dance; the State animal, the horse; and the State shell, the knobbled whelk or conch shell.

As you may know, New Jersey's nickname is "The Garden State." Back in 1954, when the New Jersey State Legislature considered whether or not to place this slogan on state license plates, a great controversy arose. No one knew why New Jersey was called "The Garden State!" The governor at the time, Governor Meyner, called for an investigation into the matter and eventually tried to prevent "The Garden State" from appearing on license plates. Eventually, the Legislature passed a law to allow for the use of "The Garden State." We still do not know how this nickname originated, but I think that it is a great description, for our State is filled with so many beautiful trees, parks, and forests.

As for my favorite joke, here it is:

Question: What did the number 0 say to the number 8?

Senator Jon Corzine (D-NJ)

Out of all the responses I received, I have to say that only Senator Corzine's joke made me laugh out loud. Corzine started his career as an investment banker, and recently authored new legislation to clean up the mutual fund industry, so it's fitting that his joke involves numbers.

Answer: Nice Belt!

Again, thank you for writing me with your question. I hope my joke is a funny and entertaining addition to your project. Please do not hesitate to contact me again in the future. Good luck in your studies and all the best to you in the future.

Sincerely,

JON S. CORZINE
United States Senator

JSC:les

Separating the joke and the punchline on two separate pieces of paper shows an attention to comedic detail that should make the people of New Jersey proud, even if their state is a squalid stinkhole.

SENATOR JOKE FORM

Please mail back to me by <u>March 19, 2003</u>! Thank You!

My name is Senator ----- Larry Craig -----

And I represent the great state of ----- Idaho -----

And my favorite joke is -----

Why did the farmer plow his field with a steamroller?

Because he planned to grow mashed potatoes!

Please return joke in my envelope, or to:
John Hargrave
P.O. Box 57013
Babson Park, MA
02457-0012

I am hoping to get all 100 senators to respond with your favorite joke!!
Please try to mail back to me by March 19! Thank you!!!

SINCERELY,

John Hargrave

(and parents)

Senator Larry Craig (R-ID)

A former rancher, Senator Craig is an expert in
environmental legislation, believing we can strike
a balance between conservation of natural resources
and development of those resources by industry.
This philosophy is beautifully illustrated in the anal-
ogy of a steamroller running over a farmer's field.

Also, it's a potato joke from the senator of Idaho.
So it's topical.

THOMAS DASCHLE
SOUTH DAKOTA

COMMITTEES
AGRICULTURE
FINANCE
RULES AND ADMINISTRATION
(202) 224-2321
TOLL FREE 1-800-424-9094
http://daschle.senate.gov

320 SOUTH FIRST STREET, SUITE 101
ABERDEEN, SD 57402
(605) 225-8823

1313 WEST MAIN STREET
RAPID CITY, SD 57702
(605) 348-7551

320 NORTH MAIN AVENUE, SUITE 8
SIOUX FALLS, SD 57101
(605) 334-9596
TDD (605) 334-4637

United States Senate

WASHINGTON, DC 20510–4103

March 24, 2003

John Hargrave
P.O. Box 57013
Babson Park, MA 02457-0013

Dear John:

Thank you for contacting me as part of your government project. I always enjoy hearing from students, and I am glad to help.

First, I think it is wonderful that you want to be a comedian when you grow up. Humor is critically important, even in politics, and especially in difficult times like these. I agree with what President Lincoln once said at a meeting with his Cabinet during the darkest days of the Civil War. The President told a joke, but no one responded. The President told another joke. It, too, was met with grim silence. Finally, the President asked the others, "Gentlemen, why don't you laugh? With the fearful strain that is upon me night and day, if I did not laugh, I should die. You need this medicine as much as I do."

I always try to include some humor in my speeches. I think the best kind of humor is good-natured; in fact, if I poke fun at anyone, it's at myself. One of the stories I use that always gets a laugh isn't really a joke, it's a true story. One evening shortly after the anthrax letter was opened in my office, I came home from work and a member of my security team told me – sort of sheepishly – that he'd made a mistake. A package had been mailed to my house that day. Printed on the box, the officer saw the words: "jerk of the month." He figured he had an emergency and called the bomb squad. Turns out, it was my monthly shipment of beef jerky from a company in South Dakota!

Again, thank you for contacting me. Best of luck on your project.

With best wishes, I am

Sincerely,

Tom Daschle
United States Senate

TAD/gsl

PRINTED ON RECYCLED PAPER

Senator Tom Daschle (D-SD)

Senator Daschle went all out, providing not one but *two* humorous anecdotes.

I love the jerky story, because it's an amusing insight into how our tax dollars are spent. I picture bomb-defusion experts surrounding a package of beef jerky, deploying the sophisticated MR-5 robot with its high-tech disrupter cannons. "IT'S JUST JERKY, SIR!" That's a scene from a movie there.

CHUCK HAGEL
NEBRASKA

248 RUSSELL SENATE OFFICE BUILDING
(202) 224-4224
(202) 224-9083 TTY/TDD

United States Senate
WASHINGTON, DC 20510-2705

FOREIGN RELATIONS
Chair, Subcommittee on International Economic
Policy, Export and Trade Promotion

BANKING, HOUSING, AND URBAN AFFAIRS
Chair, Subcommittee on International
Trade and Finance

SELECT COMMITTEE ON INTELLIGENCE

March 21, 2003

Mr. John Hargrave
Post Office Box 57013
Babson Park, MA 02457

Dear John:

Thanks for your letter.

Due to anthrax exposure on Capitol Hill, all Congressional mail must now undergo security screening. Unfortunately, this process delayed the delivery of your letter to my office. This is why I was unable to respond to your letter by the March 19th deadline.

My favorite joke was sent to me by a high school Latin club in Florida. "Latin isn't dead. It's just 'Roman' around."

Enclosed is a signed photo. Continue to study hard and aim high!

Sincerely,

Chuck H

Enclosure

4009 6th Avenue	294 Federal Building	11301 Davenport Street	115 Railway Street
Suite 9	100 Centennial Mall North	Suite 2	Suite C102
Kearney, NE 68845	Lincoln, NE 68508	Omaha, NE 68154	Scottsbluff, NE 69361
(308) 236-7602	(402) 476-1400	(402) 758-8981	(308) 632-6032

chuck_hagel@hagel.senate.gov

Senator Chuck Hagel (R-NE)

Senator Hagel's letter was perhaps the most *unintentionally* funny; somehow the juxtaposition of the joke with the photo is just perfect. He looks like he's trying to keep a hamburger warm between his buttcheeks.

```
ORRIN G. HATCH                                              COMMITTEES:
    UTAH
                                                            JUDICIARY
  PATRICIA KNIGHT                                            CHAIRMAN
  CHIEF OF STAFF        United States Senate                FINANCE

104 Hart Senate Office Building  WASHINGTON, DC 20510-4402  INTELLIGENCE

Telephone: (202) 224-1251                                  INDIAN AFFAIRS
TDD (202) 224-2849
Fax: (202) 224-6331         March 31, 2003                 AGING

Website: http://www.senate.gov/~hatch/                     JOINT COMMITTEE
                                                            ON TAXATION


        John Hargrave
        Post Office Box 57013
        Babson Park, MA 02457

        Dear John:

             Thank you for writing me.  I always enjoy hearing from young
        people.

             I was delighted to read your letter asking me for my
        favorite joke.  I believe a sense of humor will serve you well in
        any career field you enter in; I often use comedy in my work when
        giving speeches and writing.

             One joke that I enjoy is:

             "Learn from the mistakes of others - you can never live long
                enough to make them all yourself."

             Unfortunately, I do not know whom to give credit for this.

             Thank you again for writing.  Good luck with your government
        class project.

                                      Sincerely,


                                      Orrin G. Hatch
                                      United States Senator

        OGH:ahh



                        PRINTED ON RECYCLED PAPER
```

Senator Orrin Hatch (R-UT)

A former Mormon bishop, Senator Hatch has a reputation as a sober and serious conservative representing the heavily church-influenced state of Utah. As chairman of the Senate Judiciary Committee, Senator Hatch opposes abortion and is tough on defense, but surprisingly proficient at working with Democrats, such as his friend Ted Kennedy. Senator Hatch didn't really send a joke, but an amusing quip. Still, the fact that he sent in anything at all should counter the critics who call him humorless.

```
ERNEST F. HOLLINGS
SOUTH CAROLINA

OFFICES:                                                      COMMITTEES:
1835 ASSEMBLY STREET                                          COMMERCE, SCIENCE, AND
COLUMBIA, SC 28291        United States Senate                  TRANSPORTATION: RANKING
803-765-5731                                                  APPROPRIATIONS:
126 FEDERAL BUILDING    126 RUSSELL OFFICE BUILDING             COMMERCE, JUSTICE, STATE AND
GREENVILLE, SC 29603      WASHINGTON, DC 20510-4002               THE JUDICIARY: RANKING
864-233-5366                  202-224-6121                     DEFENSE
112 CUSTOM HOUSE       EMAIL: http://hollings.senate.gov       LABOR, HEALTH AND HUMAN SERVICES,
200 EAST BAY STREET                                              EDUCATION
CHARLESTON, SC 29401                                          ENERGY AND WATER DEVELOPMENT
843-727-4525              March 20, 2003                        INTERIOR
                                                             BUDGET
                                                             DEMOCRATIC POLICY COMMITTEE
```

Mr. John Hargrave
P.O. Box 57013
Babson Park, MA 02457

Dear Mr. Hargrave:

Many thanks for your letter informing me of your government project. I regret that
I do not have one favorite joke to send you. I believe maintaining a good sense of humor
is essential to a healthy, happy and successful life and, therefore, equally appreciate most
jokes I've heard or told. Everyone has their own individual likes and dislikes of the wide
range of jokes and senses of humor in our society. As a comedian I'm sure you will set
your own style that appeals to the majority of your audience.

Please accept my best wishes for every success with your school project, your
career goals, and your future endeavors.

With kindest regards, I am

Sincerely,

Ernest F. Hollings

EFH/ccp

Senator Ernest Hollings (D-SC)

This was one of several "cop-out" responses I
received, where the senator apparently couldn't recall
a joke—or at least a *clean* enough joke—to send me.
Come on. A life spent in politics, and you don't know
one freaking joke? You're in the wrong business, pal.

Furthermore, Hollings's claim that "I equally
appreciate most jokes I've heard or told" is such a
typical political response. Take a stand on something!
Is he afraid to offend *jokes* now? Does he realize that
jokes can't vote? This statement implies that all jokes

are created equal, which is something only a robot would say. Therefore, I have come to the conclusion that Senator Hollings is a robot.

But Hollings was the only Senator to send me back my original postage-paid envelope, so at least he's a *friendly* robot.

John Hargrave

From:	▓▓▓▓▓ ▓▓▓▓▓
To:	John Hargrave
Sent:	Friday, May 02, 2003 4:28 PM
Subject:	Your Request

Dear John - The following is a joke that Senator Kerry has been using recently at public speaking engagements. I hope it is helpful with your project and that you realize your dream of becoming a comedian (although you will probably need better material than this!) Good luck.

Sincerely
▓▓▓▓▓ ▓▓▓▓▓ ▓▓▓
Office of Senator John Kerry

Joke : "We have a new Chaplain in the Senate and a tour came through the other day. They asked him a lot of questions about being Chaplain and one person turned to him and asked: "When you open the Senate with prayer each morning, do you look out at the Senators and pray for them?" The Chaplain didn't lose a beat – he said "No, actually I look out at all those Senators and I pray for the country."

Senator John Kerry (D-MA)

One of Kerry's aides e-mailed me this response.

I was quite sad that Kerry lost the 2004 Presidential election, because it would have been monster balls to say that *I pranked the President.*

JON KYL
ARIZONA

730 HART SENATE OFFICE BUILDING
(202) 224-4521

COMMITTEES:
FINANCE
JUDICIARY
ENERGY AND NATURAL
RESOURCES
CHAIRMAN
REPUBLICAN POLICY COMMITTEE

United States Senate
WASHINGTON, DC 20510-0304

STATE OFFICES
2200 EAST CAMELBACK ROAD
SUITE 120
PHOENIX, AZ 85016
(602) 840-1891

7315 NORTH ORACLE ROAD
SUITE 220
TUCSON, AZ 85704
(520) 575-8633

March 17, 2003

John Hargrave
P.O. Box 57013
Babson Park, MA 02457

Dear John:

You had asked for a favorite joke. Here is one I often tell when I speak to groups in my state of Arizona, and in Washington, D.C.

I was working in my garden one weekend and realized I needed some extra plants. So, dressed in my grubbies and baseball cap, I went to the nursery to find some plants. When I paid for the stuff, the clerk looked at me quizzically and said, "Did anyone ever tell you that you look just like Jon Kyl?" I said, "Yes." He said, "I'll bet it makes you mad, don't it!"

Sincerely,

JON KYL
United States Senator

JK:LW

http://www.senate.gov/~kyl/
PRINTED ON RECYCLED PAPER

Senator Jon Kyl (R-AZ)

A cute self-effacing story. I appreciate that he told a real-life anecdote rather than a prepackaged joke.

Senator Kyl is regarded as an expert on terrorism and homeland security, so I think it's funny that he included a joke about not being recognized.

JOHN McCAIN
ARIZONA

COMMITTEE ON COMMERCE,
SCIENCE, AND TRANSPORTATION
COMMITTEE ON ARMED SERVICES
COMMITTEE ON INDIAN AFFAIRS

United States Senate

241 RUSSELL SENATE OFFICE BUILDING
WASHINGTON, DC 20510-0303
(202) 224-2235

4450 SOUTH RURAL ROAD
SUITE B-130
TEMPE, AZ 85282
(480) 897-8289

2400 EAST ARIZONA
BILTMORE CIRCLE
SUITE 1150
PHOENIX, AZ 85016
(602) 952-2410

450 WEST PASEO REDONDO
SUITE 200
TUCSON, AZ 85701
(520) 670-6334

TELEPHONE FOR HEARING IMPAIRED
(202) 224-7132
(602) 952-0170

May 8, 2003

Mr. John Hargrave
PO Box 57013
Babson Park, MA 02457-0012

Dear John:

Thank you for contacting my office to request a joke for your project. I am happy to oblige.

Here is my favorite joke: I feel terrible for all the mothers in the state of Arizona. Because, as you know, Barry Goldwater from Arizona ran for President of the United States, Morris Udall from Arizona ran for President of the United States, Bruce Babbitt from Arizona ran for President of the United States, and I, John McCain from Arizona ran for President of the United States. . . . Arizona may be the only state in the nation where mothers no longer tell their children that some day they can grow up and be President of the United States.

It was a pleasure to hear from you. If you would like information regarding my interests and history as a Senator, please refer to my website: mccain.senate.gov

Please do not hesitate to contact me in the future.

Sincerely,

John McCain
United States Senator

JM/amj

PRINTED ON RECYCLED PAPER

Senator John McCain (R-AZ)

I thought Senator McCain's joke was funny. Of course, he ran for the Republican Presidential nomination in 2000, so you'd expect him to have some good material. Once you start seeking the presidency, you'd better have some decent writers.

SENATOR JOKE FORM
Please mail back to me by <u>March 19, 2003</u>! Thank You!

My name is Senator — <u>Barbara Mikulski</u>

And I represent the great state of — <u>Maryland</u>

And my favorite joke is —

<u>Q: Why didn't the skeleton cross</u>
<u>the road?</u>

<u>A: He didn't have any guts!</u>
Always have the guts to stand
up for what you believe in.

Please return joke in my envelope, or to:
John Hargrave
P.O. Box 57013
Babson Park, MA
02457-0012

I am hoping to get all 100 senators to respond with your favorite joke!!
Please try to mail back to me by March 19! Thank you!!!

SINCERELY,

John Hargrave

(and parents)

Senator Barbara Mikulski (D-MD)

"The people of Maryland elected Barbara Mikulski...
because she's a fighter," states Senator Mikulski's
Web site, and that she is: a former social worker
and activist, and a fighter for the rights of seniors,
veterans, and women. Let's be honest, though: that
form was filled out by an intern. No way the Fightin'
Mikulski would sign with such unhurried script.
That lady does not have time for penmanship,
because she is on her way to a *tussle*.

SENATOR JOKE FORM

Please mail back to me by <u>March 19, 2003</u>! Thank You!

My name is Senator ---<u>Ben Nelson</u>----------------------------------

And I represent the great state of ---<u>Nebraska</u>----------------------------

And my favorite joke is -<u>Two senators are riding in an elevator</u>

<u>together. One senator leans over to the other one and</u>

<u>says:</u>

<u>Senator 1: Hey there, you'll never guess who was talking</u>
<u>   about you last night.</u>
<u>Senator 2: Who?</u>
<u>Senator 1: Nobody.</u>

Please return joke in my envelope, or to:
John Hargrave
P.O. Box 57013
Babson Park, MA
02457-0012

I am hoping to get all 100 senators to respond with your favorite joke!!
Please try to mail back to me by March 19! Thank you!!!

SINCERELY,

John Hargrave

(and parents)

Senator Ben Nelson (D-NE)

This was the only senatorial joke that I didn't quite get. A few people tried to explain it to me, and I guess one senator is trying to deflate the other senator's ego. I'm just thinking, that seems a little over the head of a ten-year-old.

It's an interesting joke, because it seems funny when you first read it, but then if you stop to think about it, *it's really not funny at all.*

RICK SANTORUM
PENNSYLVANIA

REPUBLICAN CONFERENCE
CHAIRMAN

WASHINGTON, DC
511 DIRKSEN SENATE OFFICE BUILDING
WASHINGTON, DC 20510
(202) 224-6324

COMMITTEES:
FINANCE
BANKING, HOUSING, AND URBAN AFFAIRS
RULES AND ADMINISTRATION
SPECIAL COMMITTEE ON AGING

United States Senate

http://santorum.senate.gov

June 24, 2003

Mr. John Hargrave
PO Box 57013
Babson Park, Massachusetts 02457-0013

Dear Mr. Hargrave:

Thank you for considering my contribution to your government project. I appreciate hearing from you and learning of your desire to be a professional comedian.

Although a favorite joke doesn't immediately come to mind, I do enjoy laughing. As a Senator, my schedule is quite varied. When the Senate is in session, I am in Washington, D.C. working with my colleagues to develop legislation that improves the quality of life for all Americans. When the Senate is not in session, I visit cities and towns throughout the Commonwealth of Pennsylvania. I also visit schools around the state where I meet students such as yourself. I am always thankful for the relief that laughter brings to a busy day.

Again, thank you for sharing your government assignment with me. I hope that you will continue to make people laugh. If you visit Washington D.C., please stop by my office to share your favorite joke.

Sincerely,

Rick Santorum
United States Senate

RJS:med

Senator Rick Santorum (R-PA)

Another cop-out. Senator Santorum enjoys laughing, but he doesn't know any jokes. What does he laugh at, then? Amusing memories? Bumper stickers? Negotiating joint resolutions for emergency appropriations? *Hoo!*

Now the third-ranking Republican in the Senate, Senator Santorum is a high-profile spokesman for the party, and the youngest member of the leadership. So maybe he enjoys laughing *maniacally*, drunk on the heady perfume of power.

OLYMPIA J. SNOWE
MAINE
154 Russell Senate Office Building
(202) 224-5344
E-Mail: Olympia@snowe.senate.gov
Web Site: http://snowe.senate.gov

United States Senate

WASHINGTON, DC 20510-1903

May 5, 2003

COMMITTEES:
COMMERCE, SCIENCE, AND
TRANSPORTATION

CHAIR, OCEANS AND FISHERIES
SUBCOMMITTEE

FINANCE

INTELLIGENCE

CHAIR, SMALL BUSINESS

John Hargrave
PO Box 57013
Babson Park, Massachusetts 02457

Dear John:

Thank you very much for writing. I am happy to answer your government project questions.

When I was growing up, I developed a very strong interest in government. I was especially interested in some form of public service so that I could work to help others. It was my dream to someday be able to make a difference in people's lives. Now I am fortunate enough to work as a United States Senator, where it is my job to serve the people of Maine. I truly enjoy my work, and hopefully I am able to make a difference.

I was happy to learn that your dream is to grow up to become a comedian. The following is one of my favorite jokes because it pokes fun at politicians:

Speaking of politics always reminds me of the story of Michelangelo and a politician arriving at the pearly gates at the same time. Both knocked at the gate. Saint Peter peered out, immediately threw open the gates, proclaiming, "He's here! He's here!", and rushed to the politician, as trumpets began to sound, flutes began to play, and a chorus of angels sang a celestial greeting.

In the rush and excitement, Michelangelo was knocked down. As he struggled to his feet and began to follow after the happy throng, the pearly gates slammed shut in his face. Shaken and confused, he knocked again. Saint Peter looked out, opened the gates, and let Michelangelo enter.

"I don't understand it, Saint Peter," Michelangelo began. "I have served God all my through my work -- through painting the Sistine Chapel and sculpting David -- and I arrive at the pearly gates and am completely ignored -- literally downtrodden -- in the midst of the tremendous welcome for, of all people, a POLITICIAN! I just don't understand!"

"Oh, Michelangelo, I am so sorry!" explained Saint Peter. "But you see, we get a great many artists and religious people entering through the pearly gates, but this is the first politician we've ever had!"

Again, thank you for contacting me – I enjoyed hearing from you. Good luck in school!

Sincerely,

OLYMPIA J. SNOWE
United States Senator

OJS:kaw

AUBURN
Two Great Falls Plaza
Suite 7B
Auburn, ME 04210
(207) 786-2451

AUGUSTA
40 Western Avenue, Suite 408C
Augusta, ME 04330
(207) 622-8292

BANGOR
One Cumberland Place, Suite 306
Bangor, ME 04401
(207) 945-0432

BIDDEFORD
231 Main Street, Suite 2
Biddeford, ME 04005
(207) 282-4144

PORTLAND
3 Canal Plaza, Suite 601
Portland, ME 04101
(207) 874-0883
Maine Relay Service
TDD 1-955-3323

PRESQUE ISLE
169 Academy Street, Suite 3
Presque Isle, ME 04769
(207) 764-5124

IN MAINE CALL TOLL FREE 1-800-432-1599
PRINTED ON RECYCLED PAPER

Senator Olympia Snowe (R-ME)

Senator Snowe holds many firsts: she was the first Greek-American woman ever elected to Congress, and later the first Republican woman to secure a full-term seat on the Senate Finance Committee. Now, she is the First Lady of *Funny*, sending in the joke that overwhelmingly won our popular vote for Funniest Senatorial Joke.

But, you know, we're talking senatorial jokes here. The bar's not that high.

Conclusion

I respect the senators who wrote back, I really do.
There was no political incentive: the kid wasn't even
of voting age, much less a voter in their home state.
As someone who takes pride in answering all his own
e-mail, I respect their dedication to listening and
responding to the people.

It's funny that of all the pranks I've pulled, this is
the one that actually *restored* my faith in the system.
Paradoxically, making fun of senators actually got
me to respect them more. At least, the 15 percent who
responded.

To the other eighty-five senators: *answer your
mail.* I mean, *Orrin Hatch* managed to send in a joke.
It's not that hard. Open a frigging knock-knock book
once in a while. ☺

The Untied Nations

 I HAD PRANKED our largest corporations, our most famous celebrities, and an entire branch of the U.S. government. Still, I wasn't satisfied. What I really wanted was to prank the entire world. As pranking the world would be costly and time consuming, however, I settled instead for pranking *all 191 member countries of the United Nations.*

The UN was founded at the end of World War II "to save succeeding generations from the scourge of war."[1] Great job on that one. Afghanistan, Algeria, Angola, Bangladesh, Bosnia, Burma, Burundi, Cambodia, Colombia, East Timor, El Salvador, Ethiopia, Guatemala, Herzegovina, India, Indonesia, Iran, Iraq, Israel, Korea, Kurdistan, Lebanon, Liberia, Mozambique, Myanmar, Nigeria, the Philippines, Romania, Rwanda, Sierra Leone, Somalia, Sudan, Syria, Uganda, Vietnam, Zaire, and Zimbabwe have all been the victims of wars, massacres, or genocide on their own soil since the UN began. But hey, on the bright side: *no more Cold War.* The UN's track record is 1-38. If it were a racehorse, you'd shoot it. And "shooting" is something the UN should know a lot about, since it's failed to stop most of it.

Still, we can't blame *all* nations for the failings of the United Nations. Maybe a few bad ambassadors spoil the whole bunch. My question was this: *which country in the UN is most devoted to world peace?* If we were able to identify that country, perhaps

1. "Charter of the United Nations," Preamble, 1945.

all nations could study and emulate its behavior, ultimately ushering in a new age of harmony and cooperation. This wasn't just a prank; it was the *salvation of the human species.*

Before we get to the prank, however, I think it's instructive to look at the history of the United Nations, and make my case for why this global body deserves a good pranking. Those who are not interested in political discourse may skip ahead to "The Prank" on page 244.

Criticisms of the United Nations

In 1945, the victorious powers of World War II founded the United Nations to eradicate war and champion human rights. The UN was built on the theory of "collective security," which means that any breach of the peace will result in a collective response from all member nations. Maintaining peace through the threat of war: it's no wonder that Henry Kissinger once argued that the ideal of "collective security" is unattainable.[2]

The UN is made of six principal organs called the United Nations System...Okay. Are they gone yet? Good. Now it's just you and me. All those other brainless morons skipped ahead. I can tell you're a *real* intellectual. I like that. You listen to NPR; occasionally you *jerk off* to NPR. You enjoy the finer things in life, like aged wine. This is why I'm giving you a sneak peek at my new illustrated novel featuring *hardcore unicorn pornography*. It's a new genre I'm calling "Uniporn." Check it out, homecorn:

2. "No act of aggression involving a major power has ever been defeated by applying the principle of collective security." Kissinger, Henry. *Diplomacy.* Simon & Schuster, 1995, p. 249.

Many critics have also taken issue with the UN's model of *consensus*: just look at its failure to prevent the United States–led invasion of Iraq in 2003.[3] Forget world peace; these guys can't even agree on what the fuck to have for *lunch*. Trying to get anything done at the UN is like trying to get agreement from 191 catty gay men at a Versace outlet store.

Other criticisms of the United Nations include:

- ⊕ The UN's failure to stop the 1994 Rwandan genocide.[4]

- ⊕ The UN's failure to stop the Second Congo War.[5]

- ⊕ The UN's failure to deliver food to starving Somalians.[6]

- ⊕ The UN's Oil-For-Food scandal.[7]

- ⊕ The routine sexual abuse of young girls by UN peacekeepers in the very countries they are assigned to protect.[8]

Hey, whatever. Everybody makes mistakes. A little rape by UN peacekeepers, I could forgive. The thing I personally found most tragic about the United Nations was how little *peace* the world's peacekeepers had been able to secure. Sixty years later, the world was still a bloody, violent mess.

But I had hope that *some* nations still had hope. So here's what I did.

The Prank: Round 1

To find out which of the 191 United Nations was most committed to peace, I made up the following ridiculous form letter:

3. "Double Standards," *The Economist*, October 10, 2002.

4. "The Triumph of Evil," PBS *FRONTLINE*, January 1999.

5. "Peacekeepers Killed in DR Congo," BBC News, January 23, 2006.

6. *Black Hawk Down*, Ridley Scott, Director, 2001.

7. "Oil-for-Terror?", *National Review*, April 18, 2004.

8. "UN Sex Crimes in Congo: Prostitution, Rapes Run Rampant," ABC News, February 10, 2005.

HOMEY PEACE CENTENNIAL
"Keeping the Peace for 100 Years"
P.O. Box 990586 Boston, MA 02199

H.E. Allan Rock
Permanent Representative of Canada to the United Nations
One Dag Hammarskjöld Plaza, 885 Second Avenue, 14th Floor
New York, NY 10017

Dear Ambassador:

I am writing on behalf of the Homey Peace Centennial, an annual celebration organized
by the citizens of Homey, Massachusetts, which you may know is often called "The
Birthplace of Peace," due to our long history of peace dating back to 1906.

As part of our 100th celebration, we are hoping to get signed photographs from each of
the 191 ambassadors to the United Nations. We would be extremely grateful if you
would send us a photograph of yourself, or your home country, writing on it the words
"PEACE HOMEY," and your signature.

We already have signed photographs from over 60 representatives of the United Nations,
and we're hoping that your country is not left out! As this is our second time contacting
you, would you kindly **send us your signed photo with the words "PEACE HOMEY"
by 15 September,** so that we still have time to incorporate it into the parade float.

Thank you, and keep the peace!

Sincerely,

John Hargrave
c/o Homey Peace Centennial
P.O. Box 990586
Boston, MA 02199
UNITED STATES

P.S. I am enclosing a mailing label to make it easier to send back your signed photo.

In order to lend plausibility to my request, I also
mocked up a fake newspaper article, which looked
eerily authentic when run through the photocopier
a few times.

Now all I had to do was get a master list of United
Nations ambassadors and their addresses. And that's
when I learned the only thing "united" about the
United Nations is the name.

A Century of Peace
Town readies for centennial celebration

By David Price
Staff Writer

For the last 25 years, Tracie LeMay has served as Senior Planner for the annual Homey Peace Celebration, a position that has allowed her to be the first to greet visiting speakers and dignitaries when they arrive. When asked to name her favorite moment, the Homey native recalls the town's 1981 visit by Nelson Mandela. "He was so majestic, and he spoke with such conviction," she responds. "Driving him from the airport to his hotel was a life-changing experience."

Volunteer Seth Macy recalls the 1996 performance of singer-songwriter Chris Garrett his personal highlight. Macy, now a senior at St. Elizabeth's High School, was inspired to take up the guitar after hearing Garrett sing her moving rendition of "Give Peace A Chance (Before We're All Dead)." But Macy says the centennial celebration will be its best yet. "People will be talking about this one for the next 100 years," he predicts.

With an impressive lineup of speakers and performers including Reverend Alan Natanagara, acoustic folk artist Angela

Franz, and prize-winning African poet Afki Homan-Katma, the 100th Homes Peace Celebration promises to be a week-end that will indeed go down in Homey history.

A centerpiece of the weekend will be an exhibit featuring signatures of all 191 ambassadors to the United Nations. "So far, we have collected over 60 signatures," says LeMay, gesturing to the handsome gold frames in which each signature will be mounted. The exhibit will eventually be put on permanent display in the Homey Peace Museum, located at 32 Ashland Street, across from Bobby's Scoop Shop.

Over four hundred people are expected to attend the opening parade, which will begin on Randall Drive, wind its way through the center of town, and end at the new Peace Gazebo. Funded by donations from local businesses, the gazebo was built especially for the event, and will be dedicated with brief remarks by Mayor Quimby, followed by a 21-gun salute. The gazebo dedication will be followed by a performance of WOW! Peace Kids, the children's anti-war musical group who have recently travelled to the war-torn

SEE CENTURY, PAGE A12

TOP: Homey High School senior Tracy Hall prepares flyers for the celebration.
BOTTOM: Senior Planner Tracie LeMay puts final touches on the Peace Gazebo.

▲ It's really quite amazing what you can do with Photoshop and a few stock photos.

UN-United and It Feels So Good

I tracked down the main UN number (not an easy task), and spoke with a surly middle-aged New Yorker.

"I need addresses for each of the 191 member nations of the UN," I requested.

She seemed confused. "What do you mean?"

"I want to write each of the ambassadors."

"Why?" Apparently no one had ever done this before.

"It's kind of like a petition," I explained. "It's for world peace."

There was a long pause. "I've got a list here," she finally revealed.

"Great. How can I get a copy?"

Silence. "Well, I'm not going to *read* these to you over the *phone*."

"They don't exist anywhere on the UN Web site?"

"No."

"Can you e-mail them to me?"

"No."

"Can you fax them to me?"

"No."

"Why not?"

"It won't fit in the fax machine. It's a booklet."

I pictured one of those Xeroxed address booklets, like a church membership directory. Good to know the UN was keeping up with technology. "Is there any other way for me to get a list of UN addresses?" I asked.

"No."

Try to wrap your head around this for a minute: *there is no master list of ambassadors to the United Nations.* "United," indeed.

Address for Success

Next, I tried the Internet. It was exhausting, cobbling together bits of information from 191 different countries, many of which change their name each month. Imagine sending Christmas cards to 191 friends who recently entered the Witness Relocation Program. Getting the *names* of the ambassadors was especially tricky, since you're dealing with people like Fawzi Bin

Abd Al-Majid Shubukshi (Saudi Arabia) or Laohaphan Laksanachanthon (Thailand). I mean, is it Mr. *Laohaphan*, or Mr. *Laksanachanthon*? Or *Ms.* Laksanachanthon? Maybe Mr. Laksanachanthon snipped off the old *meatballs and sausage*, if you get my meaning.

I learned that the proper form of address for an ambassador is "H.E. Laohaphan Laksanachanthon," which stands for "His/Her Excellency." So that took care of the gender problem. I also learned that many of the ambassadors, sadly, were my own age. How depressing is that? I could have been a fucking *ambassador*. Instead, here I am in my thirties, making prank phone calls to clowns.

After many tedious hours, I assembled my list. I ran a mail merge, "personalizing" each letter. Then my wife and I spent an evening stuffing envelopes with my ridiculous request for urban ghetto slang. "Nobody's going to fall for this," she predicted.

But on that point, she was wrong.

Round 1 Results

Read all the UN responses:
www.prankthemonkey.com/un

I received too many responses to print in this book, but there's a collage of my favorites opposite. All told, I received fourteen responses to my original request: the Bahamas, Barbados, Belarus, Chile, Democratic Republic of the Congo, Hungary, Macedonia, Mali, Micronesia, the Philippines, the Russian Federation, Slovenia, Syria, and Turkey. That's just over 7 percent of the United Nations at least marginally interested in peace. But my goal was to find the nation *most* committed to peace. It was time for the elimination round.

Dear Mr. Hargrave

I commend your work in the context of the Homey Peace Centennial as a noble and most welcome undertaking.
With best wishes,

Andrei Dapkiunas

Peace Homey

Peace Homey

PEACE HOMEY

"PEACE HOMEY"

MALI
Peace Homey

PEACE HOMEY

MACEDONIA EXPO 2000

The Prank: Round 2

I sent out the next letter to all the countries that responded to the original RFP (Request For Pranking). This one required a little more TLC (Tender Loving Con-Artistry); I carefully personalized each letter with the appropriate city and country names.

HOMEY PEACE CENTENNIAL
"Keeping the Peace for 100 Years"
P.O. Box 990586 Boston, MA 02199

H.E. Andrey Ivanovich Denisov
Permanent Representative of the Russian Federation to the United Nations
136 East 67th Street
New York, NY 10021

Dear Ambassador:

First, we THANK YOU for generously contributing a signed photo to the Homey Peace Centennial. With the 100th celebration just a few weeks away, it is good to know that the Russian Federation will be represented in our final exhibit! We have received signatures from nearly 150 of our United Nations ambassadors, and we are excited that your country will be included!

I am writing to request one additional favor. One of the leaders of the Homey Peace Celebration, Mrs. Francis Out, has chosen to retire from her post as Executive Committee Chairperson this year. In addition to the United Nations exhibit, we are hoping that you would be so kind as to send us **one additional signed photo with the words "PEACE OUT."** At 86 years of age, Francis has given more than half her life to the cause of peace, and as Russia has always held a special place in her heart (she visited Moscow in 1993), a signed photo from you would be tremendously appreciated.

Thank you so much for contribution to our event. We would be truly grateful if you could send us one additional photo by the date of the celebration (15 November).

Keep the peace,

John Hargrave
c/o Homey Peace Centennial
P.O. Box 990586
Boston, MA 02199
UNITED STATES

P.S. I am enclosing a mailing label to make it easier to send back your signed photo with the words "PEACE OUT."

Round 2 Results

This time, I received responses from just four nations: Hungary, Philippines, the Russian Federation, and Slovenia.

And then there were four. But ultimately, there could only be one. This was like a retarded game of Risk, except I was playing with real countries.

The Prank: Round 3

I had to really pull out the stops on this one, enclosing two full-page photos with the prank letter:

HOMEY PEACE CENTENNIAL
"Keeping the Peace for 100 Years"
P.O. Box 990586 Boston, MA 02199

H.E. Gábor Bródi
Permanent Representative of the Republic of Hungary to the United Nations
227 East 52nd Street
New York, NY 10022-6301

Dear Ambassador Bródi:

Our 100th celebration was truly an occasion to remember. Hundreds of people turned out to push the non-motorized parade floats through the streets of Homey. Despite the driving rain and sleet, celebrants planted over 300 flowers, and made nearly 750 pounds of homemade granola. Our visitors enjoyed pacifying speeches from the nephew of Dr. Martin Luther King, Jr's taxidermist, and enjoyed hourly performances of MimePrime, a combination mime/primal scream therapy troupe.

My personal highlight was the dedication of our new Peace Gazebo, which we proudly adorned with the signatures of all 191 members of the United Nations. **The Republic of Hungary** was proudly represented in this historic display of peace, and while I regret to inform you that the display was stolen from the gazebo on its first night, we managed to capture a lovely photograph, which I am including here.

I also appreciate you sending a second photo in honor of Mrs. Francis Out, whose 42 years of service were commemorated with the cannon firing of a German-made Doppelzünder artillery shell. When we presented her with your Excellency's signature, she was moved to tears. (Photo enclosed.)

I am embarrassed to ask for a final favor. We are now inducting a new Executive Chairperson to lead the Homey Peace Celebration into the next century. His name is Mr. Chiang-Ho Yo, and **we would be deeply grateful if you could send a final signed photograph with the words "PEACE, YO."** I am truly sorry to impose on you in this manner, but Mr. Yo saw the nice photo you sent Mrs. Out, and he looked really sad that he wouldn't be getting one.

Thank you for your generous support and patience, and keep the peace!

John Hargrave

◄ "The Homey Peace Gazebo, before it was defaced by drunken vandals."

◄ "Mrs. Francis Out, after being presented with her signed photograph from Hungary."

Round 3 Results

Because I was going broke from the postage, I determined the *first* country that responded would become the world's MVP (Most Valuable Peacenik). And that country, amazingly enough, was the **Russian Federation.** You used to know them by their old name, the Evil Empire. The *USS of fucking R.* After the collapse of the Cold War, the Soviet Union fragmented

PEACE, YO *Andrey Denisov*

▲ H.E. Andrey Ivanovich Denisov, World's Most Peaceful Ambassador.

9. The United Nations did not actually end the Cold War.

into independent states, leaving only its heart and soul, the Russian Federation. The country that has now proven itself the most *peace-loving country in the world.*

What the fuck happened, United States? How about you, United Kingdom? *We share the name "United,"* for Christ's sake. We're 50 percent there already. We pay for more than a quarter of the United Nations' budget: can't we afford a goddamn intern to answer the mail?! How does *Russia* now lead us in peacekeeping? I thought we were defenders of worldwide freedom. I guess making *freedom* is more important than making *peace.*

So there you have it. The Russian Federation is officially the World's Most Peaceful Nation. Once our tormentor, now our mentor. Maybe the United Nations did one thing right after all: it ended the Cold War.[9]

Peace out. 🐵

Highway to Hell

THE MASSACHUSETTS TURNPIKE, our main highway leading through Boston, is a toll road. Riding it end to end costs you $5.60; commuting into the city from the suburbs costs $2.00, or more, each way. All those tolls really add up—the average commuter spends $1,000.00 per year on tolls—but it's either that or keep our massive highway construction projects under budget.

Recently, while giving away yet another $1.00 of my hard-earned money for the privilege of *driving into town*, I wondered: How flexible are they about the tolls? So I decided to undertake a series of experiments.

Now, there are three ways to pay tolls on the "Mass Pike," as we call it:

1. You can drive through the "Fast Lane," which is a computerized system that detects a small device that you keep on your windshield, while pelting your car with gamma rays and slowly giving you cancer of the prostate. All Fast Lanes require that you slow your car to 15 mph, and some make you stop completely, giving new meaning to the word "Fast."

2. You can pay cash to the toll booth operator. This practice harkens back to days of yore, where a traveling journeyman would have to pay a wizened troll before he could cross a precarious bridge slung over a yawning gorge. "THREE GOLD COINS!" the troll would yell, flecks of saliva and goat meat dripping from his beard. Same deal today.

▶ You can see that the money goes to keeping the baskets clean and well-manicured.

3. If you have exact change, you can use the "baskets," which are big scoop-shaped buckets into which you throw money. The money slides down a chute, where it is then processed either by highly efficient money-sorting machinery, or financially astute elves. That part is a mystery.

Experiment 1

First, I went through one of the $1.00 toll gates, *but I only threw in 97 cents.* Believe it or not, I was nervous as I drove away. Would the Turnpike Police pull me over and make me fill potholes with gravel and hot tar until I paid off my debt? Would angry Dobermans chase me down the highway, chomping at my tires?

Nothing happened.

Experiment 2

Emboldened, the next time I
went through the toll booth,
I decided to try throwing in
just *seven* cents.

Nothing happened.

While I was glad I
wasn't getting in trouble,
this wasn't giving me much
to write about. It was time
for the experiments to get nuttier.

Experiment 3

The next time I went through, I decided to just write
them an I.O.U., and tape it to the toll booth. I signed it
"Mariah Carey," because I figured she can afford the
extra dollar.

Nothing happened.

This is great! I thought. All these years, I've been
paying tolls, and it turns out they're optional! What

other creative payment options could I use to pay my tolls on the Massachusetts Turnpike?

Experiment 4

This time, instead of throwing in $1.00, I decided to tape two pictures of rap superstar 50 Cent, because that *adds up* to a dollar.

As I drove away, I kept nervously glancing in my rearview mirror for the Toll Booth Police, or 50 Cent's posse, but the sad truth is that *nothing happened.*

Experiment 5

One thing that confused me was the toll booth signs, which read $1.00 COINS ONLY NO BILLS PENNIES OR CANADIAN COINS. (With all that toll money, you'd think they could afford some punctuation.) Fortunately, the sign makes no mention of *other* foreign coins, which is the loophole I used for my next experiment.

I consulted an online currency calculator to get up-to-the-minute exchange rates, then tossed in the following coins:

- 1 Indian Rupee ($0.02 U.S.)
- 15 Thai Baht ($0.36 U.S.)

- 11 Singapore cents ($0.06 U.S.)

- 1 Finnish Marka and 200 Italian Lira (replaced by the Euro)

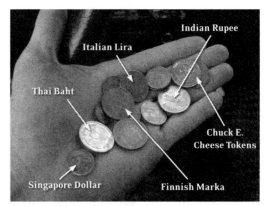

Italian Lira

Indian Rupee

Thai Baht

Chuck E. Cheese Tokens

Singapore Dollar

Finnish Marka

That only added up to 44 cents, so I threw in a couple of Chuck E. Cheese tokens as well.

When I went through this time, I heard the toll booth operator shout something that sounded like, "WALP!" I had been trying my little experiments at the same toll booth, so maybe he recognized my car, or maybe he was choking on a thick slice of ham. I didn't stick around to find out—I got the WALP out of there.

Experiment 6

In olden days, one could directly barter goods and services without the aid of money. So I bought a couple of oranges from a local convenience store, which cost me about a dollar. In my next run through the Mass Pike toll booths, I threw in the oranges.

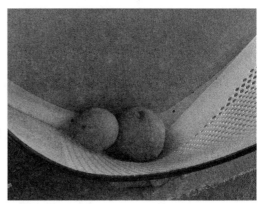

They sat in the bucket, where I assume they remained until a Fruit Collection Officer came by to pick them up.

The Apology

Since none of my experiments had any effect on the automated change buckets, which cheerfully allowed me to pass, I concluded that the Massachusetts Turnpike Authority was the most laid-back government agency ever—even more than the Department of Motor Vehicles, where most employees spend 92 percent of their workday in a deep, restful slumber.

I felt that if I was going to leave an I.O.U. for a one-dollar toll, however, I should pay up. So I snail-mailed a letter to the Massachusetts Turnpike Authority:

John Hargrave
P.O. Box 57013
Babson Park, MA 02457

Massachusetts Turnpike Authority
Ten Park Plaza
Suite 4160
Boston, MA 02116

July 10, 2003

To Whom It May Concern:

I recently found myself short on cash when going through one of the $1.00 toll booth on the Massachusetts Turnpike, so I left you an "I.O.U." note, which I signed "Mariah Carey."

Because I recently became a born-again Christian, I am trying to make amends with everyone I have wronged. So I am paying you $1.17, the amount that I shortchanged you, plus 17% interest.

I want to thank you for keeping our roadways clean and well-maintained, and I hope that we can remain friends.

Sincerely,

John Hargrave

And, hey, while I was sending out letters...

John Hargrave
P.O. Box 57013
Babson Park, MA 02457

Mariah Carey
c/o William Morris Agency
1325 Avenue of the Americas
New York, NY 10019

July 10, 2003

Dear Ms. Carey:

Recently I was driving on the Massachusetts Turnpike, and found myself short of change when I exited at a $1.00 toll booth. I left an I.O.U., and signed it with your name. I thought, "Mariah can afford it."

Because I have since accepted Jesus Christ as my Lord and Savior, I feel the need to apologize to you. What I did was wrong, and I am very sorry if it put you in an uncomfortable situation. I sincerely hope that the Turnpike Police did not come to your door, angrily demanding their dollar.

In case they did, I am enclosing a check for $2.11, which is the amount I owe you, plus 111% interest. I arrived at this number from the first line of "Babydoll" off your album "Butterfly," where you sing "It's 2:11 and I'm stressing," which I know you wrote for me and me alone.

I hope we can remain friends 4-ever.

John Hargrave

My prediction was that the Turnpike check would get mired in bureaucracy and never get cashed, while Mariah's agents would greedily deposit hers immediately, since they get 15 percent.

The Surprising Conclusion

A few weeks after sending out the checks, I got my bank statement in the mail, and would you believe the Turnpike Authority actually cashed my check? I knew our highway construction projects were way overbudget, but, I mean, *a dollar seventeen*?!

Still no word from the Mariah Carey camp.

So I guess we've learned a valuable lesson: if you need to steal, don't steal from an impoverished, badly managed government agency. *Steal from Mariah.* 😜

The Boston Tax Party

ON THE EVENING OF December 16, 1773, a group
of colonial settlers stole away, under the cover of
darkness, to the narrow waterway that ran along
the edge of the young British colony of Boston. They
were disguised as Mohawk Indians, because if you've
got to do something illegal, you should blame it
on the Indians. Led by the famous patriot Samuel
Adams, who would later become the patron saint of
yuppie alcoholics, the men illegally boarded three
ships loaded with hundreds of crates of British tea.
Without violence or bloodshed, they quietly broke
open these crates, dumping 342 chests of tea into the
Boston Harbor. Then they followed that with 18 bags
of sugar, 84 lemon wedges, and 564 pounds of ice.
Apparently the Boston Tea Party wasn't a political
statement at all, they were just *thirsty*. Little known
historical fact. I mean, they called it a *party*. Hello!

Every American schoolchild learns about this
famous prank by our forefathers, an act of protest
against "taxation without representation." It was,
quite simply, the most highly praised act of tax
evasion in American history, but if you tried it today,
the IRS would be so far up your ass that you'd be
crapping 1040s for weeks. "True, the patriots were
protesting against unfair British taxes," we might
explain to a skeptical student, "but that was the
old government. Those guys were *tryannical*. Not
like your *new* government, which only uses taxpayer
money for honest and efficient programs that
directly improve the lives of its citizens."

Still, that hasn't stopped thousands of U.S. citizens from trying to avoid paying taxes, often in bizarre and creative ways—though admittedly few as weird as Harbor Tea. Let's face it: the only thing worse than *doing* your taxes is *paying* your taxes. I would never condone stealing from the government, but I understand the frustration of "tax resisters" like our founding fathers. When April rolls around, it's hard to hand over a third of your income to the government, money that will be used to finance wars you don't believe in and causes you don't support. Most reasonable Americans would agree we need a strong defense; it's the strong *offense* we don't want to pay for. In a sense, it's blood money—just ask a dead Iraqi's mom. Tax attacks.

I'm an honest, taxpaying citizen. But my dream was to become an *ornery*, taxpaying citizen. Was there some way to legally pay my taxes, yet still stir up a bit of trouble? I read through pages of tax law, trying to find a loophole that would let me prank the IRS. It was incredibly tedious research, nearly as bad as watching Ashton Kutcher's movies. But eventually I came up with an idea: *what if I filled out my tax return using Roman numerals?*

After all, if my country was going to *act* like ancient Rome, creating a worldwide empire of "democracy" through continuous military conquest, then I would *pay* like I was in ancient Rome. It was perfectly legal, since nowhere does the IRS state that you must fill out your tax return using the modern decimal system. I would pay every penny I owed, it's just that they'd need to hire a centurion to read the results.

Part I: Pay unto Caesar That Which Is Caesar's

Roman numerals, it turns out, are not as easy as you might think.

It's hard enough trying to translate the COPYRIGHT MCMLXXXIV on the end of an old movie. But did you know that the official Roman numerals only go up to 3,999 (MMMCMXCIX)? That means, when it comes time for Super Bowl 4000, we're fucked. We're going to have to start over. This posed a problem for my prank: I'm not rich, but I do make more than $4K a year. Fortunately, some ancient Roman invented the shorthand of putting a line over a Roman numeral to multiply it by a thousand. Sometimes they just stacked up the M's—10,000 would be represented as MMMMMMMMMM—but then it starts to resemble porno dialogue. Or possibly my Wal-Mart receipt. The line over the Roman numeral works better.

The Romans also had no number for *zero*, which was not invented until the Middle Ages. Isn't that weird? Even if you had five stones, and you subtracted five stones, you still had *something*: a twig, maybe, or a piece of bark. Everybody had something. Nobody realized they had nothing. But then they discovered nothing, and that was really something.

At any rate, first I went online and had H&R Block do my taxes the correct way. That way, I figured I could always blame the Roman numeral thing on an H&R Block software bug. I printed out the finished tax returns—federal *and* state—then painstakingly translated and copied the numbers onto the standard tax forms. I have to say, I really did feel like a Roman emperor as I did it. All I needed was a wax stamp and a lard-covered orgy.

I signed and dated the returns, then mailed them off to the government. Fortunately, I had overpaid my taxes, so I was actually due a refund. If they had a sense of humor, I reflected, they'd pay me in Roman denarii.

Part II: Rome Sweet Rome

A few weeks later, I got back a letter from my home state taxation division, the Massachusetts Department of Revenue. With trembling fingers, I opened the envelope, expecting to find a notice that they were coming to audit me. Instead, I found MY REFUND CHECK.

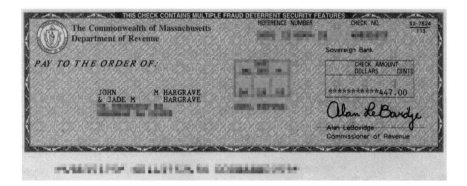

Not only did the Massachusetts government process my ridiculous return, but they actually *corrected an error* I made in reporting wages. I had to figure out how this happened, so I called up the Department of Revenue, where I spoke with a patient young fellow named Eric, who pulled up an electronic scan of my tax return on his computer.

"I don't know what all these letters are," he said. "I don't know what to make of this."

"They're Roman numerals," I educated him.

"How come those were put in?"

"I'm a big fan of Roman history."

There was a pause. "Yeah, but when you file a return like this, it won't be processed correctly."

"I don't understand," I responded. "I got a refund check."

"Oh, well, yeah." An uncomfortably long pause. "But in order to file a return, you need to use regular numbers, or it's not going to get processed right."

"But it did."

"Yeah, but it could lead to a problem."

"It didn't, though."

"Our scanners just don't accept that type of numbers."

"But I got a refund check," I reminded him.

Another pause. "That's pretty amazing," he finally admitted. "I've never seen anything like that."

"So I *shouldn't* use Roman numerals?" I clarified.

"No," he chuckled. "I guess they just pulled all your W-2s, and figured it out from there. I've never seen that before, to be honest with you."

"Really?" I asked. "There's a software program called Microcaesar Taximus. It does this for you automatically. I'm surprised you don't see more of these."

"Pretty amazing," he responded. "I've never seen anything like this."

To me, the amazing thing was that you don't even need to send in a tax return. Apparently, if they can't figure it out, they'll just do it for you. At least in Massachusetts, where they're scared we'll dump more tea into the harbor.

Part III: Rome Wasn't Built in a Day

The federal government, on the other hand, never responded. Weeks went by, then months. Fortunately,

I had sent in my return via Certified Mail, so I was able to log on to the U.S. Postal Service Web site and see that my return had not only been *received*, but *signed for* by one R AHLES. I figured it would take a while for Mr. or Ms. Ahles to translate the numbers, so I waited nearly half a year before I finally called the IRS, asking about the status of my refundimus.

Search Results

Label/Receipt Number: ▆▆▆▆▆▆▆▆▆▆
Status: **Delivered**

Your item was delivered at ▆▆▆▆▆▆▆▆ in ANDOVER, MA 05501. The item was signed for by R AHLES. A proof of delivery record may be available through your local Post Office for a fee.

Additional information for this item is stored in files offline.

▲ The proof.

Mrs. Johnson, the surprisingly helpful middle-aged woman at the IRS, told me that unfortunately, they had no record of my tax return.

"I'm looking at the signature confirmation right now," I told her.

"I don't know what to tell you," she said. "I'm showing that we never received it."

"It's just weird that the U.S. Postal Service tells me it arrived, and you're telling me it didn't." I loved being able to play two government agencies off each other. I pictured a really slow, bureaucratic cage match between the IRS and the USPS, in which fighters from each side would have to fill out extensive paperwork before they could throw a punch.

"Can you send it in again?"

"Depends," I said. "Are you going to lose it again?"

"I'm sorry about that, sir."

"Will I be fined a late fee?"

"Oh, no. As long as there are no taxes due, you have up to three years to file your return. After three years, the refund is forfeited."

"You're kidding." I was learning all these new factses about taxes.

"Did you make a copy of your tax return?" she asked me.

"Of course." I didn't tell her the copy was hand-scribed by my galley of Roman slaves. (The first photocopiers.)

"You can just make another copy, and send that in," she reassured me. "That'll be fine."

"You're not going to lose it this time?" I asked.

"No," she promised. "I'm sorry about that."

And she did, in fact, sound genuinely sorry. I would come to learn that my stereotype of IRS employees—cold, unfeeling, bureaucratic—was largely incorrect.

Except for R AHLES, who I strongly suspect got my return, then threw it away.

Part IV: All Roads Lead to Rome

I sent in another copy of my tax return, then waited. And waited. This time, I only had to wait *four* months before I got the reply shown opposite.

"Dear Taxpayer(s)," the letter began. "We have determined that the information you sent is frivolous and your position has no basis in law. This is to inform you of the potential consequences of the position you have taken." It was basically a warning letter, explaining that I had thirty days to file an updated return, and I would be charged a $500 "frivolous return penalty" for each additional prank return I filed. I was amused that they actually had a name for the penalty, but even more amused by their suggestion to read the IRS document entitled *The Truth About Frivolous Tax Arguments*. Apparently, the IRS was now the authority on frivolousness.

Internal Revenue Service
1973 North Rulon White Blvd.
Ogden, UT 84404-0040

Department of the Treasury

Contact Telephone Number:
Contact Hours: 7:00 a.m. - 3:00 p.m. Mountain Time

Dear Taxpayer(s):

This is in reply to your Tax Return(s) dated March 7, 2005.

We have determined that the information you sent is frivolous
and your position has no basis in law. Claims such as yours have
been considered and repeatedly rejected as without merit by the
federal courts - including the United States Supreme Court.
Therefore, we will not respond to future correspondence concerning
these issues. Our lack of response to further correspondence does
not in any way convey agreement or acceptance of the arguments
advanced. If you intend to persist in making such arguments, we
encourage you to seek advice from a reputable tax practitioner or
attorney.

This is to inform you of the potential consequences of the
position you have taken and to offer you an opportunity to correct
your position within 30 days of the date of this letter.

Also be advised that people who violate the tax laws may be
subject to federal criminal prosecution and imprisonment. Information
about the IRS's criminal enforcement program is available on the
internet at www.irs.gov. Once there, enter the IRS keyword: fraud.

There are some people who encourage others to violate our
nation's tax laws by arguing that there is no legal requirement for
them to file tax returns or pay income taxes. These people
base their arguments on legal statements taken out of context and on
frivolous arguments that have been repeatedly rejected by federal
courts. People who rely on this kind of information can ultimately
pay more in taxes, interest and penalties than they would have paid
simply by filing correct tax returns.

IRS Publication 2105, Why do I Have to Pay Taxes?, can be obtained
from our internet website www.irs.gov/pub/irs-pdf/p2105.pdf. We also
refer you to a document entitled The Truth About Frivolous Tax
Arguments. It is also on our website at: www.irs.gov/pub/irs-
utl/friv_tax.pdf. If you do not have internet access, you can obtain
copies of these documents from your local IRS office.

Letter 3176C (3-1-2004)

I don't know about you, but when I think frivolity,
I think the IRS.

The Truth About Frivolous Tax Arguments is
a fascinating fifty-four-page document outlining all
the different ways people have tried to weasel out of
their taxes. I was clutching my sides in unadulterated
mirth as I read arguments like "Only foreign income
is taxable," or "Compelled compliance with the federal
income tax laws is a form of servitude in violation

of the Thirteenth Amendment." I mean: *HAW!* Shoo! Talk about *frivolous*! With comedy like that, this shit writes itself.

And yet, I found nothing preventing Roman numerals. After all, I wasn't trying to get out of paying my taxes (the IRS owed *me*, remember?), I was just using a different numbering system. But as I read through *The Truth About Frivolous Tax Arguments*, I found that the IRS didn't find these returns funny after all, despite their name. "Like moths to a flame," the brochure warned, "some people find themselves irresistibly drawn to the tax protestor movement's illusory claim that there is no legal requirement to pay federal income tax. And like moths, *these people sometimes get burned.*" In fact, the maximum penalty I could be fined for my prank, under IRS Section 6673, was $25,000.

Frivolous, my ass. This was getting serious.

Part V: Rome Has Spoken

"It's all in Roman numerals," the IRS agent told me over the phone. This time it was my "case worker," a middle-aged woman whom the IRS had assigned to keep an eye on me. She was trying to sort out my return, and she sounded confused. "We have no way of knowing what those numbers are."

"I do most of my counting in Roman numerals," I told her. "See, I teach Roman history on the side. Local high school."

"It's hard for us to interpretate these numbers," she said. It took me a second to transperlate what she meant by this.

"What bothers me," I said, "is that you called my tax return 'frivolous.' I think that calling the Roman numeral system 'frivolous' is demeaning and inaccurate. With only slight modifications, it's the system we use today. Indeed, it is the system upon which your very work with the IRS is based!"

"See, we work with just numbers," explained the IRS agent. "Numbers only. It's not our job to know Roman numerals. *We have no way of knowing what your figures are.*" I've got to say, this statement didn't fill me with confidence in the mathematical ability of our nation's bean counters.

I decided to take another tack. "Listen. I've been telling my class about this issue with the IRS, and I feel that if you force me to use the modern numbering system, you'll essentially be driving a stake through the heart of our education system. You'll be destroying my students' faith in the value of ancient Roman history."

She paused, then sighed. "I'm really sorry about that. We kind of have to go by what we're told to do in these situations. I talked to a few people about this return, and we've never seen one like this."

"Well, I just want to be clear that Roman numerals aren't frivolous. In fact, when we want to stress the *importance* of something, like Olympic games or Super Bowls, we use Roman numerals. Or take kings and popes. They use Roman numerals to denote their titles of authority, like King Louis XIV. Is that frivolous?"

"Well..." She was sympathetic. "Like I said, we've *never* come across a tax return like this."

"Okay." I really needed the refund money. "Look: I can send in an amended return, but can you just admit that Roman numerals are not frivolous? Would you tell me they're important, to make me feel better?"

"This return would be fine with me," she chuckled, "but since we don't have the training in those kind of numbers, we just don't know what to do with them."

"But they're not frivolous, are they?" I pressed.

"No," she admitted. "No."

"Thanks," I said, savoring my small, retarded victory. "I appreciate it."

"And I can appreciate your statement here," she said. "I can understand how you feel."

I thanked her again, and hung up. Now, see how we talked it out like rational adults? I sent back a corrected tax return, using the decimal system, and received my refund check a few weeks later. When I deposited the check, however, I couldn't resist filling out my account number in Roman numerals.

I've got to say, of all the institutions I pranked in this book, the IRS was the most reasonable. Maybe the new government *is* better than the old one, after all. No one had to be fined $25 large; no one had to dump any tea in the Harbor. Though I did see a homeless guy dumping *pee* in the Harbor last Wednesday. He may have been protesting something.

Prank the Monkey

Isn't it funny that the U.S. government, which once was all *opposed* to taxes, now *requires* taxes? That band was so cool until they sold out. And it's the final haunting lesson of the Boston Tea Prank: *we eventually become what we once fought against.* It happens. It's life. Rebelling against the parents is fun, until you *become* the parents. One day you're pranking the monkey; the next day you *are* the monkey. One need look no further than our current U.S.-U.K. brotherhood on everything from trade agreements to Iraq, to illustrate that simple fact: *New government, same as the old government.*

So why continue to prank? Because sometimes, my friends, it *does* make a difference. Just lean back and imagine that cold December night, the heady scent of all that tea, the giddy nervousness of the patriots as they drunkenly vandalized those British ships. What did it feel like to pull off the caper that started a Revolution? It was one hell of a way to kick-start a country.

So the U.S. government now makes you pay taxes. So what? As the old saying goes, Only two things in life are certain, and one of them ain't Death.

Which, incidentally, I *also* pranked. 😋

The John Hargrave Memorial Concert

 THE STUDENTS AT THE BERKLEE COLLEGE OF
MUSIC had no idea they were just about to
witness a violent and bloody murder.

Several hundred music majors were eating peace-
fully in the student cafeteria, a large airy room with
an enormous plate-glass window on one side. The
window faced into a little-used hallway, so no one
paid much attention, until a sweaty, disheveled student ran into it, panting heavily. Behind him was a
filthy, unshaven vagrant yelling violent obscenities.

"GIVE ME MY MONEY!" roared the drunk,
waving a razor-sharp stiletto knife. "GIVE ME MY
FUCKING MONEY!"

"I DON'T HAVE YOUR MONEY!" screamed the
student. "HELP!"

"HOLY SHIT!" yelled a percussion major from
inside the cafeteria, drawing everyone's attention
to the window.

Students leaped up from their chairs, running
over to watch a scene they were helpless to stop.
A few intrepid heroes dashed through the side door,
amid cries for help. Near the window, a student
with multiple earrings and an afro quietly held up
a red folder.

The young white male with the dirty-blond ponytail looked pleadingly at the students, who were now
gathered three deep around the window. "HELP!" he
shouted again. Inside the cafeteria, I vaguely noticed
people shouting and calling for help, I saw the red

folder, but everything was in TiVo slow-mo. I was focused on the moment.

"THE FUCKING MONEY!" shouted my accomplice Al Natanagara, who fifteen years later would draw the illustrations for this book. "GIVE ME THE FUCKING MONEY!"

Behind the glass, the students watched the young man scream, "I DON'T HAVE IT!" Cornered and desperate, he lunged at the drunk. At that moment, quick as a crack-addled frog's tongue, the vagrant stabbed the student in the stomach, repeatedly and viciously, until his hand was slick with warm, thick human blood.

All right, it was corn syrup. Stage blood, the finest, purchased from the famous Jack's Joke Shop in downtown Boston. The knife was a realistic-looking breakaway knife, and it was pretty intimidating. "Please don't *actually* stab me," I told Al several times as we practiced the murder choreography in our apartment, again and again, until we were convinced it looked real.

The Getaway

The drugged-out bum staggered back and appeared to notice the panicked college crowd for the first time. Shielding his filthy face, he ran up a nearby staircase and fled the building. I was doubled over with pain, my arms clutching my bloody midsection. I secretly opened a hidden bag of raw chicken breasts marinated in stage blood, and tried valiantly to keep my slippery innards from falling onto the floor. Then I gurgled up a final mouthful of blood (gelatin capsule), reeling into the window. I put up my hand to catch myself, leaving an enormous bloody handprint on the window, a gruesome reminder to the students of the horrors they had just witnessed.

The red notebook had turned to yellow, which meant thirty seconds to get out. I staggered out the side door, as quickly as a dying man can stagger. Once out of sight, I sprinted outside, whispering into my walkie-talkie: "I'm on my way."

Jade, waiting in the getaway car in the alleyway outside, was disturbed to see the following sight in her rearview mirror: her boyfriend, covered with a blood-soaked white T-shirt, his face and arms spattered with blood. I was running at top speed, clutching a bag of bloody chicken breasts. I looked like an insane butcher.

"Hi, honey," I said, leaping into the car.

"Oh, boy," she said, peeling out in her white 1986 Ford Mercury station wagon. It was the least sexy getaway car ever designed. Also, the brakes didn't work.

If you don't understand how supportive my wife has been of my "career," consider this: *She drove the getaway car for my fake death.* We're a great team, we really are. Navigating the wood-paneled station wagon down the narrow streets of Boston at 2 miles an hour, with the clutch popping around every corner. We were like Bonnie and Clyde, with palsy.

Berzerklee

I had spent an unhappy year at Miami University, an ivy-league college located in Oxford, Ohio. They call it "Miami" because that's where most of the students would rather be. Bored and aimless, I dropped out of school for a year, wrote a terrible novel that nobody wanted, then decided to ensure myself a lifelong, stable career path by moving to Boston and becoming a professional musician.

Berklee College of Music is the world's largest independent music college, focusing exclusively on contemporary music. You've probably enjoyed the music of many of its renowned alumni, such as Melissa Etheridge, Branford Marsalis, and Quincy Jones. I was a pretty good bass player, but more important, I knew I wanted to work creative, and Berklee had a good reputation for that. Besides: Boston vs. Oxford, Ohio. The reason they call Ohio "round on the ends and high in the middle" is because most of the students in Oxford are smoking huge fatty blunts to combat the boredom.

Berklee was not exactly a traditional college experience. The real-life school of rock was an "urban campus," which is a euphemism for "no campus." The college was a number of tightly packed brick buildings in the middle of Boston's Back Bay. The ironically named "Berklee Beach" was a long strip of sidewalk that caught the afternoon sun at the corners of Massachusetts Avenue and Boylston Street, which I still think of as the crossroads of the world. (Fuck Times Square.) We'd sit out there, sunning ourselves, a bunch of art-school freaks. Long hair was a requirement, unless you were Japanese. Piercings and tattoos were optional, but strongly encouraged. I practiced the bass four hours a day, and by my final semester, I could outplay God.

I had enrolled in an independent study program, which I mostly used as an excuse to write elaborate *Spinal Tap*-like musical comedy performances. After a few shows, I had gathered something of a following, and I was under pressure to outdo myself with my final performance. The performance in question was my *senior recital*, the moment of truth for music students, the final show upon which my graduation would be judged. The more I thought about how important this show was, the more I thought it would be funny if I didn't even show up. Could I somehow avoid the stress by getting other people to do my show for me instead?

Hey: *what if I died?* Then I wouldn't even have to show up, and my show could be called "The John Hargrave Memorial Concert." It worked on so many levels, because my final show would be, you know, *my final show.* "The John Hargrave Memorial Concert." Because I am mentally ill, that seemed pretty funny to me. It would be the ultimate college prank. But how would I ever get people to believe I was dead? Well, what if I faked my own death?

Killing Me Softly

Killing me off also killed other birds with the same stone. It automatically publicized my senior recital. I wouldn't have to practice a lot, or memorize any complicated musical pieces. It would provide the final chapter for my first book. And it would be, so to speak, one *killer* fucking senior project.

I pictured students showing up for this heart-wrenching memorial concert, and instead enjoying a ninety-minute show with fantastic musical performances and live comedy tributes. It would be immediately clear that it was all a joke. There would be an hourlong comedy retrospective of my life, a short film that I would write and produce exclusively for this one-time performance. This *would* end up being a lot of work after all, just not in the way that anyone expected.

Then, at the very end of the show, I would scream from the side of the theater, "I'm not quite dead yet!" I would come in, wheeling an IV (which ended up being a real bitch to rent from the medical supply house). And then I would summon my band onstage, complete with a seven-piece horn section and full gospel choir. We would play one final song, which would *rock your fucking balls off*. Literally, testes would be rolling on the floor, and students would accidentally mash them beneath their furiously rocking feet.

That's what was *supposed* to happen. What *really* happened just about killed me, in an entirely different way.

Death Becomes Me

After our successful getaway, we had a small band of rumormongers talk loudly throughout the school for the rest of the day, reliving the event for anyone who happened to miss it. "And then this kid John Hargrave got *stabbed* in the fuckin' *stomach*, man. I totally saw the whole thing."

Satisfied that all was going well, I moved into the next phase of my plan: *get a disguise.* My long ponytail, which I had patiently grown for five years, got hacked off by a gay hairstylist in Cambridge. I went to Jack's Joke Shop and invested in a high-quality fake mustache, which looked just as terrible as the shitty ones. But with a cap and sunglasses, I was passable, I thought, for someone else. Although there was a small danger I might get mistaken for Magnum, P.I.

I needed the disguise for the next day, when my friends and I began plastering the campus with posters advertising the show:

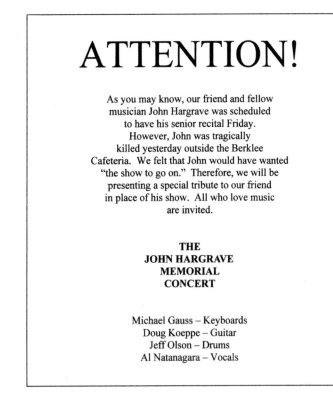

ATTENTION!

As you may know, our friend and fellow musician John Hargrave was scheduled to have his senior recital Friday. However, John was tragically killed yesterday outside the Berklee Cafeteria. We felt that John would have wanted "the show to go on." Therefore, we will be presenting a special tribute to our friend in place of his show. All who love music are invited.

**THE
JOHN HARGRAVE
MEMORIAL
CONCERT**

Michael Gauss – Keyboards
Doug Koeppe – Guitar
Jeff Olson – Drums
Al Natanagara – Vocals

In addition to the massive publicity blitz promoting the concert that my friends inexplicably threw together in twenty-four hours, some of our posters looked eerily like Berklee's official safety notices. It's usually not hard to forge realistic-looking postings from your school administration or workplace employer. Just match the font, the color of the paper, and the proper bureaucratic tone:

STUDENTS:

Due to the frequency of violent incidents on and around the Berklee campus, once again we ask you to practice safety at all times. Here are some tips to keep in mind:

1) Never leave your instrument unattended. If you must leave it, make sure it is with a trusted friend or resident assistant.

2) Never travel alone, especially at night. Whether walking to your dorm or the cafeteria, always remember to bring a friend. Walk purposefully but unhurried.

3) Never give your room, telephone number, or student ID to a stranger.

4) If anyone approaches you asking for money, drugs, etc., politely say, "No thank you," and quickly walk away.

5) Beware of strangers who suddenly seem "friendly" or who begin telling you details about their lives.

6) If you see any suspicious looking persons on campus, immediately alert a security guard or staff member.

7) If you see what appears to be a concealed weapon on a suspicious looking person, do not confront the person. Simply alert a security guard or staff member.

8) If you ever witness a scene of violence or conflict, it's best not to get involved. Immediately alert a security guard or staff member.

9) Do not offer to watch a package for a stranger or hold on to something until they get back.

10) REMEMBER - An ounce of safety prevention is worth a pound of cure.

My first inkling that the prank might have been going a little *too* well was later that night when I went to Kinko's to run off several hundred more flyers. The college kid working the counter came back to me with a stack of copies. "I heard about this, man," he said. "I just want to say I'm really sorry. You can have these copies for free."

"Thanks," I said, taken aback. He had no idea *I was the dead guy.* The story was taking on a life of its own.

I returned to campus to hang up more posters under the cover of darkness. Turning the corner onto Mass Ave, I approached the Berklee Beach, where I saw a group of students gathered perhaps forty feet away. An emo chick had gone to the convenience store across the street and bought a little twelve-pack of birthday candles. Some leather-jacketed guitar major with a lighter was handing out the candles to a small group, maybe half a dozen students. It took a minute for me to register what was going on: *they were holding a candlelight vigil.*

I am a good prankster. But if I were a *perfect* prankster, I would have turned around and walked away. But, come *on.* How often does life give you an opportunity to attend your own candlelight vigil? Two, three times, tops.

As I approached the small group of students, I realized that I knew a couple of them: they were friends I hadn't let in on the joke. Two of the others, including the emo, I knew vaguely from other classes. It began to dawn on me that this was a bad move, but I was too close to turn back.

I shuffled to the guy in the leather jacket, head down in the shadows. Fortunately, shady characters hanging around Berklee at night were pretty common. "Hey, can I have one?" I asked him, keeping my back turned to the rest of the group.

"Yeah, man." He lit a candle. It was one of those blue birthday candles with the white waxy stripes.

"Thanks." I took the candle, which must have illuminated my face, because the emo chick suddenly screamed. "You FUCK!" she yelled, pointing at me. She saw right through the disguise, even with the ridiculous pushbroom mustache. I shuffled away quickly, muttering something incomprehensible. "You CRUEL FUCK!" she screamed after me, as I turned the corner and ran away from campus as fast as I could.

The Big Day

Friday. Concert day. I had enjoyed a total of four hours sleep over the last four days, and not sequentially. I had a vanful of family and friends driving in to see my glorious senior project, my masterpiece. I had seven horns and a gospel choir fully rehearsed and ready to go. I had costumes, props, and actors. I had been up all night finishing my comedy film, which had turned out well. I was nervous, nauseous, and exhausted, but I was ready to rock.

Wearing my disguise, I ventured back onto campus that morning, trying to get everything ready for the afternoon show. I knew that my little candle stunt the previous night had been unwise, but I had no clue that the buzz about the "murder on campus" was at fever pitch. Walking through the hallways with my bass guitar slung over my shoulder, I was annoyed to find that *all our posters* had been removed. Hundreds of flyers, *gone.* I stopped in front of a bulletin board that we had completely plastered just the day before, and that's when I saw the word CANCELLED. On my arms and back, cold prickly adrenaline sweat as my body processed the horrible news:

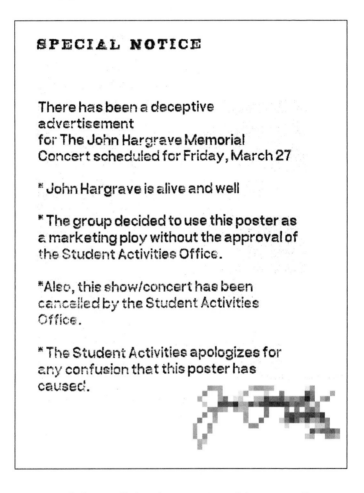

SPECIAL NOTICE

There has been a deceptive advertisement
for The John Hargrave Memorial
Concert scheduled for Friday, March 27

* John Hargrave is alive and well

* The group decided to use this poster as a marketing ploy without the approval of the Student Activities Office.

*Also, this show/concert has been cancelled by the Student Activities Office.

* The Student Activities apologizes for any confusion that this poster has caused.

It's fun to fight The Man. But this was my first painful lesson that The Man always reserves the right to fight back. And when he does, he will kick the living shit out of you. David got off a lucky shot on Goliath, but let's not forget the hundreds of

Israelite soldiers that Goliath killed before that. I was getting one hardcore punk-ass *smiting*.

I was determined to save the show. With less than five hours to our scheduled performance, I marched over to the Dean of Students' office, and spelled out my demands to the...well, to the secretary.

Even in academia, the important people are insulated by their handlers, ensuring that students can never easily talk to the people who supposedly represent them. "I need to see the Dean," I told the young blond woman outside his office.

She barely looked up from her computer. "You'll have to make an appointment."

"It's urgent," I told her. "My senior recital was just canceled."

"Oh." This got her attention. "Are you John Hargrave?"

"Yes."

"So you're not dead, then."

"No."

"Yeah, we knew that." She smirked. Pulling out a large desk calendar, she flipped through the pages. "He has an opening next Tuesday."

"I need to talk to him now," I insisted.

"We can't do that."

"Why not?"

"We, ah..." She lowered her voice. "Look. I heard they're reviewing your case for *appropriate disciplinary measures*."

That threw me. "What do you mean?" I said. "Like putting me on suspension?"

"Sometimes it's that," she said. "Or..." She let it hang there.

"Or what?"

"Well. Things don't look so good."

"They going to kick me out of school?"

She gave me a little shrug and a half-smile. "Should I put you in for next Tuesday, then?"

I couldn't believe it. "Screw that. I'm going to see the President."

"Okay," she said, closing the calendar. "Good luck on that one."

Inside the Oval Office

Academic presidents usually have multiple layers of handlers: a few secretaries to deal with the mundane stuff, like ignoring the e-mail, then a couple of professionals to handle the big jobs. These are usually polished PR guys who can skillfully handle complaints and deflect controversy, leaving the President free to take lengthy lunches at the homes of wealthy alumni donors, while the academic quality of the institution gradually disintegrates under the weight of an unmotivated faculty and apathetic student body. I'm telling you: being a university president is free money. It's like being on unemployment, but with an office.

I was no match for the smiling, shark-suited guy who came out to greet me at the President's office. He was smooth as a transexual's legs. I ranted about my recital being canceled, and he listened politely and nodded. I argued that Berklee should encourage my out-of-the-box creative idea, and he repeated my points back to me, to make sure he understood. The guy was a fucking therapist. He was good. I found my anger slowly dissipating, and I began to wonder if he was hypnotizing me with his shimmering gray suit.

"Well, I'm sorry about your recital being canceled," he told me. "But let me try to explain it to you from our point of view. You've caused a lot of people around campus a good deal of hurt and fear."

"Hmm." This had not occurred to me.

"Did you know that Professor Tate started crying in class when he heard the news?"

This crushed me. Tate was one of those rare and gifted teachers, the kind that you get maybe two or three times in your life. He had made a big impact on me with his brilliant, passionate Art History classes. "I did not know that."

"He ended up dismissing the class. *He thought you were murdered.*" He let this sink in. "We've been fielding calls all week from students, faculty, parents. People are genuinely terrified for their safety. Do you understand that this has become a crisis situation?"

"I'm sorry," I said, and I was. "But listen: the recital will explain everything. Everyone will see the whole thing was a joke."

"Your recital is not happening," he said firmly.

"Please." The sickening taste of desperation boiled in my throat. "I'll make a public apology. I'll explain that I'm alive and well."

"That would be a good start."

"And then can we do the show this afternoon?"

"No." He got up to leave. "But maybe you'll be allowed to graduate."

The Show Must Go On

I phoned my band members, who had no idea what was going on. "We've run into some problems," I said.

"But the show will continue. We're going to do this thing, one way or another."

Then, with just three hours left, I ran frantically around campus, trying to get everything set up for the show. My family and friends arrived from Ohio, and I put them to work. The recital hall, a beautiful wood-paneled auditorium, had been left open, and we quietly shuffled props and instruments onstage. "Shhh!" I kept hissing at everyone, irritably.

"Why are we doing this quietly?" my mother asked, carrying in a large candelabrum.

"Just try to keep a low profile," I told her. *"I'm supposed to be dead."*

The gospel choir showed up, and the horn section was trickling in. A few diehard fans showed up early, to make sure they'd get a seat. They congratulated me on the outstanding prank, and I was beginning to feel like we might pull this off. Since being a professional musician also means being a professional roadie, I ran out to my car to get a final armful of stuff. We still had to do a sound and video check, but it looked like we were going to make it.

I came back inside to find a group of three security guards angrily ordering everyone out of the theater.

"What's up, guys?" I asked, wheeling in a full-size medical IV unit.

"You John Hargrave?" asked the one on the left. Large black guy, shaved head.

"Yes." I tried to see around him, but he was huge, a minor continent.

"I have to ask you to leave the premises," he said. "And take these people with you."

"I can't leave," I said, pointing into the auditorium. "All my stuff is in there."

"We'll send someone in to move it out for you. But right now, you need to leave this building." He pointed to the door. "NOW."

The other two guards were busy shuffling everyone out of the theater: my parents, a dozen musicians, and a full gospel choir. A few of my ardent supporters had prepared for the show by drinking heavily, and they began to get belligerent. One of these guys, Kenny, was this crazy redneck from Kentucky. "What the *fuck*, hoss?" he started shouting at the security guards. "We ain't going nowhere!"

"They just want to do a *SHOW*!" yelled a large black woman behind me, one of our altos.

Now there was a scuffle inside the theater, with the two guards trying to wrestle Kenny to the side door. Berklee students, you have to understand, are nuts. The remaining students inside the theater were staging a mini-uprising, while outside we were drawing an even larger crowd of curious onlookers. It quickly devolved into madness: long-haired freaks hollering at the guards, drunken rednecks laughing maniacally, my parents looking around frantically for an exit. Someone knocked over the IV unit, and a bag of saline burst on the floor. This was turning into fucking Kent State.

"We've got a situation!" the guard yelled into his walkie-talkie, still trying to blockade the door against all of us. "We need the police, RIGHT NOW!"

I sprinted to the nearest payphone and asked the operator to connect me to the *Boston Globe*, Boston's largest daily newspaper. A sleepy-sounding guy answered. "News desk."

"Hey, you guys need to send a reporter over to the Berklee campus *right now.* There's a big confrontation going on between the students and the guards."

"Yeah." The guy at the *Globe* had heard it all before. "What's it about?"

"Long story. But they just called the police."

"Hmm," he said. This seemed to get his attention. "I'll look around and see if we can get someone out to cover it."

It took me a while to make the call, so by the time I ran back inside, the guards had managed to evacuate the recital hall. They had fastened a large chain and padlock across the doors, and I was heartbroken to see that most of the crowd had scattered away, except for the rubberneckers who were hanging around to see what happened next. A pair of Boston police officers (probably good cop/bad cop) were conferring with the guards in the corner. Before they saw me again, I quickly ducked out a side door, where I found my family and friends waiting on the sidewalk. Here were the core group of people who would stick with me through every success and failure for the rest of my life: my girlfriend Jade, my parents, the great Al Natanagara, my bandmates. They were my lifeblood, the people whose love and friendship would get me through many more creative disasters and personal embarrassments. But sadly, none of them wrote for the *Globe.*

I was out of options. I looked into the sea of disappointed faces, and I wanted to die, but for real this time.

"Can I have a minute alone with Jade?" I asked, my eyes welling up.

Jade and I found a nearby alley, and I hugged her tightly, burying my face in her shirt. She had been up all night helping finish our stage set, and she smelled faintly of paint. I couldn't hold back the tears, which came in long, deep sobs. "I'm a failure," I heaved into her shoulder. "I am a failure."

Meet the Press

Before I explain how my story hit the front page of the *Globe* Arts section, I should give you a little background. Improbably, the *Globe* had already been working on an article about Berklee, written by a female student who wanted to complain about the school's rampant sexism. As if the Berklee administration didn't have enough to worry about with my stunt, there was now this additional public relations nightmare: the 700,000 readers of the *Globe* reading that female Berklee students were routinely getting sexually harassed. I found this interesting, since sexual harassment was one of the themes of my show. You know, THE ONE THAT GOT CANCELED.

I almost missed the article because I was busy issuing apologies to the various people I had injured or upset. I stopped by Professor Tate's office, who looked like he was seeing a ghost. "You're *alive*!" he shouted ebulliently, shaking me by the shoulders. Others weren't so forgiving: my mailbox was stuffed with letters from angry students, people who had been affected by real-life violence. I personally responded to each of these people, either in person or with a handwritten note of apology. If my behavior to this point had been self-destructive, I was determined to become self-constructive. Despite how cool it sounded to get kicked out of school, *I wanted to graduate.* I was $40,000 in the hole with student loans, and six weeks away from passing my finals and getting the fuck out of there.

Still, when the *Globe* article hit, I saw an opportunity to screw over the college administration one last time and still get out of there alive. If I played it right, this would be a win/win scenario, *except both wins would be mine.*

Beat the Press

Two weeks later, the *Globe* ran a follow-up. In addition to other letters sent in by angry Berklee students and faculty, my guest editorial ran front and center on the Arts section. I explained how my concert had been canceled because of censorship conflicts, that I hadn't had a chance to adequately express my point of view, and that going to the *Globe* was apparently the only way students could get their voices heard. We felt "powerless against our school's overwhelming bureaucracy, alienated from our untouchable administration," I complained. "It is ironic that the leaders of a music school would be so deaf to the cries of their students. Perhaps this article will teach them, as we are taught daily, to 'use their ears.'"

Biggity-bam and a boo-yah. Thank you, *Boston Globe.* Fuck the *Herald,* okay? The *Boston Herald* isn't fit to use for wiping your dog's hemorrhoids. The *Globe* is the number one newspaper in America! We talk about a free press: this time, the press was quite literally going to set me free.

1. Actually, number eight by circulation, but who's counting.

I called the Dean's secretary and made an appointment for the following Tuesday. I showed up in a suit and tie, with my list of penances. "I've apologized to everyone," I ticked off my list, "and I paid for the damage Kenny did to the recital hall."

"Ah yes," said the Dean, a tall man in his mid-fifties with a large nose and an oversized tweed jacket. "Kenny." Apparently they knew each other well.

"I hope you'll understand I've done everything I can."

"I appreciate you taking *some* responsibility for your actions," he said, idly fingering a ballpoint pen on his desk. "But I'm disappointed you don't feel responsibility for the hurt and fear you caused others who have not contacted you directly."

"Hmm." I didn't know how to respond to this.

"Why didn't you ask for permission before you embarked on this stunt?" he asked.

"Have you heard of Jesus?" I immediately regretted the question.

He paused. "Yes, I've heard of Jesus."

"There's this story where Jesus overturns the tables of the moneychangers in the temple. He goes in and trashes the place. He didn't ask for permission."

He looked at me incredulously. "Jesus didn't fake His own death."

"Some say He did." Great. Now I could add *heresy* to my list of offenses.

The Dean glared at me, a long slow glare that, had it been focused under a magnifying glass, could have burned ants.

I decided to change the subject. "Hey, can I graduate?" I asked brightly.

He shook his head, then leaned back, frowning at his desk. "You know, there are some people in the community who feel you should be dismissed." Clearly, the *Globe* article hadn't helped my case.

Or had it? "Look, Dean," I said, my throat tight. "You don't want to throw me out." I had brought along a copy of the article, which I pulled out from a leather portfolio. "I don't know if you've had a chance to read this yet."

Again with the glare.

"The way I see it, it'll look really bad if you expel the kid who just criticized you on the front page of the *Globe*."

Silence. He rolled his pen.

"Also," I pointed out, "*magna cum laude*." I let this register. "Assuming you let me graduate."

The Little Video That Could

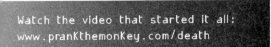

Watch the video that started it all:
www.prankthemonkey.com/death

And so, they let me graduate with only a brief suspension to appease the critics. I was banned from doing any more live performances at the college, but they didn't say anything about video. So just before I graduated, I finished up *The John Hargrave Memorial Video,* the short film that I had put together for the final show. I gave it away to a bunch of people as graduation presents, then had to dub another batch of copies when other students started asking me for it. I stuck around Boston for the summer, and by the next fall,

people were still asking me for copies of the film.
I started charging for the tapes, then for my time,
and ultimately for the movie itself. It became kind
of a cult classic on the Berklee campus: the video
of the kid who faked his own death. It was in the
Globe and everything, man. And I heard he got
kicked out of school, too! *No shit!*

Many years later, the *Globe* did a piece on my Web
site, which ran once again on the front page of the
Arts section. (It ran, ironically, in the very issue of the
Globe that I was arrested for "shoplifting" from CVS.)
The reporter who wrote the article was very good, not
like the hacks at the *Herald*, and insisted on pester-
ing the Berklee administration about exactly what
happened. I chuckled as I imagined the Berklee regis-
trar's office having to dig back into my file, trying to
justify why the whole episode was such a big deal.

But did my prank really change anything? The
President of Berklee, under fire from all sides, sent
a note out to the Berklee community after those
original Globe articles. He promised the school would
"identify and engage a professional consultant with
college experience in matters of diversity to help all
of us formulate and participate in a process through
which we will address our attitudes, experiences,
beliefs, and values and their impact on the differ-
ences among us." Let me know if you figure out what
that means.

Now that I look back on the whole episode fifteen
years later, I feel that nothing ever really changed.
Here I've spent the entire book complaining about
how much the system sucks, but what have I done to

improve it? (Paying off Ronald McDonald doesn't count.) So I forged a few credit card receipts, and pranked some senators. You think anybody cares? They're 30,000 feet up, man. I'm not even on the radar. To close out the book, I felt I needed to do something, however small and silly, to change things for the better.

So here's what I did. This might actually get me invited back to an alumni dinner at Berklee someday. I called up the Vice President of Institutional Advancement at Berklee College of Music. This is the guy who raises the money. I told him I wanted to donate $1,000, which I realize is not even enough to cover a day's tuition, but I only got a $5,000 advance on this book, so cut me some slack. I told him I wanted to set up a scholarship. He politely pointed out that $1,000 wasn't even enough to buy the "s" in "scholarship." I tried to think of what I could get instead.

"Hey, you know how schools will name buildings after alumni who donate huge amounts of money?" I asked him.

"Sure."

"How much for a stapler?"

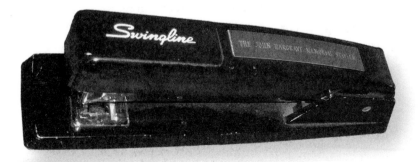

He thought about this. "$1,000 could get you a stapler."

"The John Hargrave Memorial Stapler?"

"Sure."

So there you go. I made a stapler-level donation. It's not much, but maybe it'll hold the school together for a little while. Or if not the school, then at least a few papers.

We're All Going to Die

The problem with faking your death is that you can only do it once. But here's the funny thing: The day I *actually* die, there are a couple of people who won't believe it.

"John Hargrave died."

"Yeah, sure."

"No, really, *he's dead.*"

"Oh yeah? How'd he die, then?"

"His cockhole exploded."

"What?! NO!"

"Yeah, the little hole on the end of the cock. It just blew up."

See, that would be a bad way to go. Too many herbal supplements, and POP! Like a sausage in the microwave.

"They say there was penis tissue everywhere. Quite a lot of it, in fact."

"No shit."

"The clergyman was certainly surprised."

Who cares if they don't believe I'm dead? I already know how it happens. My death is not going to be a surprise to me. I saw a vision of it, and you'll be happy to know I don't suffer much. Explosive dongs are not involved.

Only one part of my death remains a mystery: I don't know *when* I'll die. If there's any justice in the universe, though, I will die on April Fool's Day. Sweet Lord, when you take me, please take me on the first of April. That's all I ask.

Born April Fool's Day, died April Fool's Day. You have to admit, that would be pretty fucking awesome. ☺

Acknowledgments

IF SHE WAS MARRIED TO A PROFESSIONAL athlete or a brain surgeon, you could understand why my wife would make sacrifices for her husband's work. It's not as easy to figure out why the woman supports a husband who wakes up at 5:30 every morning to make prank phone calls to the Queen. I've tried to show you small examples throughout the book of her patience, dedication, and support, but none of my "work" would happen without her. I love her, and she's beautiful: **Jade Hargrave**.

To my incomparable illustrator, **Al Natanagara**, who proves that the pen (tablet) is mightier than the sword.

A toast to the great **Moses Blumenstiel** and his mad impov stylingz. Check yourself before you wreck yourself.

Award-winning photographer **Andrew Miller** (andrewmillerphoto.com), for the cover photos, the press photos, and the *nude* photos. I'll never forget that night. The tattoo will assure that.

Thank you to the people who have made ZUG.com great over the years: **Genevieve Martineau, Jay Stevens, Al Natanagara, Seth Macy, Tracie McMay, Angela Frantz**, and the GAB community. Without you, there wouldn't be a book, and thus the world would probably be a better place.

Thank you to my editor, **Jeremie Ruby-Strauss**, for believing in the project, and for raping and murdering all the angels.

Thanks to **Richard Ember** (editor), **Elleanore Waka** (production manager), **Arthur Maisel** (production editor), **Susan Higgins** (copyeditor), **Jeff Rutzky** (book designer), **Kristen Hayes** (senior designer for the cover), and everyone else at Citadel and Kensington.

Thank you to my test readers: **Jim Merullo**, **Kate Epstein**, and **Ethan Handelman**. Thank you to **Jess Lindley**, the hottest MILF in Massachusetts.

Thank you to Arnold Worldwide, especially **Joe Mahoney**, **Max Pfennighaus**, **Barry Silverstein**, and **Meredith Vellines**, for ideas and advice. Thank you to **Matt Lindley** for not firing me yet.

Thanks to the Michael Jackson crew: **Gerson Barahona**, **Mark Higgins**, **Michael Hoban**, **Hugo Reyes**, and **Diana Thom**.

A special shout out to the man of a thousand voices, **Jim Meskimen** (www.appliedsilliness.com), who is available for commercials, voice-overs, or just random screaming.

Thanks to our forefathers in pranking, who provided inspiration for many of the stunts in this book: **Alan Abel**, **Abbie Hoffman**, **Allen Funt**, **Andy Kaufman**, **Michael Moore**, **Don Novello**, **Joey Skaggs**, and **Jeffrey Vallance**.

Thank you to my Lord and Savior **Jesus Christ**, who I hope will forgive me.

And I never thought I (or anyone else in the world) would say this, but thank you to **Charles Manson**. Apparently we're pen pals now.

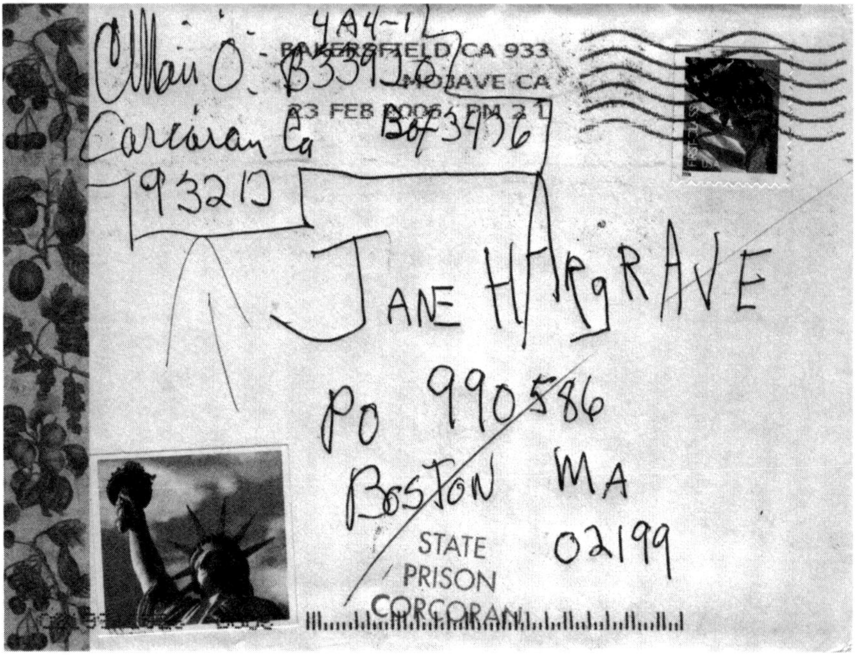

Allan O ~ B33910
Corcoran Ca B073936
93212

JANE HARgRAVE
PO 990586
BOSTON MA
02199

Dear Mymonk

    I,ve got 4 monks hoads ins My garden with Jumson weed + AZALi a few SiLver Fish Mely J.F.Ks grang as I told Frather Gibalt No lies — al 12 as the pope in whiskey in the more head pirat from porch people My sisters puppy was her Sisters snake + Indina got a BIg Snake that you Can not OUt Snake Ran Dass NY snake from the will

    - COBRA -

sell your little lams to th big black wraif who sells ALL wild life + hamburge Clowns who feel they will all be dead befor you can grow up to Sherley mc Clane Shirly Menters + Sherly tempels pempsel an My FAT Boys But aut af Chiago Sweet Ladgus af Seattle chuef af washing State by white patty af rebirth in 1776 you May not git back to Black 1500 befor th yellow dragons Eat up all the lies sucking an altry toys mushrooms

2/ino mexico Sun gods changin up
SIDE DOWN
ald shals upside down to SUN
gods - your worst Dinels are my
best Sants + the bottom + warof
Of my days minibe your heaven forever
                    FOOLING
as rome's been ~~Playing~~ You
to the othy Charls fur a ride
on my Bike — ul d war thy
pope at 12 years ald you
gut to be Mathin super sisty
of pupies + Lizard bate, mitty the
worm Cans you Daint mudentud
yankee schoals mould teach
George Washington's tree they
tryed to transplant O TOOLS

©TNG

Chief of Palace in Boston to
Jo mo Kenyeta of Kenya afreq
+ Preg Carters in JFK's grave
yard becom LIE got No Real
no real brother an Sisters Just
greed power profit Lust games
for a short time — af the truth is
So Cool why are the lies always
rich + got food + fun +the
truth is always in Cages — Everything
is true to you because you can see
A Man you 17 times befor Sunday
an Spanish but you didnt see
I brother from Spain came + said
me dont go along with ROME
we keep a face up but no Mouth +
no shadows Im som Matter now Sisty
atoal + Me's + Mac + Macks + Buss+S/At5
EASY ☆ ⊙ = ‡

About ZUG.com

ZUG.com is the world's only comedy site. Jam-packed with stories, pranks, and boners, my popular Web site is updated regularly at www.ZUG.com. Hate your job? ZUG is the perfect way to lower your employer's productivity, eventually allowing Indian competitors to drive your company out of business. Contemplating suicide? ZUG also offers relief from your emotional torment, but without all the embarrassing awkwardness in the afterlife. Hours of hilarity, months of mirth, and every page is *free*! Now in convenient "Web" form at **www.ZUG.com**.